IN PERIL ON THE SEA

THE HISTORICAL SERIES OF THE REFORMED CHURCH IN AMERICA
NO. 92

IN PERIL ON THE SEA
The Forgotten Story of the
William & Mary Shipwreck

Kenneth A. Schaaf

VAN RAALTE PRESS
Holland, Michigan

© 2018 Van Raalte Press
All rights reserved

Van Raalte Press
Theil Research Center
PO Box 9000
Holland, MI 49423
www.hope.edu/vri

Printed in the United States of America

ISBN: 978-0-9891469-6-8

Library of Congress Preassigned Control Number 2018937215

To Carol

A wife of noble character

The Historical Series of the Reformed Church in America

The series was inaugurated in 1968 by the General Synod of the Reformed Church in America acting through the Commission on History to communicate the church's heritage and collective memory and to reflect on our identity and mission, encouraging historical scholarship which informs both church and academy.

www.rca.org/series

General Editor
Rev. Donald J. Bruggink, PhD, DD
Western Theological Seminary
Van Raalte Institute, Hope College

Associate Editor
James Hart Brumm, MDiv
New Brunswick Theological Seminary

Copy Editor
JoHannah Smith
Holland, Michigan

Production Editor
Russell L. Gasero
Archives, Reformed Church in America

Commission on History
James Hart Brumm, MDiv, New Brunswick Theological Seminary
Lynn Japinga, PhD, Hope College
David M. Tripold, PhD, Monmouth University
Douglas Van Aartsen, MDiv, Ireton, Iowa
Matthew Van Maastricht, MDiv, Milwaukee, Wisconsin
Linda Walvoord, PhD, University of Cincinnati

Contents

Acknowledgments   ix
Note from the editor   xiii
Preface   xv
Introduction   xix

Part I   Leaving Home   1

  Harlingen, Friesland   3
  The Cow Doctor's Son   13
  Across the North Sea   17
  The Train to Liverpool   21
  The Ship Builder   27
  Awaiting Departure   35
  The Captain   41
  To Charleston and Liverpool   47

Part II   Tossed About at Sea   53

  Week One: To Sea   55
  Week Two: Early Losses   59
  Week Three: Growing Fear   63
  Week Four: Rising Tensions   65
  Week Five: The Unbroken Horizon   69
  Week Six: New Optimism   73
  Week Seven: Channel Fever   77
  Great Isaac Rocks   83
  Abandoned   89

Part III Rescue and Healing   95

  Ascension Day   97
  In the Bahamas   105
  Nassau Town   115
  The Runaway Captain   125
  Leaving Nassau   131
  To New Orleans   137

Part IV Finding a New Home   143

    New Orleans   145
    Steamboat to Saint Louis   161
    Saint Louis, Missouri   177
    Saint Louis to Galena, Illinois   185
    The Final Ascent   191
    Frisia   199

Part V Epilogue   209

    Rescuer: Robert Sands   213
    Survivors: Hendrik Kas and Grietje Jansonius   219
    Survivors: Beinze Rienks and Metje van der Ploeg   223
    Survivors: Antje Kooistra and sons   227
    Survivor: Izaak Roorda   231
    Survivor: O. H. Bonnema, community planner   235
    Survivor: B. B. Haagsma, record keeper   239
    Survivors: Johannes Tuininga and family   245
    Seaman: John D. Best   249
    Survivors: Sjoerd Bekius and Maartje Schaaf, cousins   253
    Survivors: Sjoerd Tjalsma and family   257
    Former Captain: Timothy R. Stinson   261
    A Final Word   271

Appendix   275

    Officers and Crew of the *William and Mary*   275
    Passenger List   276

Selected Bibliography   285
Index   291

Acknowledgments

Someone once defined work as creating order out of chaos. Most certainly, the account of the *William and Mary* and the stories of her passengers could not be told without sifting through a broad field of debris that had been buried for more than a century and a half. But with the help of so many, it never felt like work; rather, it was more like a treasure-hunt expedition.

Since the research effort began at the Library of Congress, acknowledgments must begin here. I am fortunate to have Steve Herman, the library's official keeper of the general collections, as not only a colleague but also a friend. I am particularly grateful for two of his staff, Tyna Hepburn and Priscilla Cooke, who over and over placed the books I needed into my hands. I drew heavily from the inexhaustible collections of the geography and map division, thankful that reference librarian, Habte Teclemariam, was expert in providing the maps and charts relative to the study. My retreats to the quietness of the Rare Book and Special Collections Reading Room always brought a sense of awe and reverence. It was my honor to work there with chief Mark Dimunation. The Serial and Government Publications Division provided access to so much of what appeared in the nineteenth-century press concerning the shipwreck; my thanks there goes to reference librarian Megan Halsband. Letters and manuscripts were made available thanks to Jeff Flannery, reference head of the manuscript division and the expert assistance of Michelle Knowl, historian and Lincoln specialist. Finally, I express my appreciation to former colleagues Sybille Jagusche and Donald Shomette, both writers, both experts in their field, and both strong in their encouragement to finish the project and see the forgotten story told to a wide audience of readers.

I have become very fond of the reference librarians, archivists, and curators that I met over the past six years. I have had the great privilege of personally visiting many of them and seeing first hand the records entrusted to their care. For others, I am pleased for their positive responses to my calls, letters, and emails of inquiry and the wealth of information they provided.

From Maine: thank you to Elizabeth Steen and Frank Connors of the Bowdoinham Historical Society for preparing me for my visit to the hometown of Stinson and Harward. I delighted in meeting with reference librarian Peter Goodwin of the Patten Free Library in Bath, homeport of the *William and Mary*. Thank you, Kelly Page, curator/registrar of the Maritime Museum Library, for providing me access to files found in no other library and then directing me to the Pejepscot Historical Society in Brunswick. I was not prepared for the scope and depth of material that Pejepscot reference librarian and docent Rebecca Roche brought out. Thank you Daniel Hope, reference librarian at Bowdoin College in Brunswick, for making the Harward files available to me.

From Colorado: I am grateful for the personal attention given by reference librarian Bruce Hanson of the Denver Public Library, Western History/Genealogy Department, on one of the busiest days of the year. On my visit to Central Presbyterian Church, historian Joseph Martell provided a wealth of information on Stinson's church. Denver's Riverside Cemetery is now closed, but Patricia Carmody of the Fairmount Heritage Foundation has been open to all of my inquiries related to the study.

From Louisiana: thank you, Daniel Hammer, head of reader services and curator of the Historic New Orleans Collection, for providing access to the records of the Deutsche Gesellschaft and for your thoughtful translation work. I am grateful to Irene Wainwright, head of the Louisiana division/city archives at the New Orleans Public Library, for her successful photo search.

From Michigan: I must thank Dick Harms, former curator of the archives of the Christian Reformed Church, and librarian Wendy Blankespoor in particular. On my visit to Heritage Hall, Wendy worked nonstop in pulling files for me to see and did not stop bringing things to my attention even after I had left. I am grateful to Loren Lemmen for his gracious offer of sharing his files from his earlier study of the *William and Mary*. My thanks go to Dr. Dennis Voskuil, director, Van Raalte Institute, and its fellows for the welcoming reception given to *In Peril*. I am indebted to Dr. Robert P. Swierenga who planted a seed for this study in 1974 and encouraged it to publication; to Dr. Jacob E. Nyenhuis, editor-in-chief, for his early acceptance and strong support for the project; and to Dr. Donald Bruggink, general editor of the RCA Historical Series, my ever-skillful pilot/navigator throughout the publishing process. Highest regards go to VRI text editor JoHannah Smith— exacting in detail, so gracious in character. I acknowledge the effort of independent researcher Ralph Haan in successfully solving the mystery of whatever happened to Maartje, but I so wanted to be the one to find her.

From Wisconsin: thank you Bill Peterson, associate archives librarian of the La Crosse Public Library, for your help in supplying pieces of the New Amsterdam story. How grateful I am for the information on the New Amsterdam Presbyterian Church sent to me by church historian Patricia Schmidt. Although not of Wisconsin, but of Williamsburg, Ontario, thank you James Kooistra for sharing your notes on your 2006 visit to New Amsterdam and for your Frisian translation work.

From Maryland: I am grateful to Elizabeth Gray, reference specialist of the National Archives and Records Administration in College Park, who placed in my hands the original hand-written records of the American consul in Nassau, the Bahamas. It was as if I had opened a time capsule.

From the Bahamas: my appreciation to Nassau archivist T. A. A. Delaney and Hope Town historian Deb Patterson for their reach into the past.

To the descendants of the Frisian survivors of the *William and Mary* shipwreck, specifically the dozens of you whom I called and who did not immediately hang up, thank you for talking even when you had never heard the account of one of your ancestors being shipwrecked on their way to America.

Finally, thank you to my family: to my wife, Carol, for being my partner in life and my principal supporter in every endeavor; to my son, Jon Schaaf, for his expertise in graphics; to my brother, Wayne Schaaf, for double checking my sources at Heritage Hall one more time and for searching for tombstones in the snow; and to my cousin, Mark de Nooy, for his willingness to visit yet another cemetery.

Kenneth A. Schaaf

A note from the editor . . .

When I received the first draft of this fine account of a disaster at sea, I sought the advice of the editorial advisory committee for the Van Raalte Press. All of us were gripped by the compelling story of immigrants' experiences during their journey from the Netherlands to America, a story that Schaaf has constructed on the basis of indefatigable research in the Library of Congress and many other sources.

Dr. Donald J. Bruggink, a senior research fellow at the Van Raalte Institute since 2003 and the founding general editor of the Historical Series of the Reformed Church in America, was one of the readers. Recognizing the broad appeal that this story would have, he also sought the advice of the RCA Commission on History, who likewise responded to this manuscript with approbation. The result is this publication by the Van Raalte Press for inclusion in the Historical Series of the Reformed Church in America.

Relying on broad reading and focused research, Kenneth Schaaf constructs a narrative that is part detective story, part drama, and part character study as he recounts the fate of ninety-two Frisians who set out for America in 1853. He draws upon maps and charts, personal journals, letters, shipping schedules, brief newspaper accounts, and interviews with descendants of the survivors, but he also learned the process of ship building and the history of the development of the British railway in the 1830s and 1840s, studied a painting of Liverpool from that era, and traced the lives of each of the crew members and passengers. At once individual and universal, *In Peril on the Sea* should appeal to a broad audience. The epilogue, appendix, bibliography, and index also provide invaluable detail for genealogists and scholars.

I am very pleased to have the Van Raalte Press as publisher of *In Peril on the Sea.*

Jacob E. Nyenhuis
Editor in Chief, Van Raalte Press
Interim Director, A. C. Van Raalte Institute

Preface

Directly across the street from the US Capital in Washington, DC, stands the Thomas Jefferson Building of the Library of Congress. Opened in 1897, it is regarded by many to be the most beautiful public building in the city. But to visiting scholars, it is not the Beaux-Arts style classical granite exterior or sparkling marble interior passages that draw them to this building. Rather it is the institution's broad and massive intellectual collections, the largest in the world, and its ease of access to them through the library's twenty-plus reading rooms.

The most impressive of all the reading rooms is, of course, the Main Reading Room, LJ 100. Entering by way of two huge bronze doors off an east corridor, then passing through a vestibule of reference librarians and a narrow alcove, the passage suddenly opens to an enormous rotunda, the reading room. The chamber is octagonal, made up of a series of marble arches that extend four stories. Encircling the room on the third-floor level is a balustrade on which stand sixteen life-size bronze statues of Plato, Bacon, Moses, Beethoven, and others—the keepers of this temple of knowledge. Above them, a spectacular 120-foot-high dome and eight celestial lights. But this is not where the treasure lies.

Out of view and kept secure in the library's climate-controlled stacks are the institution's holdings: books, maps, manuscripts, photographs, films, sheet music, sound recordings, law materials, newspapers and journals—more than 155 million items on an estimated 838 miles of shelving. Although the stacks are closed to the public, those holding a research pass to the reading rooms can get a peek by passing through Alcove 3 in the Main Reading Room, into the open reference collection of the local history and genealogy section, a token of the unit's much larger collection.

It is on one of these reference shelves that I found a book compiled by Robert P. Swierenga, *Dutch Emigrants to the United States, South Africa, South America, and Southeast Asia, 1835-1880*, an alphabetical listing by household heads and independent persons. Starting with "Aalberts" and ending with "Zwijnenburg," it includes 21,800 names from various Dutch sources. It is an oft-used tool by those doing research in Dutch immigration and a great favorite of mine. On one of my visits to this source, my curiosity took me to find my surname, Schaaf. There were five Schaafs, and three were from Het Bildt, Friesland, the area of origin of our family. Two of the three arrived in 1847: Pieter Schaaf and Sjoerd Pieters Schaaf. In all likelihood, father and son. The last was a Maartje Pieters Schaaf, a farm servant girl who reportedly arrived in 1853, and in all probability, a daughter of Pieter and a sister to Sjoerd. I had an aunt Maartje Schaaf, born in Het Bildt many years later, as well as a cousin, Maartje or Martha; could there be some family connection? Another Swierenga source identified the ship Maartje was on as the *William and Mary*, from Liverpool, a ship that never arrived at her destination.

I next went to the *New York Times*; if there had been a shipwreck, the *Times* would have reported it. And there it was. On page three of the issue for May 17, 1853, under the caption "Disaster at Sea," was a statement from the captain of the *William and Mary*. It concluded, "The W. & M. left Liverpool with 208 passengers . . . who nearly all went down in the vessel . . . names unknown." I suddenly felt like a parent searching for a lost child. I had to find Maartje.

A genealogical study revealed two things. First, Maartje was the daughter of Pieter Schaaf who had settled in Vriesland, Michigan, five years earlier. Her mother had died in Holland, and this was her attempt to now find her father. Second, Maartje and I do have a common ancestor, a colorful figure in the Dutch Patriot movement of the 1780s, who was strongly influenced by the American freedom experience. In a failed challenge in 1787 to the weak, autocratic Dutch Stadholder Prince Willem V, Maartje's grandfather and many of his companions fled to France in a self-imposed exile. It was his son, Pieter, who left for Michigan in 1847, and his great-grandson, Jan, my grandfather, who left for New Jersey in 1910.

With this new information and so many questions, I began my search for Maartje. Did she survive the shipwreck? How was that possible? Did she find her father and brother? Did she marry and raise a family of her own? Could she possibly have descendants living today? If so, do they know her story—their story? And the others that traveled with her, what happened to them?

So the digging for information began, first in Friesland, then in England, the Bahamas, up and down the Mississippi Valley, and in towns and cities all across the country. With every passing week, the once-hidden story of the *William and Mary* and her passengers began to unfold, and I was amazed at what I found.

I uncovered accounts of great hardship and loss, a way of life all too common to those living in the mid-nineteenth century. And at the same time, even on the darkest of days, there was evidence of God's care and concern, His ever-amazing grace.

Kenneth A. Schaaf

O Holy Spirit, who didst brood upon the chaos dark and rude, who bid its angry tumult cease, and give, for wild confusion, peace, O hear us when we cry to thee for those in peril on the sea.
William Whiting, 1860

Introduction

Our life's journey sometimes takes us to places we never intended to go. We set our destination, establish our route, and make our reservations. But then the unexpected occurs, there is a delay, an accident, a reroute, a complete change of plans. This certainly was the case for a hapless band of Dutch travelers on their trip to America during the late winter and spring of 1853. A few turned back before it began. Others would soon regret not having done likewise. But like many journeys, once begun, there are few opportunities to go back or start over.

It is through a rich collection of found journals, letters, personal papers, nineteenth-century maps and nautical charts, period travel literature, and a host of newspaper accounts from both sides of the Atlantic that we follow a group of emigrant travelers on their perilous voyage, from their tightly woven Frisian heritage into a new American tapestry.

Accounts of life journeys have been around for as long as our race has felt compelled to move from one location to another, as in the Biblical account of the wanderings of the children of Israel, Chaucer's *Canterbury Tales*, Longfellow's *Tales of the Wayside Inn*, and even our contemporary travelogues. For the duration of the journey, there is an intersection of lives, a cultural exchange, a common shared experience. Then, suddenly, the trip is over, our travelers go in different directions, and their stories, repeated less and less often, are soon forgotten.

In Peter H. Wood's thorough study of Winslow Homer's painting, "Gulf Stream," he wrote, "There is no older or richer artistic image than that of a boat and its occupants at the mercy of the mighty sea." With that analogy, he went on to suggest, "We are each lost at sea in the modern world; we are ignored by remote ships and buffeted by passing squalls, and we have as much hope of controlling our fearful destiny as [Homer's] luckless mariner . . . it will take Divine Providence to save us."[1]

You and I are on our once-only life journey, traveling through time over unfamiliar seas. Our experiences, though common to all, are *our* adventures, *our* challenges. Although we sometimes think we are better equipped than generations past to handle what may come, our twenty-first century intellect and technology still appear inadequate to safely see us through what we are presented in life. We make choices along the way, and we like to believe we are in control. But where we begin, when, and with whom, are not of our volition. Our Creator, in His wisdom and knowledge, has determined the where, when, how, and with whom. Like the band of Frisian travelers who left their homes so many years ago, we are called to trust Him to pilot us through the journey, from start to finish.

---

[1] Wood, *Weathering the Storm: Inside Winslow Homer's Gulf Stream* (Athens: University of Georgia Press, 2004), 16-19.

PART I

Leaving Home

He determined the times set for them and
the exact places where they should live.
Acts 17:26[1]

Harlingen, Friesland

They began arriving at the Harlingen quay during the early morning hours—the travelers, their families, and friends—for the announced 11:00 a.m. departure. Snow had fallen during the night, and the weather that Saturday morning remained bitterly cold. Visually it was a chiaroscuro scene: clusters of darkly clad Frisians with black steamer trunks, willow baskets, wooden crates, and an assortment of carpet bags of various shapes and sizes, set against a frigid, all-white sky and ground. The contrast would have made for a great photograph, although the appearance of a camera at such an event was still decades into the future.

Emotions were also in the extreme. For some it was a day of high hopes, excitement, anticipation, and adventure. For others—

[1] Luke's record of St. Paul's address to the philosophers on Mars Hill in Athens remains as a clear statement of both God's sovereignty and his personal concern for the affairs of humankind.

mostly those with close family bonds—it was a day of dread. The possibility of ever returning and seeing their loved ones again was unlikely. These were their forever-final moments together. One traveler in the group felt a range of emotions and later wrote, "I never hovered between hope and fear more than I did during those few moments."[2]

With few-known exceptions, the travelers had little in terms of earthly goods. Emigration records testify to there being one wealthy merchant, one self-proclaimed doctor, and one teacher; all the others were occupied in manual trades typical to isolated Friesland—farm hands, farm servant girls, a rope maker, a blacksmith's helper, a tailor, a carpenter's helper, a miller's hand, and many who simply declared themselves a "workman."[3]

Holland's economy in the mid-nineteenth century was, in a word, depressing. According to Dutch scholar Jacob van Hinte, "In Friesland especially, the situation of the laborers was anything but an enviable one. A day's pay of the permanent laborers, the best situated group, was so small that it is a wonder that a laborer, who often had a large family, could even survive."[4] Those fortunate to have permanent work were under a heavy tax burden in providing welfare for those without employ.

Friesland in the 1850s had virtually no industry to speak of—a few canning factories, several brickyards, a sugar beet mill

[2] Izaak Roorda recorded his journey and published it as *Schipbreuk van het barkschip William and Mary* during the summer of 1853. It was later translated, inserted in *The Roorda Family History*, and privately published in Des Moines, Iowa, 21.

[3] Drawn in part from the compilations of Robert Swierenga's *Dutch Emigrants to the United States, South Africa, South America, and Southeast Asia, 1835-1880: An Alphabetical Listing by Household Head and Independent Persons* (Wilmington, DE: Scholarly Resources, 1983) and from the massive digital record collections of Tresoar, the Frisian Historical and Literary Center in Leeuwarden.

[4] Van Hinte, *Netherlanders in America: A Study of Emigration and Settlement in the Nineteenth and Twentieth Centuries in the United States of America*, gen. ed. Robert P. Swierenga, trans. Adriaan de Wit (Grand Rapids, MI: Baker Book House, 1985), 80.

here and there. Most men faced a future toiling the cold, damp fields or, if they lived on the coast, working its waterways, a dangerous and unreliable livelihood. So when letters arrived from those who had preceded them to America that boasted of an abundance of land and unlimited opportunities, seeds of hope were planted.

Six years earlier, many had left the Netherlands for convictions of faith, believing their passage to America would allow them the freedom they had lost in Holland. The Netherlands during the 1830s had become increasingly liberal in matters of faith. Many preachers in the state church, the Nederlands Hervormde Kerk, had turned from teaching the scriptures. In reaction, the Seceder movement rose up with a return to orthodox theology—but at a high price. The Dutch, otherwise known for their spirit of tolerance, demonstrated closed minds toward those holding scriptural values. With the abdication of autocratic King Willem I in 1840 and the ascendency of Willem II the following year, persecution of the Seceders officially ended, although in practice, it continued for some time. Rather than face an ongoing civil and cultural war, many Seceders chose to leave. This was especially true with the large number of emigrants who made their passage in 1847. In that year alone, over eight thousand Netherlanders left their homeland for the opportunity of starting over in America. But this was not the case with those gathered on the Harlingen wharf. The vast majority were members of the Nederlands Hervormde Kerk. The only exceptions were three Roman Catholic families. There was not a single professing Seceder or Gereformeerd member in the company.

For many of us living in the twenty-first century, it is difficult to fully sense the risks in mid-nineteenth-century ocean travel. Large city newspapers, such as the *Times* of London and the *New York Daily Times*, reported in their marine intelligence columns daily accounts of lost ships, and, at a time preceding wireless communication, such news appeared weeks after the fact. Nor did on-board conditions work in favor of the emigrating family. Poor food storage, limited potable water supplies, inadequate ventilation, confined accommodations, and lengthy transatlantic voyages resulted in a high loss of life. Cholera, small pox, and typhus, or as it was commonly known, ship fever, would move quickly through a ship. And although the advent of the steamship meant faster voyages, steamships were built also to move more passengers. In either case, the mortality rate was high and bears further evidence to the desperate conditions in Europe.

One of the first to appear at the ship that morning was twenty-eight-year-old Oepke Haitzes Bonnema, the organizer, leader, and financial sponsor of the group. In all probability, he had spent Friday night with Mevrouw Botje Harmens Steinfort, his maternal grandmother, in her stately brick mansion on Noordenhaven, along Harlingen's central canal. A widow and seventy-two years of age, Botje was exceptionally wealthy. As a result of her longevity and her moneyed family connections, she was beneficiary to several estates, including that of her uncle, her father—a man of independent means—both of her sisters, and her husband. During her thirty-three-year marriage to property assessor Jelle Louws Fopma, she and her husband traded in real estate—houses, gardens plots, meadowlands, and acres of arable farmland. Her access to capital allowed her to loan amounts large and small to families across Friesland over a period of four decades.

Botje and Jelle had only one child, Stijntje, who at age eighteen had married down to grain dealer Haitze Eeltje Bonnema. But Bonnema was ambitious and showed promise. Before the couple's first anniversary, Stijntje presented to Botje and Jelle their first grandchild. Setting aside the custom of naming the first son after his paternal grandfather, they instead named him

Jelle. Three years later, Stijntje gave birth to a second son, naming him Oepke, the focus of our study, once again overlooking his paternal grandfather. When the third child arrived, the baby was named Harmen, this time after his grandmother's father. Then one month after giving birth, Stijntje died; she was only twenty-four.

Left with a five year old, a two year old, and a new baby, it was not long before Haitze remarried, curiously to another Stijntje, who in time gave birth to three more children. Soon after the birth of their last child, Haitze himself died at age forty-two, leaving Oepke and his siblings in the care of their stepmother. While this situation would be rare today, in Holland in past centuries, it was a common occurrence. Just prior to Oepke's twentieth birthday, he appeared in court for the privilege of gaining majority status in making his own business decisions. In his childhood years, he must have watched his father and his grandfather, also a grain dealer, very closely. After only eight years of taking over the business, he owned considerable land in Friesland through profits made in the grain trade.

In 1852, not long after the death of his stepmother, Bonnema proposed a plan that he hoped would extend his profits even further, while also offering a means of relief for a segment of the oppressed families he saw around him. The concept was not new; American clergyman Calvin Colton had proposed a similar plan twenty years earlier.[5] The idea was this: Bonnema would arrange transportation from Harlingen, Friesland, to the new American state of Iowa, for a limited number of families and

---

5   Colton, *Manual for Emigrants to America* (London: Westley and Davis, 1832), 152. "Let every wealthy emigrant . . . collect the honest and industrious poor about them, let them set up a standard and beat for recruits on kind and generous terms; and, when they have found enough for a little colony, let them take these families and these individuals under their protection and guidance, and pass over the Atlantic, and penetrate into some of the vacant territory of the West."

singles. In exchange, once they arrived, they would establish a new community and, over a period of time, return Bonnema's initial investment. To those lacking in English skills and funds for transportation but willing to pull up stakes and eager to work, this was a golden opportunity.

Immediately applicants began contacting him. Since Bonnema lived in the village of Kimswerd, about three miles from the port of Harlingen, it is not surprising to find most of the inquiries came from towns within just a few miles of his home. One hopeful, twenty-year-old, Izaak Epkes Roorda, wrote, "After having talked with Mr. Bonnema, it was immediately decided that I was to go along as a glass cutter and farmer. I was to receive fl.4 a week [$1.60 USD] with free board and rooming. Then when we were in America, I would pay him back as I could."[6] The proposition seemed almost too good to be true. Departure was set for Saturday, February 26, 1853.

And so they came. The *Leeuwarder Courant* reported a few days later, "Great was the number of relatives, friends, and interested persons who had gathered around their relatives and fellow countrymen to see them leave the Fatherland."[7] Four families arrived from the municipality of Barradeel. First was Johannes Tuininga, forty; his wife, Trijntje; and their five children.[8] With them were their neighbors, Arijen Westerhuis, thirty-eight, his wife, Jeltje, and their five children—all close in age to the Tuiningas. Siebren Wesselius, fifty-six, was there with his wife, Marijke, and their three children. There also was Rients Sikkema, thirty-three; his wife, Ymkje; and their two young children. Their two-month-old Sikke, was the youngest child on the trip. The couple had lost

[6] *Roorda Family History*, 21.
[7] *Leeuwarder Courant* (March 1, 1853), 2.
[8] Although we have no passenger list for the *City of Norwich*, a nearly complete list is provided by Broer Haagsma in his *Lotgevallen van den heer O. H. Bonnema en zijne togtgenooten, op reis uit Friesland naar de Vereenigde Staten van Noord-Amerika* (Harlingen: S. Houtsma, 1853), 39-40.

another child the previous summer. With this group was Johannes Stienstra, thirty-eight; his wife, Riemke; and three children from nearby Franekeradeel.

Three families came from the municipality of Wonseradeel. First was Jacob Kooistra, a forty-five-year-old carpenter's helper; his wife, Antje; and their five children. Next was Sjoerd Tjalsma, forty-three, a boatman; his pregnant wife, Sjoukje; and their seven children—the largest family arriving at the ship that morning. Finally, there was Bauke Graafsma, forty, a laborer; his young wife, Klaaske; and their two children. This couple had previously lost three children.

Feye Schaafsma, forty-two, a carpenter, with his wife, Siementje, and four children, lived right there in Harlingen. So did forty-three-year-old Herke de Jong, also a carpenter, and his new wife, Anna Voortallen. With them were Herke's seven-year-old twins, Luutske and Cornelius. Finally, from Harlingen, were Jan Balkstra, twenty-nine, a rope maker, with his wife Anna, and Hendrikus de Boer, forty-three, a blacksmith helper, with his wife Anna.

It was Jan Martens van der Ploeg who had the distinction that morning of bringing his family the farthest. At sixty-five years of age, he was also the oldest of the travelers. As a widower, he lived with his two adult children, Baukje and Marten, on a vest-pocket farm near the coastal village of Ternaard, in the northeast corner of Friesland. Unskilled and illiterate, his life, as well as his children's, was harsh and severe. Yet, somehow, word of Bonnema's offer had reached their home and gave them hope for a brighter future. Quickly the three contracted themselves to the grain dealer, pulled up stakes, sold their belongings, and made their way to Harlingen.

Within this core of thirteen families were twenty-eight singles, twenty-three men and five women, ranging in age from twenty to thirty-eight, although most were in their early twenties. It was this group that, for the most part, had not established deep

Of the ninety-two Frisian emigrants that left on February 26, 1853,
eighty came from within twelve miles of Harlingen
(*map by Kenneth A. Schaaf and Jon Schaaf*)

ties to their homeland and had the least to risk in their venture. If
you could find smiles in the crowd that morning, this is probably
where you would find them.

Among the singles were cousins Maartje Pieters Schaaf
and Sjoerd Douwes Bekius, both twenty-three, both from the
municipality of Het Bildt (land built from the sea), and both eager
for change. Maartje was the fifth and youngest child of carpenter
Pieter Sjoerds Schaaf and Mettje Nammes Sybesma. In 1847

Maartje's father, sister, and brother left Het Bildt to establish themselves in western Michigan as part of a Seceder colony. Once settled, they were to send for Maartje, her mother, and another sister. But just one year later, Maartje sent word that her mother had died, and her own departure was uncertain. Now, five years later, with Bonnema's arrangements and financial help, she held new hope of rejoining her father, sister, and brother.

Maartje had invaluable companionship and assistance from her cousin, Sjoerd. He was the fifth and youngest child of innkeeper Douwe Alerts Bekius and Maartje Sjoerds Schaaf. Sjoerd's mother and Maartje's father were sister and brother. Very quickly, Sjoerd's assertiveness and his ability to pick up spoken English placed him in the eyes of the other Dutch travelers as a leader in their group.

Tensions were high that morning, and sometime between eight and nine o'clock, they got even higher. As soon as Bonnema had finished stowing baggage, the young captain, eager to be under way, had his crew cast off the mooring lines—more than two hours earlier than expected. Several persons not yet on board had to be brought out to the moving vessel in two small fishing boats. Two young people were not so fortunate; their bags left without them.

On the first leg of their journey to America, the ninety-two Frisian emigrants were booked passage on the *City of Norwich*, a seven-hundred-ton paddlewheel steamship. Its London-based owner, the newly formed North of Europe Steam Navigation Company, was offering first-class service from Harlingen to Lowestoft, England, with a cargo pick up in Amsterdam's port of Nieuwe Diep. This premiere service was estimated to take thirteen hours.

Lest one get the impression that the Frisians were about to embark on a finely appointed Victorian vessel, that view needs correction. Advertisements in the *Leeuwarder Courant* during

NIEUWE STOOMVAART tusschen **HARLINGEN** en **NIEUWE-DIEP** naar **LOWESTOFT**, in directe verbinding met de Spoorwegen naar **LONDON, YARMOUTH, NORWICH, MANCHESTER, LIVERPOOL**, en de tusschen- en omliggende plaatsen.

Overtogt van HARLINGEN naar LOWESTOFT circa 18 uren, en naar LONDON, 18, de andere Plaatsen naar evenredigheid.

Zal van HARLINGEN vertrekken op *Zaturdag 26 Februarij* 1853, Het nieuw gebouwde **IJZEREN STOOMSCHIP**

CITY of NORWICH,

groot 700 ton en van 300 paardekrachten.

Landverhuizers worden op deze gelegenheid attent gemaakt, daar zij voor *f* 12 de persoon van *Harlingen* naar *Liverpool* worden vervoerd.

Voor Goederen en Vee gelieve men zich te adresseren te *Harlingen* en *Nieuwediep* bij de Agenten

R. MUNTZ & C⁰.,

en verders Informatien te bekomen bij DE NORTH of EUROPE STEAM NAVIGATION COMPANY, 84 *King William Street London.*

Advertisement for the new steamship service from Harlingen, Friesland, to Lowestoft, England, commencing February 26, 1853. Unlike previous ads, this one appealed to both emigrant and livestock interests
(*courtesy* Archief Leeuwarder Courant)

January and February were clearly directed toward livestock interests. Attention was drawn to the relatively short time at sea, a freight deck that was under cover, and specially constructed feed and water facilities. These were all intended to reduce livestock mortality en route. Any appeal for emigration trade was given last and briefly, almost as an afterthought. For fl.12 per person, the company would provide water transport to Lowestoft and rail conveyance across England to the port at Liverpool, the point of their transatlantic departure.

*I look not for freedom from trials; they must needs be; but the
number, the kind, the form, the degree of them, I can safely leave to Him
who has ordered and will still order all things well.*

Samuel F. B. Morse

The Cow Doctor's Son

In the southwest corner of Friesland, seven miles south of
the port of Harlingen, in the clay region of Wonseradeel, lies the
small village of Schraard, whose population in 1851 was 258. A
mound village, its history goes back to the twelfth century, when
the area was claimed from the sea, drained, and transformed into
tillable farmland. Today Schraard consists of a thirteenth-century
church, a cluster of neat brick and tile homes, and several cottage
businesses, all set on six narrow lanes and one slow-moving
canal. It is one of the most beautiful hamlets in Friesland, a jewel
surrounded on all sides by acres of lush, green pastureland.

Little has changed in Schraard over the years since the
evening in May of 1831 when Broer Haagsma was born. His father,
Bauke Broers Haagsma, was a dairy farmer, as was his father before
him. There was one older sister; another sister and brother would
follow. But when Broer turned seven, his life changed forever. First

he witnessed the death of his infant brother, and then six months later, he saw the sudden death of his mother. Although we have no written record of the trauma that came with this loss, it is hard to imagine the experience without a long-lasting impact.

Other changes followed. In June of 1839, Broer's father hung up a new shingle and placed a notice in the *Leeuwarder Courant*: "Bauke Broers Haagsma, Vee-Artzenij Praktijk," (veterinary science practice). As the only son, sometimes Broer would go with his father to neighboring farms to care for sick and injured cows and horses.

It was also in 1839 that his father found a new wife and mother for Broer and his sisters. Fokeltje was young—fifteen years younger than Broer's father—and over the next six years, she would give birth to five children. But for some reason, most did not live long. The first baby lived for five months; the third child died at age six, and the fourth died at five weeks. The last one was the worst. Broer's stepmother died giving birth to the baby, and then, five months later, the baby died. For the next four years, there was no mother in the home; Broer's older teenage sister cared for him, his sister, and stepbrother. His father went on with life, with the business of caring for livestock. Municipal records show money being borrowed, agreements being made, the house in Schraard being sold.

Finally, in 1845, when Broer was seventeen, his father married yet again, this time to Baukjen, a woman who was closer in age to Broer than she was to his father. Together they had six more children. The first lived fifteen days, another four years, and still another only three days. One lived to the age of twenty-three, before she herself died in childbirth.

Despite the sadness in the Haagsma home and frequent encounters with death, Broer showed much promise as a student, receiving a better-than-average education. He was particularly gifted in handling details, numbers, facts, and information. In

1852, at the age of twenty-one, he taught in a school in Arum, a small village midway between Schraard and Harlingen. There he heard of a grain dealer in the nearby town of Kimswerd who was organizing a group leaving for America. A contact was made, and, by the end of the year, young Broer agreed to join the party, serving as Oepke Bonnema's bookkeeper.

Broer had to then approach his father and tell him of his plan, one that would mean saying another goodbye and not seeing each other again this side of the grave. From Broer's point of view, life in Friesland seemed to be going backward; this was his golden opportunity.[9] Oddly for his father, life was still going forward. Before the year was out, his wife would give birth to his twelfth child—one who would reach maturity.[10]

[9]   A similar expression came from Albertus C. Van Raalte in a letter of December 16, 1846, to his family after being in the United States for several months. He wrote, "I can easily foresee many hardships and obstacles ahead for me, but I prefer this young and budding world over the full-grown, aged, and nearly disintegrating Europe, where all plans and activities are shackled by laws and customs which are centuries old, and where both material and spiritual activity is hampered. Yes, my friends, I am glad that my generation is being transplanted to this youthful world. A log cabin and other obstacles do not deter me." Letter published in *Voices from America* (Grand Rapids, MI: Heritage Hall, 1992), 28-29.

[10]   Three more children would be born to the cow doctor and his third wife. Two would die young; one would live to maturity. The cow doctor himself remained active in his practice well into his seventies.

If God has made all these things, He guides and governs them all,
and all things that concern them; for the Power that could make
all things must certainly have the power to guide and direct them.
Daniel Defoe, *Adventures of Robinson Crusoe*

Across the North Sea

As the iron ship got underway, its passengers did their best to find comfort in what was an extremely uncomfortable setting. Although their baggage was protected from the elements in the hold below, the passengers themselves were left standing on deck, huddled together to seek warmth in their numbers. Piles of hay, not intended for them, provided meager relief for the women and children. Pelted by snow and hail through the open sides and chilled by a cold wind moving over the waves, they endured conditions on board which worsened by the moment. The Waddenzee is an exceptionally shallow watercourse and difficult to navigate even when calm. After two hours of tossing and yet still within sight of Harlingen, the captain feared running aground. The anchor was dropped, and for the next six hours, the ship was at the mercy of the storm. Understandably, most passengers became ill. Finally, about five that afternoon, with conditions slightly improved and a rising tide, the anchor was weighed, and they were once again under way on a course directly south. An hour later, the ship hit hard aground and was forced to once again lower the hook and wait for high tide.

The port of Nieuwe Diep was hardly on the way to Lowestoft. Rather, it would take them 140 miles off a direct course, to the southwest corner of the former Zuiderzee. Arriving there early Sunday morning, they found awaiting them on the pier, the rest of the paying load—a large herd of sheep and cattle. Although the agrarian Frisians were very familiar with sheep and cattle, passenger Roorda noted in his journal, this "did not improve conditions."[11] Once loaded, the ship was back on a northward course through the Zuiderzee and, after some hours, out into the North Sea.

As the coast of the Netherlands disappeared in the East, the *City of Norwich* found itself caught in yet another fierce storm. All day Sunday and into the evening, the ship tossed on the waves. Roorda notes that it was so rough that some of the cattle were pitched over the four-foot railing and into the sea. Passengers had to hold on for all they were worth. When they finally approached the English coast, the waves continued to push them dangerously close to the rocks. Fortunately, the three-hundred-horsepower steam engine allowed them to reverse and then redirect to the small fishing village of Lowestoft. It was a great relief to all when the moon suddenly broke through the clouds, and the ship safely entered the harbor. Twenty-four hours earlier, when they were being tossed about on the North Sea, the gale was so severe in Lowestoft that up to forty vessels were damaged to the point of being disabled.

Some of the Frisians had to wonder if the order of unloading the ship was determined logistically or by the value of its cargo.

---

[11]   *Roorda Family History*, 22.

Immediately on landing, the sheep and cattle were taken off the ship and moved onto the train. Next, all baggage was removed from the hold and sent to the customs house for examination. Finally, at three o'clock in the morning, forty-two hours after leaving Harlingen, the passengers, exhausted from lack of sleep, numb with cold, and famished, were permitted to leave the now littered and smelly deck and make their way to the warmth of the railroad station and its pots of hot coffee.

Somebody told you the railroad was a bad thing. That was a lie.
It may do a bit of harm here and there, to this and that;
and so does the sun in heaven. But the railway's a good thing.[12]
George Eliot, *Middlemarch: A Study of Provincial Life*

The Train to Liverpool

If Bonnema had disappointed any in the group with the arrangements made for the first leg of their journey, he did his best to make amends. Early Monday morning, Bonnema made his way through the snow-covered streets of Lowestoft and found a supply of woolen blankets, one for each person in the group. Although the stations they would enter would be heated, mid-nineteenth-century train cars were cold and drafty. By eight o'clock that morning, the weary passengers, with their few possessions, were all on board, wrapped in their blankets, and once more moving generally westward.

---

[12] Not everyone, however, felt kindly toward the railroad and its intrusion across the British countryside. Dickens wrote, "away with a shriek and a roar and a rattle, and no trace to leave behind but dust and vapour: like as in the track of the remorseless monster, Death." *Domby and Son* (London: Bradbury and Evans, 1848), 276.

At this point, a brief history of the British railway is in order.[13] The first successful railway was established between Manchester and Liverpool in the 1830s. Since it was built to transport primarily manufactured goods, it was a surprise to railway investors when the general public began using the service. In fact, interest was so strong, that the 1840s became known as the decade of railway mania. By 1846 there were over six hundred individual railways scattered across the country. With varying track widths and little cooperation among the companies, long-distance travel required orienteering skills. A passenger would purchase his or her ticket for the first line, ride it to the end of the line, leave the train, purchase another ticket for the next line, travel it for several miles, exit and repeat the process numerous times, depending on how far one was traveling. And since there was no recognized standard time, schedules meant little; each station established its own time. By the end of the decade, fierce competition among the lines brought about a period of amalgamation, and that resulted in a standard gauge, a standard time, and a clearinghouse for smoother trans-Britain travel.

Despite improvements, for our band of unseasoned travelers crossing England in the dead of winter, conditions were still primitive. Oil lamps, known to leak, smoke, or go out, and the body heat of fellow travelers provided the only warmth in the cars. Numbness would start at one's feet and work its way through the entire body. The first dining car was still some twenty-six years into the future, and perhaps just as well. The lavatory was also a thing of the future. Seats were arranged, not along a central

---

[13]   Three very good sources are: Leslie James, *A Chronology of the Construction of Britain's Railways, 1778-1855* (London: Ian Allen, 1983), providing excellent maps of the various rail lines; Philippa Bigeli, *Taking the Train: Railway Travel in Victorian Times* (London: Her Majesty's Stationery Office, 1978), with very good illustrative material; and *Victorian and Edwardian Railway Travel*, with introduction and commentaries by Jeoffry Spence (London: B. T. Batsford, 1977).

corridor, but in rows of facing seats that extended the width of the car. There was no getting up to stretch your legs, no going for a stroll. Although some comforts were available in first class—lap and foot warmers, upholstered seats, and better lighting—our travelers were certainly not in first class.

In 1853 the route from Lowestoft to Liverpool, two hundred miles as the crow flies, was more like 275 miles the way the track lay. From the Lowestoft station, the Frisians traveled northwest, through the little village of Reedham, on to Norwich, then southwest. By noon, the train entered the town of Ely, once the home of Oliver Cromwell. Here the section destined for London, with its supply of mutton and beef on the hoof, was disconnected. From the station, the Frisians would have seen the towers of the Ely Cathedral, one of the seven wonders of the medieval world. Taking the opportunity for a quick walking tour of the city, the travelers—most dressed in their native garb and wooden clogs—were surprised at the attention they received. This happened repeatedly. By 2:30 p.m., the train was reconnected; all were on board once again, and, at the speed of thirteen miles per hour, they rattled on toward Peterborough, some thirty-three miles distant. Here, from the right side of the train, our travelers would have seen the magnificent Cathedral Church of St. Peter, St. Paul, and St. Andrew with its multiple spires and Norman arches. For some reason, Broer Haagsma, the twenty-two-year-old former schoolteacher now serving as Bonnema's record keeper, missed this entirely in his journal, instead commenting that the railway station there was 160 feet in length. He also quaintly comments on how startled they all were when they encountered their first tunnel, how suddenly they were thrust into darkness, not knowing what had happened, and then suddenly seeing daylight again.

By the time they reached Nottingham, its legendary Sherwood Forest was enshrouded with evening mist; no one got a glimpse of the band of merry men. On through the night they lurched along, tired, chilled, hungry, in need of a rest room, uncertain as to what was ahead, children crying, small ones needing diaper changes. All were oblivious to what they passed— former homes of Isaac Newton, Lord Byron, pilgrim father William Brewster, and more; old manses of brick, stone, tile, and timber, abbeys and chapels, hedge-bordered fields, and rolling brooks.

It was at five o'clock in the morning on Tuesday, March 1, when the company of Frisians passed though the long city tunnel and entered Liverpool's waterfront Victoria Station. Having made it to this point, hopes were high for departure on the steamship *City of Philadelphia*, leaving for Philadelphia the next day. Since British law permitted boarding twenty-four hours before departure, they optimistically prepared to board immediately. Soon, however, Bonnema brought the disappointing news that their delayed arrival in Liverpool resulted in the loss of space on the *City of Philadelphia*. They would need to remain in Liverpool until another ship could be found. In the meantime, decent accommodations were made in a rooming house operated by a German family. At the cost of two shillings per room per day ($.48 USD), they could remain there as long as necessary. Haagsma noted that it looked like they might need to remain two or possibly three weeks.

For the Frisian group, it should not have been difficult to find another ship. The twice-weekly, eight-page *Liverpool Mercury* carried a full page of advertisements by shipping companies in each issue. Between March 2 and 18, there were twenty ships leaving for American ports. While several of the steamship companies gave prices of £15 to £20 for second-class accommodations, there were also less expensive sailing vessels, many of which even posted fixed departure dates. The delay should not be long.

As the Frisians settled into their temporary quarters, a new American president was moving into his temporary home in the executive mansion in Washington, DC. On March 4, 1853, Democrat Franklin Pierce was sworn in as the fourteenth president of the United States. Although a New Englander by birth, he leaned decidedly to the South on the country's most dividing issue of the mid-nineteenth century—slavery. Although slavery had been abolished in England some twenty years earlier, when Pierce delivered his inaugural address, he promised no interference with the Southern custom. To his way of thinking, involuntary servitude was an American right recognized by the Constitution. Vice president William King was from North Carolina; secretary of the treasury James Guthrie was from Kentucky, and attorney general Caleb Cushing would become known as "the crusher of abolitionists." The secretary of war was Mississippi slave owner and future president of the Confederate States of America Jefferson Davis. For Pierce, the question of slavery was settled.

For our Frisian travelers, slavery was never a question for consideration. Admittedly there was slavery in the Dutch colonies but not in Friesland. Now over the course of their journey, again and again, they would be confronted with the matter of race and the question of equality.

Erelong we will launch a vessel as goodly and strong
and stanch as ever weathered a wintry sea.
Henry Wadsworth Longfellow

The Ship Builder

If you were to sail up along the rocky southern coast of Maine, around the bouldered twins—Wood Island and Pond Island—and into the mouth of the Kennebec River, you would encounter one of the most rugged yet beautiful regions of the country. For the European settlers of the early 1720s, coastal Kennebec, although attractive to the eye, had little to offer by way of tillable farmland. It was not until reaching the Merrymeeting Bay region, some twenty-five miles upstream, that the colonials found tillable soil suitable for farming.

Encroaching on the land of the native Abenaki and Penobscot tribes, however, came at a high price; many of the early settlers paid with their lives. Recorded in history are accounts of six wars over a period of ninety years—the Indian Wars—waged between those who had freely hunted and fished the region for generations past and those who wanted ownership for their heirs and assigns forever.

It was in 1762 that the town of Bowdoinham was organized near the western shore of Merrymeeting Bay. Most of its frontier residents had started out working the land as farmers. As the land was cleared of its trees, some turned their attention to harvesting and processing its lumber. With this great abundance of timber and access to the sea, it was only a short time before some began building ships. Despite duties imposed by the British Crown to restrict manufacturing of this type, in 1768 the first vessel slipped out of Merrymeeting Bay, down the Kennebec River, and on to the Atlantic. Appropriately named *Merry Meeting*, over the next century she would be followed by almost two hundred others.

Here we meet John Harward, shipbuilder. It was Harward's great-grandfather, Thomas Harward, who first entered what was then the colony of Massachusetts.[14] Born in 1700, in Guildford, Surry, England, he received bachelor's and master's degrees from Oxford and a medical degree from the Royal College of Physicians and Surgeons. In July of 1730, Harward was appointed to serve as lecturer at King's Chapel in Boston. As a young clergyman/ physician, he arrived in the Bay Colony with his wife, Letitia, and their two sons, William and George. The reverend doctor appeared to possess great promise in the colony and had a particular burden for the Mohawk nation, to learn their language and to share the gospel. His ministry, however, was cut short at age thirty-six, leaving his widow and two young sons with an estate in which his debts more than doubled his inventoried assets.[15]

---

[14] Biographical data on the Harward family resides in the Special Collections and Archive of the Bowdoin College Library, Brunswick, ME, and in the collections of the Pejepscot Historical Society, Brunswick, ME.

[15] We do have a record of his writings—two of which are today in the Rare Book and Special Collections Division of the Library of Congress in Washington, DC. In 1732 he published his *Electuarium novum alexipharmacum*, a small, 26-page book of notes and opinions of more than 50 herbs, extracts, powders, syrups, gums, seeds, etc., used in his medical practice. Also published that year was a sermon he had previously delivered in the Royal Chapel in Boston, titled, *The Fulness of Joy in the Presence of God*, a message on Psalm 16:11.

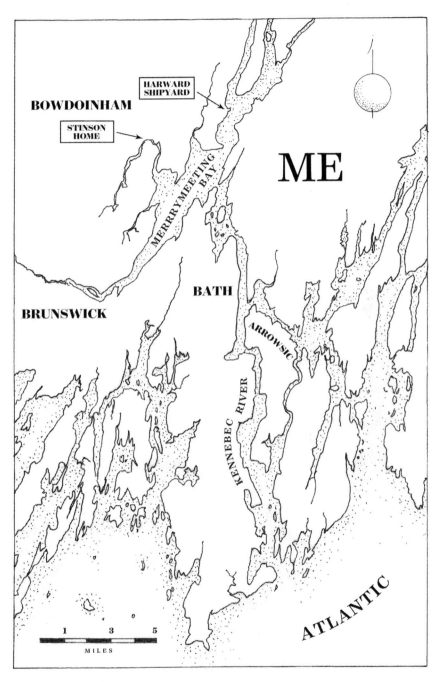

Kennebec River Valley, Maine
(*map by Kenneth A. Schaaf and Jon Schaaf*)

Despite the family's impoverishment, both sons received commendable educations. William attained a law degree and relocated to Jamaica. There he served as an attorney, an assistant magistrate for the Parish of St. Thomas-in-the-East, and briefly, a lieutenant general in the militia. He particularly prospered as the owner of a large coffee plantation. His brother, George, became a teacher, married in Boston, and then settled in Brunswick, Maine, where he built a house on a high hill overlooking the Androscoggin River.

George and his wife, Hannah, had only one son, Thomas. And it was Thomas who made a particular imprint in the Merrymeeting Bay region. Frequently identified as a mariner, he built a large Federal-style home on River Road (later Pork Point Road) in Bowdoinham.[16] Facing east and the Kennebec River, it was a home befitting a sea captain; sheathed in clapboards in the Greek Revival/Italianate style, with Colonial Revival elements, it rested on a foundation of huge granite blocks. Thomas and his wife raised thirteen children in their house on the Kennebec, seven of whom went down to the sea. Three of their sons, William, Captain David, and Captain Otis, lost their lives at sea.

It is no surprise that Thomas stepped into the shipbuilding trade and established a yard on the Kennebec, just a short walk from his home to the water's edge. His first effort in 1786 was a 130-ton schooner he named *Vassalborough*, after the town of that name, located thirty-five miles north of Bowdoinham. When his youngest son, John, joined him in the craft of shipbuilding, the business flourished. Over a fifty-two-year period, the Harward yard completed thirty-two, ocean-going vessels, more than any other yard on the river.

The period from 1848 to 1852 was a particularly active time for the Harward yard. In 1848 the ship *John and Albert* was added

---

[16]   On September 27, 1996, the Harward House was added to the National Register of Historic Places by the US Department of Interior, National Park Service.

Harward house on Merrymeeting Bay (*courtesy Betsy Steen*)

to the fleet. The following year, two ships went into service, the *Rhine* and the *Wabash*, followed immediately by the *Naples* in 1850. In 1851 the keel was laid for the 407-ton ship *Tonquin* and the next year, a 513-ton ship that John would name after his youngest son and youngest daughter: the *William and Mary*. This ship, his tenth, would be 137 feet in length, 28 feet in beam, with a draft of 17 feet. When completed, it would be placed in service as a North Atlantic packet and, hopefully, return a profit for the Harward family.

William Avery Baker, in his *Maritime History of Bath, Maine*, makes the point that few records documenting the construction of the Kennebec fleet are extant. Ship plans, itemized expense accounts, and wage records, all stored in shops, tool sheds, and attics along the river, were eventually lost to fire or neglect. To date, no records on the construction of the *William and Mary* have been found. Baker, however, does give a thorough shopping list of what would have been needed, and John Harward, as the master ship builder, would have been the one to place the orders.

Shipbuilder John Harward in midlife (*collection of Pejepscot Historical Society*)

Harward would start with his extensive lumber order, shipments of oak (white, red, and gray) and pine (pitch and hard), all of which were carefully surveyed prior to use. Soon the yard would echo the cacophony of the trade: saws ripping through timber, planes shaving and shaping, mallets pounding tree nails, rattling chains, and shouts among the workmen. Teams of horses and drivers were engaged to maneuver the cumbersome loads into position. A blacksmith was hired to forge the ship's ironwork, and a founder for casting metals was on site. Anchors and reels of anchor chain were purchased from the ship chandler Zina Hyde & Company in Bath, the city that was designated as the ship's homeport. Barrels of black tar were delivered. A master caulker and his helpers were assigned to close the seams and gaps. Painters were hired to coat the hull and cabins, varnish the deck and brightwork, and gild the name boards. The *William and Mary*'s three masts, each over sixty feet in length, her spars, and bowsprit were prepared. Her sails were cut, sewn, and delivered. Magoun and Clapp of Bath supplied spools of cordage. Four boats were ordered: a long boat, a lifeboat, and two small boats.

Two large hand pumps were purchased and installed in her bulge. Water casks of various sizes were purchased and installed. Cabin furnishings were ordered, delivered, and put in place. The cook's galley for the crew was installed and a deck camboose for immigrant passengers. Tools and supplies for every kind of repair at sea were brought on board. The latest charts were ordered for the eastern and Gulf ports and for entering British harbors. The sixteenth edition, the most recent, of Edmund March Blunt's *American Coast Pilot, containing directions for principal harbors, capes and headlands on the coasts of North and South America, etc.,* was an essential for the captain and his mates. Tallow was ordered to grease the launch ways.

On Wednesday, September 1, 1852, the *William and Mary* was released into the Kennebec River. Neighbor Wilbur F. Decker noted that on the day of a launch, crowds would assemble to witness the event.[17] Once in the water, the ship would be moved to the wharf where, over a period of weeks, riggers would step the masts, raise the spars, and complete the standing rigging. In early November of 1852, just prior to going to sea, the *William and Mary*'s water casks were filled and food provisions stocked, at least enough to make its first port of call.

It is estimated that the cost of constructing and outfitting the *William and Mary* was approximately $23,000.[18] Harward covered his investment by selling shares of the vessel. While he retained ownershp of five-sixteenths of the ship, lesser fractions were purchased by eight men in the Kennebec community.

Insurance was arranged with three Boston providers: Hope Insurance Company, City Fire Insurance Company, and New

---

[17] Decker, "The Ship Yard Next Door," *Decker Papers,* MS 435, 1, Maine Maritime Museum, Bath, ME.

[18] Bowdoinham shipbuilder S. V. Given constructed his 656-ton ship, *Shanghai,* at a cost of $30,000 ($45/ton) during the same period the *William and Mary* was under construction; St. Vincent Given to Capt. John O. Given, Oct. 27, 1852.

John Harward's vessel, *Albert*, rigged here as a bark, was
nearly equal in its dimensions to the ship *William and Mary*
(*courtesy Maine Maritime Museum Library*)

Inland Mutual Marine Insurance Company. Together the three
insurers provided $26,000 worth of coverage.[19] A contract of
affreightment was made with J. C. Nichols in Charleston, South
Carolina. Arrangements were made locally for a pilot and tow
service to navigate down the narrow Kennebec River and to the
sea. The only remaining item was the appointment of the ship's
master and his selection of officers and crew.

[19] *North American and United States Gazette*, Philadelphia (May 19, 1853), 1.

There was the rattling of wheels, a clattering of hoofs, a clashing of iron, a jolting of cotton and hides and casks and timber, an incessant deafening disturbance on the quay, that was the very madness of sound.
Charles Dickens, *The Uncommon Traveler*

Awaiting Departure

Liverpool lies on the northwest-flowing River Mersey, its twenty-plus docks spread along a seven-mile stretch on the northwest bank. In a large, full-color lithograph, constructed and drawn by John Raphael Isaac during the 1850s, we get a bird's-eye view of a city bustling in maritime trade.[20] In this image, the Mersey is crowded with vessels of both sail and steam. Along the river's edge is a long series of cleverly engineered docks or half-tide basins, built to compensate for the Mersey's thirty-foot tidal variation and named after elements of the empire: Victoria, Waterloo, Prince's, George's, Albert's, King's, and Queen's—to name but a few. Separated from the river by bridge gates, which opened only during high tide, dock masters were thus able to maintain all vessels in an upright position, even when the river dropped at low tide.

[20] John Raphael Isaac's low-angle, bird's-eye view was published in Liverpool in 1859. Image size: 58 x 87 cm.

35

Parallel to the docks is a wide, busy strand or connecting road and on the inland side of that, row after row of monumental warehouses, some as high as thirteen stories. Built of fireproof brick and iron, under the firm direction of dock engineer Jesse Hartley, many remain in existence today. Cotton and sugar cane, although primary imports during the 1850s, were but a fraction of what passed through their doorways each week. The *Liverpool Mercury* weekly listed the diverse markets; in the corn exchange alone were wheat, barley, malt, oats, beans, peas, corn, and flour. In the butter exchange were tubs of grease, lard, and, of course, butter. There were markets for salt, rum, tea, coffee, black pepper, linseed oil, jute, dry goods, timber, iron, and so on—imports from exotic cities around the globe and exports from the mills of nearby Manchester and the factories of Birmingham. Radiating like a fanfold from the river's floating landing stage—the city's ferry terminus and central to the rows of docks—are streets that lead up into the interior and more elevated portions of the city. Scattered across Isaac's cityscape are numerous church steeples, smoke stacks, and surprisingly, about a half-dozen windmills very similar to those the Frisians would have known.

But there were elements to the landscape that did not appear in Isaac's bird's-eye view. Nathaniel Hawthorne, when appointed as United States consul to Liverpool in 1853, after being there only a few weeks, wrote, "Liverpool is the most detestable place as a residence that ever my lot was cast—smoky, noisy, dirty, pestilential . . . the streets swarm with beggars by day and by night."[21] Emerson, who visited Liverpool on several occasions, saw the city as "the least agreeable [stop for] the traveller in all England."[22] Melville thought no better and remarked, "Of all

---

[21]   Hawthorne, *The Letters, 1853-1856*, ed. Thomas Woodson et al. (Columbus: Ohio State University Press, 1987), 119.

[22]   Emerson, as quoted in Rupert Christiansen, *The Victorian Visitors: Culture Shock in Nineteenth-Century Britain* (New York: Atlantic Monthly Press, 2000), 91.

seaports in the world, Liverpool, perhaps, most abounds in all the varieties of land-sharks, land-rats, and other vermin which makes the hapless mariner their prey."[23] Dickens, who targeted urban social ills in his novels, was known to roam the docks and alleys of Liverpool to gather material for the *Uncommercial Traveller.*

From their offices at No. 3 Water Street, Liverpool shipping agents John Pilkington and Henry T. Wilson advertised only their Australia-bound service, making no mention of their service to American ports. With the discovery of gold in Australia, Pilkington and Wilson, under the name of White Star Line, chose to concentrate their advertising in that direction. In time the White Star would develop an Atlantic fleet, even placing a ship called the *Titanic* into its service, but that was still decades away. In the 1850s, the fledgling company owned no Atlantic vessels but did lease ships to several East Coast ports. We do not know why Oepke Bonnema, in search of a westbound ship, went to Pilkington and Wilson and passed on so many ships guaranteeing to leave sooner. One would think that with a group of ninety-two, he could have bargained for a good rate. Perhaps he did consider others but found Pilkington and Wilson to have the lowest possible transatlantic fare.

Whatever the case, Bonnema informed the group that he had located a sailing vessel, reported to be new and fast, and that it would be leaving for New Orleans on March 16, two weeks away. From New Orleans, they could take a steamboat up the Mississippi River and then select an area to establish their community. On returning to the brokers and meeting with Messrs. Vos and Brown, Bonnema signed a contract for the group but was told there would be a slight delay. It was the nature of packet ships to accommodate both passengers and freight, but ships would not leave the dock until their holds were completely

---

[23] Melville, as quoted in George Chandler, *Liverpool and Literature* (Liverpool: Rondo Publications, 1974), 66.

filled. Some brokers would favor passenger service and might even post a firm departure date, with notice to freight haulers that shipments would not be accepted dockside after midnight preceding the day of departure. Pilkington and Wilson, however, made no such statement. On March 11, with their arrangements now in place, Broer Haagsma got off a brief letter to inform his family and friends in Friesland. "There will only be 160 passengers on board this well-equipped boat," he wrote, "so we shall not be crowded. Since travel is slow, it may take 6 weeks."[24]

What do you do for two weeks in a foreign city, with its strange language, currency, food, and customs? There were some basic provisions that everyone was expected to purchase for the crossing, such as bedding, cooking utensils, tin plates, and flatware. This could be completed in less than a day, just before sailing. For the unencumbered singles in the group, it became an opportunity to explore the city and to go sightseeing, something that most of them had never done before. Haagsma filled four pages of his journal with the things he and some of the others experienced in Liverpool. There was a visit to a horse race and attendance at a concert; to his ears, English music was "harsh." He visited the city's parks and commented on the statues of Sir Walter Scott and Lord Nelson. One day, Haagsma and his companions rented a horse-drawn coach and visited the city of Aigburth, some three hours distant. On another, he took a ferry across the River Mersey to the old, vacated Brighton fortress. This was the Liverpool of a twenty-two-year-old visitor.

We can be certain that for the married couples in the group, those with several children to care for, like the Kooistra, Tjalsma,

---

[24] Haagsma, letter reprinted in *The Roorda Family History*, 28. An analysis of the maritime record shows that forty-two sailing vessels left Liverpool for New Orleans during the spring of 1853. Only six made the journey in six weeks; eight took seven weeks; fourteen took eight weeks; and another thirteen took nine or more weeks to arrive.

Tuininga, and Westerhuis families, Liverpool was not a vacation. It is doubtful if in their years of work they had ever taken a vacation. It would have been uncomfortable for them to wait day after day, watching others go about their work while they were idle. For the women, caring for children in a rooming house environment had to be extremely difficult. Roorda comments that although the food there was good, the entire group had to eat in one room and at two tables. He makes no mention of its bathroom facilities.

Wherever they walked, with their Frisian dress, they attracted attention. The city was such a contrast to their home villages that some were hesitant to even cross the street, lest a coach or wagon run them down. The soot from thousands of coal furnaces coated the city gray; in fact, publisher George H. Putnam wrote in his memoirs, "In Liverpool, it usually rains black."[25] Poet journalist William Cullen Bryant remarked that the public buildings "appear almost of a sooty hue."[26] The weather during their stay was gloomy—cold days of cloud cover, periods of snow, sleet, hail, and rain. Seldom did the sun make an appearance. From Roorda's point of view, "Our stay in Liverpool wasn't pleasant."[27]

For Feye and Siementje Schaafsma, the difficulty of getting to Liverpool, as well as the long delay in leaving, prompted them to reconsider their decision to go to America.[28] Their change in plans, however, was not without some difficulty. Once again they crossed England by rail, this time to the northeastern port of

---

[25] Putnam, *Memories of My Youth, 1844-1865* (New York: G. P. Putnam, 1914), 30.

[26] Bryant, *Letters of a Traveler; or Notes of Things Seen in Europe and America*, 2nd ed. (New York: G. P. Putnam, 1850), 146.

[27] *Roorda Family History*, 22.

[28] Haagsma, *Lotgevallen*, 9, does not mention Feye Schaafsma by name but rather "a man and his wife and four children." It is Herman De Jager who references a "Veijer Schaafsma, his wife, and four children" returning to their hometown of Harlingen in a letter published on July 13, 1853, in *De Hollander*, Holland, MI. His letter was then republished on August 11, 1853, in Friesland, where it appeared as Frije Schaafsma.

Great Grimsby. Here they boarded the paddle-wheel ship, *Jupiter*, which, rather than taking them back to Harlingen, made a direct course for Hamburg, Germany—double the distance Harlingen would have been. And upon entering the River Elbe, they found the waterway still blocked by winter's ice. It would take several days for the river to open and permit them the final leg on their homeward journey.

In the written accounts that we have from the group, no one mentions what was done for Sunday worship on the three Sundays they were in Liverpool. In Friesland, most people would not miss a service. Yet in a strange city and with a language few could follow, xenophobia may have kept them outside of any Liverpool church. Or perhaps not; there were almost 150 congregations in the city, 58 being the state Church of England, beside several Methodist, Presbyterian, and Baptist churches. Haagsma does remark how absolutely quiet the city became on Sunday and how all commerce ceased.

As March 16 approached, the group learned that the ship was not fully loaded and that their departure would be delayed yet another eight days. There were no cranes or steam derricks in the 1850s; every item placed in the ship's hold had to be lowered by block and tackle from a spencer gaff or carried on the backs of dock stevedores. Once below, the head stevedore and ship's mate would direct its precise placement for optimal ship balance.

He never used to swear, though, at his men, they said, but
somehow he got an inordinate quantity of cruel,
unmitigated hard work out of them.
Herman Melville, *Moby Dick*

The Captain

Having met Oepke Bonnema, the organizer of our Frisian band of travelers; Broer Haagsma, the primary chronicler of their journey; and John Harward, the builder of the ship that would convey them across the Atlantic, we now meet the ship's captain. Because of his prominent position in our story, it is worth our investigation into his background to see what influenced him to go to sea and perhaps something of what had shaped his character.

Bowdoinham, Maine, hometown to shipbuilder John Harward, could boast to have twenty-six men declare their occupation as sea captain in 1850. Another sixty-two men claimed their livelihood as seaman or sailor. But it is unlikely that Harward had a long list of candidates for the position of master of the *William and Mary*. As the ship's owner, Harward had much at stake. He would appoint someone he knew and trusted and in whom he had complete confidence to handle his ship well in whatever conditions may occur. His choice as captain for his tenth vessel was thirty-two-year-old Timothy R. Stinson.

On August 4, 1718, another ship named *William and Mary*, of no connection to John Harward's later ship of the same name, entered Boston harbor. It would be the first of six vessels to fulfill the dream of Puritan minister Cotton Mather, the relocation of persecuted Protestant families from Ireland to locations throughout New England. Mather, a prolific author, with some 450 books and pamphlets on topics of spiritual, social, political, and scientific concerns, had great sympathy for fellow Protestants in Ireland.[29]

The last ship to arrive, the *Maccallum*, from Londonderry, was of particular interest to Mather. On September 1, he wrote in his journal,

> This day a ship arrived from Ireland wth 20 odd familys; they were first bound for N. London [Connecticut] but having a long Passage, the M^{rs}. [Master] perswaded y^{m} to putt in here, so the poor Creatures are left in ye Lurch.[30]

Included in the list of "poor Creatures" were thirty-nine-year-old James Stinson, his wife, Jane, and their six children, ranging in age from twelve down to one. As Presbyterians, they were in the minority in Tyrone County, Ireland. After one week, the *Maccallum* resumed its voyage, not south to New London but instead north to the mouth of the Kennebec River.

---

[29]   Mather wrote in his diary on August 7, 1718, "But what shall be done for the great numbers of People that are transporting themselves hither from the North of Ireland? Much may be done for the Kingdome [*sic*] of God in these Parts of the World by this transportation." *Diary of Cotton Mather* (New York: F. Unger Publishing Co., 1957), 2:549.

[30]   Mather, in Charles Knowles Bolton, *Scotch Irish Pioneers in Ulster and America* (Boston: Bacon and Brown, 1910), 142.

From this point, the Stinsons and their companions moved inland, eventually purchasing property in the newly established settlement of Pejepscot Company on the Androscoggin River, the present location of Brunswick, Maine. Homes were built and property cleared; the location showed much promise. But during the summer of 1722, the Abenaki tribe, under the influence of the French, attacked the settlement and burned the village to the ground. Were it not for the refuge they found inside the walls of Fort George, the Stinsons and their neighbors would all have lost their lives. James and his sons, William and James Jr., spent the next three years battling the Abenaki.

At the war's conclusion, the Stinsons sold their home site and moved southeast to Arrowsic Island. Although the land was rocky and hardly ideal for farming, the wide and deep slack water location on the river was highly valued. As the Stinson children grew and married, the Stinson name became well known through the Kennebec region.

William, the oldest son, and his wife, Elizabeth, raised eight children: three sons and five daughters. Their oldest son, John, continued in his father's footsteps farming on rocky Arrowsic. There he and his wife raised a large family, eleven children, most with Bible names. John was witness to the transition from obligation to the Crown to allegiance to the newly established Unites States of America. His younger brother, James, however, was a Loyalist and fled northward to New Brunswick. There he remained, separated from his family for the rest of his life.

Twenty-five years after the Revolutionary War, the Kennebec River Valley found itself once again threatened by war. In December of 1807, the US Congress, in response to the British impressment of American sailors, passed the Embargo Act. The law restricted American ships from leaving port and had an immediate crippling effect on the regional economy. Support for another war with England was difficult to muster, especially in backcountry areas. In 1808 John Stinson's youngest son, David, his wife, Mehitable, and their infant daughter, left Arrowsic Island and ascended the Kennebec River nearly one hundred miles. Here they settled first in the wilderness village of Embden and later in nearby Concord. While we are not entirely certain as to what compelled the young father to move so deeply into the woods, we know that at the conclusion of the War of 1812, David and his family moved downriver and settled in Bowdoinham.

It was in Bowdoinham on June 14, 1820, where Mehitable gave birth to her seventh child, Timothy Reirdan. Growing up on the west bank of the Cathance River had a significant pull on the boy. He knew the Cathance flowed northward into Merrymeeting Bay, that the bay fed into the Kennebec River, that the Kennebec emptied into the North Atlantic, and on the North Atlantic, one could go in whichever direction one chose to set their sail. Bath historian, William Avery Baker, leads us to believe that for over a century of Stinson men, an association with the sea was more the rule than the exception, providing a partial list of twelve Stinsons who went to sea.[31] A Stinson genealogy prepared by Fred and Ethelyn Pinkham also shows a significant number of men going to sea and, unsurprisingly, a high incidence of drowning.[32] While some Stinson men were content to remain at home and till the soil, Timothy was not one of them.

Timothy Stinson's early career as a seaman is obscure. Most boys who went to sea began when they were about fifteen, and we may assume this to be the case with Timothy as well. Regretfully, records of his early assignments are not to be found. We know a Stinson was captain of the riverboat *Flushing*, with service between Bath and Augusta, but it is not clear if Timothy was the master in question. In July of 1848, a brief marriage announcement

---

[31] Baker, *A Maritime History of Bath, Maine and the Kennebec River Region* (Bath, ME: Marine Research Society of Bath, 1973).
[32] Pinkham, *Stinson Genealogy* (Bath, ME: F. D. Pinkham, 1975).

appeared in the *Maine Cultivator and Hallowell Gazette*: "In Bowdoinham, by Rev. C. C. Cone, Capt. Timothy R. Stinson, to Miss Thankful Purrington [*sic*]." Thankful was twenty-nine, the daughter of Bowdoinham farmer Nathaniel Purington and his late wife, Fanny, and a member of the Methodist-Episcopal Church in Bowdoinham, where they were married. Although the Stinsons were traditionally Presbyterian in confession, we are given no information as to Timothy's faith, convictions, or values in his early life.

We see the couple again in the 1850 federal census for Bowdoinham. In this enrollment, Stinson is twenty-nine, a "mariner" by occupation, with Thankful, now thirty-one, and son, Charles Nathaniel, age one. They are believed to be living on Pleasant Street, a short lane of ten homes on a hill, at the top of which was the village school and at the bottom, a shipyard on the Cathance River. Thankful's father and stepmother lived on Pleasant Street, and it is possible that the couple had a house on their property. Two years later, Stinson and his wife purchased a small house, a barn, and a lot in Bowdoinham.

Haagsma notes in his journal that Stinson was "a man with a fine seaman's appearance."[33] Beyond this somewhat ambiguous description, we have no idea if he was tall or short, slim or stout, bearded or beshaven. But once at sea and on his quarterdeck, we will see his character more defined.

Stinson's first task as master was that of raising a crew. Like Harward, he looked to those around him, men he already knew. Samuel Welsh of Boston was signed on as first mate, and Loami Ross of nearby Litchfield, Maine, was made second mate. Stephen W. Purington, Nicholas Card, John Best, Edward Weeks, Isaac Ridley, and Lemuel Prebble, all Kennebec men, signed ship's articles as seamen. Henry Moore, of New York; Samuel Harris, of

[33] Haagsma, *Lotgevallen*, 9.

Providence, Rhode Island; William Ward, of Philadelphia; and Thomas Allen, of Baltimore, Maryland, were also added to the crew for her maiden voyage.

The *William and Mary* was ready for service in the fall of 1852, with Charleston, South Carolina, designated as her first port. Since an empty ship sails sluggishly and earns no money, before leaving Bath on November 15, the *William and Mary* was loaded with hay and containers of smoked herring. At last she slipped out of the mouth of the Kennebec and into the broad Atlantic on her southbound voyage.

They that go down to the sea in ships, that do business in great
waters, these see the works of the Lord and his wonders in the deep.
Psalm 107:23-24

To Charleston and Liverpool

Edmund Blunt's *American Coast Pilot* is as authoritative as
it is thick. Its full title is sixty words in length; between its hard
covers is a full two inches, "containing directions for the principal
harbors, capes, and headlands on the coasts of North and South
America." Blunt notes five channels into Charleston harbor, but
only one is deep enough for vessels with a draft like that of the
William and Mary. His directions for the ship channel are explained:

> Standing in for the Bar, having the Beacon to appear, a
> handspike's length to the N. of the lighthouse, and you will
> soon make the Bar Buoy lying in 3 fathoms water, and which
> may be passed on either side. Nearly in the same range lie
> two other Buoys; the first on the south point of the North
> Breaker, and the other on the inner south point (or S.W.

Point) of the same breaker. These buoys are to be left on the starboard hand, at the distance of a ship's length.[34]

Fortunately, Blunt includes a trifold chart showing the channel, its surrounding water depths, and markers.

On December 1, fifteen days after leaving Bath, the *William and Mary* entered Charleston's main shipping channel and, with a pilot, slipped between Fort Moultrie to starboard, then Fort Sumter to port, around Fort Pinckney, and onto the Cooper River. Shortly after, she tied up at the Boyce and Company wharf at the foot of Elliot Street. To the surprise of the crew, the 398-ton *Wabash* was tied at the very next pier. The *Wabash* had been built three years earlier by John Harward but was now owned by David C. Magoun and also in Atlantic service. Recently arrived from New York, she would be loaded and sent off to Liverpool. Port Charleston in the 1850s was a major trade center; in the harbor that day were twenty-six ships, eighteen barks, and nineteen brigs, besides schooners and smaller vessels. Three other ships tied up at the Boyce Wharf were being loaded with cargoes destined for Liverpool. Shipping agent/broker, James C. Nichols, was responsibile for unloading and selling her cargo. Nichols, thirty-six, was a native of Maine and may have known Harward and Stinson from previous transactions. Despite his Yankee roots, he took a bride from Beauford, South Carolina, fathered a family of five in Charleston city, adopted the southern custom of slave ownership, and built a brisk business on the waterfront. He immediately placed an advertisement in the *Charleston Daily Courier* for "100 boxes of fine English smoked herring, per ship *William & Mary*, and a small lot of Eastern hay." As soon as the hold was emptied, Nichols arranged her next haul, 1884 bales of Upland cotton destined for British manufacturers. There would be no eastbound passengers.

[34]   Blunt, *American Coast Pilot*, 16th ed. (New York: Blunt, 1850), 240.

> **H**AY.—For sale, 800 bales of prime Eastern HAY,
> just received per ship Ontario, from Wiscasset, Me.
> **ALSO,**
> 100 boxes of fine English SMOKED HERRINGS, per
> ship William and Mary.
> **AND,**
> A small lot of Eastern HAY, in lots to suit purchasers,
> by   JAMES O. NICHOLS, Agent,
> D 6   Boyce & Co.'s wharf.
>
> **S**ALT.—500 Sacks Liverpool SALT. For sale by
> JACOB BROCK, 2 Boyce & Co's wharf.
> D 6

Advertisement for the cargo of the
*William and Mary (newspaper collection
of the Library of Congress)*

With the approach of Christmas, Charleston turned its attention to celebrations. The city's two newspapers, the *Charleston Mercury* and the *Charleston Daily Courier*, carried advertisements of toys and other gifts.[35] Importer J. Spear advertised "fine watches, sterling silver-ware, and fancy goods." John Marion posted:

> A fine assortment of fancy boxes, toys of every style and variety, fancy baskets [*fancy* was the word of the day], French confectioneries, ornaments, JuJube paste drops, candied fruit, etc. Preserved fruits in bottles and tin canisters, strawberries and raspberries in their own juices, and a large assortment of fire works.

The last item must have been to celebrate the New Year. Charleston's book dealers, with access to domestic and international publishers, offered a large selection of folios; floral books; books on birds, fruit, music, poetry, British literature, and antiquities; and books by contemporary authors. But the fastest selling book of 1852, Harriet Beecher Stowe's *Uncle Tom's Cabin*, was not to be found in this city. What was advertised, however,

---

[35] Unlike merchants of today, ads for Christmas gifts were not placed in Charleston newspapers until just five days before Christmas and took up less than one half of one page.

was *Aunt Phillis's Cabin,* by Mary H. Eastman, a firm advocate of slavery from Virginia.[36] And then there was gun dealer Charles Dunn's advertisement of his "anti-abolitionist guns and rifles."

On December 22, the schooner *Time,* of Nassau, the Bahamas, tied up at the Atlantic Wharf next to the *William and Mary,* bringing two passengers and a cargo of fresh fruit for the Christmas tables of Charleston. For Stinson and his crew, although far from home at Christmas, the days spent in this southern port had to be a pleasant break. But immediately after the New Year holiday, Stinson was ready to leave port for his first transatlantic voyage as master. The *Charleston Mercury* reported on January 4, 1853, that the *William and Mary* was cleared to sail. As she passed Fort Sumter, no one on board had any thought that in just eight years, this would be where the first shot of the Civil War would be fired and begin a four-year war, in which some six hundred thousand people would lose their lives.

Although many captains avoided winter crossings and the treacherous North Atlantic storms, Captain Stinson, or perhaps John Harward, the ship's primary owner, chose otherwise. Fortunately, the *William and Mary* had an uneventful crossing, albeit rather slow. On January 10, she was seen by another ship at latitude 33° N, longitude 73° W—384 statute miles from her starting point. On February 4, near latitude 50° N and longitude 11° W—some 415 miles southwest of Liverpool—Stinson recorded in the log passing a ship, name unknown, all three of her masts

---

[36] *Charleston Daily Courier* (December 22, 1852), 4. It was Eastman's view that abolition was "born in fanaticism [and] nurtured in violence and disorder." With Stowe's release of *Uncle Tom's Cabin* in early 1852, Eastman quickly responded with her account of Aunt Phillis and Uncle Bacchus, a slave couple living on the plantation of their benevolent master in Virginia, *Aunt Phillis's Cabin, or Southern Life as it is* (Philadelphia: Lippincott, Grambo, 1852), 24.

having been cut and no sign of her master or crew. Soon thereafter, the *William and Mary* encountered contrary winds from the SE and NE and could make little eastbound progress through St. George's Channel between Ireland and Wales. Finally on February 21, the *William and Mary* reached the lightship *Formby* and awaited a pilot to take them through the Crosby Channel and up the River Mersey. Several days later, it was reported in the *Liverpool Mercury* that the vessel had entered Liverpool harbor and was ready for unloading. Pilkington and Wilson of the White Star Line were listed as the ship's agents.

During the eighteenth century, Liverpool merchants turned a strong profit on the African slave trade. Now in the mid-nineteenth century, with slave marketing in Great Britain and her colonies a thing of the past, raw cotton was the primary source of the city's income—ironically, still at the expense of America's slave labor force.

The *William and Mary*'s 1884 bales, once unloaded, would be fed to the spinning and weaving mills of nearby Lancashire and Manchester and made into dry goods. In time, a portion of that craft would be placed on ships returning to the United States.

PART II

Tossed About at Sea

The fair breeze blew, the white foam flew, the furrow followed free.
Samuel Colleridge

Week One: To Sea

Monday, March 21: After a full three-week delay, the day for boarding the ship had finally come. As the Frisians walked from their boarding house down to the quay, drays were loaded with their trunks, bags, and bedding and delivered to the dock. There she lay; the three-mast sail ship *William and Mary*. People scrambled about, trying to identify luggage and carry it into the steerage hold. To add to the clamor on deck, stevedores continued to lower cargo into the ship's hold: heavy railroad iron, bulky crates or barrels of crockery, and cartons of dry goods—a great improvement, the Frisians thought, over the cargo of their previous voyage.[1] But then a new reality presented itself; in

---

[1] Unknown in port, but once at sea, it would become apparent that the *William and Mary* was dangerously overloaded. A half century would pass before the British Unseaworthy Ships Bill would be amended to require all foreign-owned vessels trading in England to have their hulls marked with a Plimsoll line or International Load Line to prevent overloading.

55

addition to their own number, there were other nationalities on board and more of them—mostly Irish, some English, a few Scots, a dozen Germans, and one Frenchman—a total of 208 passengers, plus a crew of sixteen. The Frisians, of course, had hoped to have their own accommodations but soon found that they would need to share with the Germans. Roorda points out that there was only a thin wall between them and the Irish. Bunk beds were arranged in two rows along the sides of the chamber, and an assortment of trunks and suitcases were arranged in the center to serve as tables and seats.

First mate Welsh called up the head of each family and made the first food distribution. This included just enough for each family for one week, and it was up to them to see that it lasted. Someone with a large appetite would be a threat to the rest of the family over the course of a week. In addition to the weekly distribution, there would be a daily water allotment.

The following day, now officially spring, presented a weather mix: clear in the morning, but snow, sleet, and rain in the evening. The ship did not move but remained in dock all day. For many it offered an opportunity to explore the ship. On deck were several cabins reserved for the captain and his officers or the ship's engineers, plus storage of sails and deck supplies. All others were housed in steerage below.

It was on Wednesday, a clear-weather day, when the ship finally moved, although not very far. At high tide, the vessel was towed by a steam tug over to the inspection dock to check compliance with the Passengers Act of 1852. Here a doctor boarded, examined each passenger, and certified all were clear for passage. At the same time, a government safety inspector went over the ship, checking water, food supplies, below deck conditions, and the like. It was then noted that the long boat stowed over the cabin was not in usable condition; it lacked caulking and, if placed in the sea, would be of little use. Despite this deficiency,

Steam-powered towboats were employed in moving ships
up and down the River Mersey. This woodcut by F. Piercy
shows a ship being taken to sea during the winter of 1853.
In the background are Fort Perch Rock and the New Brighton
Lighthouse (*courtesy Library of Congress*)

and likely with the captain's word that this would be cared for
once underway, the ship was released for passage.

Finally on their fourth day on board the ship, under cloudy
skies, a steam tug arrived to tow the *William and Mary* up the River
Mersey and out the Crosby Channel. The mouth of the Mersey
is narrow with sand bars on either side; between the outflowing
current and the periodic incoming tide, maneuvering the channel
can be dangerous and requires a towboat and a seasoned pilot.
Once reaching the lightship *Crosby*, identified by a single mast,
light, and red ball, the channel is in a direct line to the lightship
Formby, with its twin lights and masts and single, high red ball.

Beside the *William and Mary*, the sail ship *Northampton* also
left that day for New Orleans. Both had a fresh breeze from the
east to carry them along the chalk cliffs of England and out into
the Irish Sea and south. Haagsma made special note in his journal
of the grand sunset over the sea.

Good Friday, March 25: As the winds diminished, the ship slowed and began rocking uncomfortably. Many on board became seasick once again and took to their bunks. That night, the Frisians were startled out of their sleep by eight of the young men in the group. At three o'clock in the morning, they woke up everyone by yelling, "Lord, we perish! To the life rafts! To the life rafts!"[2] The names of the jokesters were not mentioned. Had anyone taken the alarm seriously, it would have been discovered that not even half of the souls on board could be accommodated in the ship's four boats, one of which was still unsealed.

On Saturday, their sixth day on board, they lost sight of the coasts of England and Ireland and entered the broad Atlantic. This was also the day that one of the Irish women gave birth to a baby girl. A Frisian, Dr. van der Veer, and a midwife assisted.[3]

[2]   Haagsma, *Lotgevallen*, 10.
[3]   Although noted as a doctor by Haagsma, there is no evidence that Johannes Koenraads van der Veer, married and the father of eight, had earned a medical degree. His vocation changed as frequently as his Leeuwarden address—beard shaver, saddlemaker, veterinarian, lab assistant, and instrument maker. While attending to the Irish passenger with her delivery, he is never mentioned in connection with any of the subsequent medical needs on board. In fact, Haagsma never mentions him again.

They reel to and fro, and stagger like a
drunken man, and are at their wits' end.

Psalm 107:27

Week Two: Early Losses

Walking on the deck early Easter morning was an exhilarating experience for Haagsma. People began greeting each other, the Frisians, the English, the Germans, the Irish, and the Scots. He wrote in his journal: "The immeasurable expanse of water appeared calm and smooth and [how] it seemed nature was making every effort to add to the luster of the Lord's resurrection."[4] But by evening, the wind increased, and the weather turned stormy.

By Monday morning, the waves had become mountainous and brought fear to the nonseamen. Crew member Stephen W. Purington, a relative of the captain's wife, was of the opinion that "The ship being loaded very deep with iron, and all that being in the lowest hold, caused her to roll very badly; indeed, sometimes it was impossible to get about the deck with safety."[5] Tiete Kooistra,

[4] Haagsma, *Lotgevallen*, 11.
[5] Purington, statement published in the *Weekly Herald*, New York (May 21, 1853), 1.

eleven at the time of the voyage, recalled seventy-one years later, "Once the ship would be atop a high wave, and one could look out across the sea, and then the next minute, the tiny craft would be almost buried between two rollers, which splashed on the decks of the ship. Most of the time, passengers walked in two or three inches of water."[6]

Both Haagsma and Roorda recorded the next day that conditions below deck had turned considerably worse. Ships are said to move with six degrees of freedom. One movement is a *rolling* action, the side-to-side rocking motion that makes walking in a straight line from bow to stern sometimes impossible. Another is *pitching*, the alternate rising and falling of the bow and stern. Yet another is *heaving*, the vertical up and down motion on sea swells. There is also *surging*, the forward (or backward) movement of the ship that hopefully moves the ship from one port to the next. *Swaying* is a sliding motion, in which wind or wave action moves the ship sideways. And finally, there is the *yawing* movement, the turning of a ship to the right or left. This constant motion for those unaccustomed to the sea left many sick in their bunks, some losing all hope of survival. But cholera or ship fever was also apparently on board. Twenty-six-year-old Dirk Hofman, one of the Frisian singles, was delirious with fever and repeatedly cried out for his mother's help. Cabin mates shook their heads, some in compassion, others irritated by his continuous moaning.

On Wednesday, March 30, the Dutch passengers awoke to the mournful sobbing of Johannes and Trijntje Tuininga and their children. For days they had watched their youngest child, Gerrit, grow listless and weak. Sometime during the early morning hours, the three-year-old drew his final breath and lay still. The reality was shocking to all. Trijntje, by age thirty-six

---

[6]   "82 year old man recalls wreck of ship 70 years ago," *La Crosse Tribune and Leader-Press*, October 5, 1924.

had given birth to five children, all of whom had been healthy. Now the crew stood before her to remove the child's body. The parents protested, believing they could hold the child's body for a land burial, but the captain knew that was not possible. Haagsma notes the "crying of both parents, brothers, and sisters was too heart-rending for my pen to describe."[7]

There was no private place for the Tuiningas to grieve; the common cabin was open to those sympathetic to their loss and suffering and to those embarrassed by their sobs. To add to their grief, they now saw their ten-year-old daughter, Antje, showing the same symptoms experienced by her brother a few days earlier. By the end of the day, the body of Dirk Hofman was also borne away for burial between the waves.[8]

If the sea was responsible for the two deaths on the *William and Mary*, it showed neither remorse nor appeasement. The next morning, a new storm rolled in. By afternoon, it changed direction but soon increased to hurricane force. Conditions on deck were so hazardous that all immigrants were forced to remain below out of the weather but in air now foul and stale. Preparing food for those who still had an appetite was difficult; those without an appetite grew weaker by the day.

On Saturday, April 2, Hendrik Spanjer, thirty-five, succumbed to the fever. The Frisian group was now down to eighty-three.

---

[7]   Haagsma, *Lotgevallen*, 12.

[8]   None of those who kept a record of the crossing make mention of Captain Stinson taking responsibility for a ceremonial committal of the deceased, although such a duty would have been expected. According to Henry Howe, author of *Life and death on the ocean*, the usual wording would have been, "Forasmuch as it hath pleased Almighty God, in His wise providence, to take out of this world the soul of our deceased brother [or sister], we therefore commit his body to the deep, to be turned into corruption, looking for the resurrection of the body, when the sea shall give up her dead" (Cincinnati: H. Howe, 1855), 376.

You hear every kind of odd noise in the ship—creaking,
straining, crunching, scraping, pounding, whistling,
blowing... each of which to your unpracticed ear
is significant of some impending catastrophe.
Harriet Beecher Stowe, *Sunny Memories of Foreign Lands*

Week Three: Growing Fear

Sunday, April 3: As the *William and Mary* sluggishly sailed westward across the Atlantic, the coal-burning steamship *Canada* moved steadily and quickly eastward. Having left Boston on Friday, April 1, the *Canada* was expected to arrive in Liverpool ten days later. Included on her passenger list were members of the Stowe family of Brunswick, Maine. Mr. Calvin Stowe was professor of biblical literature, first at Lane Seminary (Ohio), then at Andover Theological Seminary (Massachusetts), and finally at Bowdoin College, his alma mater. His wife, Harriet, a woman of determined character, was incensed at the passage of the 1850 Fugitive Slave Law, so much so that she began a writing effort that would soon change the conscience of America. Written just a few miles from where the *William and Mary* was constructed, her book was published the same year the ship was launched. In ten months' time, three hundred thousand copies of *Uncle Tom's Cabin* were sold in the United States alone. Waiting for her at the Liverpool dock would be a large crowd of enthusiastic supporters, although such support was far from universal. Queen Victoria refused to see her and was critical of anyone who would. The press, both at home and abroad, was often vicious in attacking her writing and her character. From Rome Pope Pius IX found *Uncle Tom's Cabin* so incendiary that he issued a papal ban on its reading.

On board the *William and Mary*, sickness continued to take its toll, especially on the children. On Sunday the Tuininga's lost their second child, ten-year-old Antje. Two days later, the Graafsma family suffered the loss of their one-year-old daughter, Trijntje, and after another two days, the Sikkemas saw their four-month-old Sikke taken from them. Although childhood mortality was common in Friesland, death on board ship seemed so much more cruel, and it certainly brought regret and guilt to the parents for their decision to leave home. If they had been content to stay, as bad as things were, their children would be alive.

Fear increased throughout the ship; no one was secure in his or her health. With the death of the Sikkema baby, Haagsma inquired as to the position of the ship, in effect asking, "We've been at sea for two full weeks. We've lost six of our number. How much longer will it take to reach New Orleans? Where are we now?" The response: latitude 45° N, longitude 20° W. "From this," he stated, "you can infer that our trip was not too prosperous."[9] Of the 5,000 miles between Liverpool and New Orleans, they had come only 958 miles. At this rate, it could take another eight weeks, longer if the winds failed or turned contrary. Haagsma's quick mind had to calculate how long their food and water supply might last and how many more losses they were likely to see before they arrived.

[9]   Haagsma, *Lotgevallen*, 13.

The waves of the ocean, whose hoarse and hollow voices are ever speaking in the sailor's ear—not only showing him, but telling him in tones louder and more distinct than all homilies ever delivered, the Lord God Omnipotent reigneth.
John Codman, *Sailors' Life and Sailors' Yarns*

Week Four: Rising Tensions

If those on the *William and Mary* felt their voyage was taking longer than it should, those on board the US Steam Frigate *Mississippi* must have felt that even more so. Put to sea on November 24, 1852, with stops in Madeira, St. Helena, Cape Town, Mauritius, and Point de Galle, Ceylon, the *Mississippi* had been away for four and a half months—with still another two-and-a-half months to go before reaching her destination. She was built in 1841, and in her twelve years of naval service, she had logged the equivalent of eleven trips around the globe. Her current mission, under the command of fifty-nine-year-old commodore Matthew Calbraith Perry and with a letter from former president Fillmore, was to sail to the port of Yedo (Tokyo) and persuade the Japanese to abandon their long-standing position of isolationism and enter into a trade agreement with the United States.

By the second week of April in 1853, having just spent a week of ship maintenance in Hong Kong, she was once again under steam for the port of Macao to take on a supply of coal. The *Mississippi* was a hermaphrodite vessel: steam powered by way of her coal-burning furnaces and boilers and also fully rigged for sailing. To save on coal—she had burned an average of twenty-six tons per day on her transatlantic crossing—her paddle wheels could be disassembled, her stack lowered, and her spars hung with canvas if the winds were blowing.

Robert Danby, first assistant engineer, faithfully kept a journal of voyage details. Included were the daily miles covered between ports, the course taken, the amount of coal consumed, weather data, and information on activities on board. Written on light blue paper, each entry appears in a straight line and in perfect script. One wonders how Danby maintained such a controlled hand under the ship's constant motion.[10]

As the officer responsible for the success of the mission, Perry ran a tight ship. Referred to as "Old Matt" by some of the sailors, he had his rules. Sunday worship was observed on his flagship—with prayers, Psalms, and sermons. His insistence on the crew's consumption of fresh fruit proved to be a valid prevention for scurvy and, although his burning of smudge pots was a bizarre antidote for yellow fever, his record of maintaining a healthy ship in the otherwise unhealthy regions of the Eastern Hemisphere cannot be argued.

On board the *William and Mary* in the Western Hemisphere, Captain Stinson also ran a tight ship, although with very different results. Almost half the age of Perry, Stinson did not have the benefit of the commodore's years of leadership experience. The

---

[10]   *Robert Danby Journal, 1852-1855*, in the manuscript collection of the Library of Congress, Washington, DC.

passengers noted his concern when one of their number fell ill, but his recommendations for cures came from a book of remedies that could hardly be called medicine. When someone suffered from a fever, for example, his instruction was to eat bacon.

Stinson had his standards. Presbyterian in background, he prohibited the use of alcohol on the ship. And while he did not establish a worship service on Sundays, he did relax crew work routines on the day of rest. But in matters of discipline, like many commanders of his day, he was rigid in authority. When the ship's cook was found taking some of the captain's meat to some of the passengers, he was severely beaten, and his position was given to another.

On Monday, April 11, it was noted that the ship was near the Azores. The following day, those on deck counted fourteen whales playing in the ocean. Stinson announced that the ship had covered nine hundred miles in five days, spreading hope and speculation that New Orleans would be reached soon. But it could not be soon enough; on that day, the Kooistras lost their two-and-a-half-year-old daughter, Bauke.

Tensions ran high that week, and a fight broke out between the crew and some of the Frisian passengers. The agreement made in Liverpool between Stinson and Bonnema was that the passengers would take responsibility for half of their provisions with the other half coming from the ship's supplies. But some of the Frisians noticed crew members were helping themselves to the Frisian allotment. On Wednesday, April 13, during the weekly distribution of food, one of the Frisians accused First Mate Welsh of thievery. Welsh responded with a punch, bringing in another Dutchman, this one with a knife. Other sailors joined in defense of the mate. Women began screaming, finally drawing Stinson's intervention. Haagsma noted that in the melee, when attention was on the combatants, several young Dutchmen took advantage to raid the sugar barrel. We are not privy to how Stinson settled the matter with the Frisian passengers, but we can assume that tension between the two groups continued for the duration of the voyage.

Week Five: The Unbroken Horizon

When the Cunard transatlantic ship *QEII* left Le Havre, France, on May 2, 1969, for her maiden voyage, she carried 1,600 paying passengers and a crew of 963. Four days, sixteen hours, and thirty-five minutes later, she reached *Ambrose* lightship, at the entrance to New York. During that remarkably brief time, her guests dined sumptuously in her five restaurants and two cafes; they swam in her four pools, shopped in her duty-free promenade, partied in her night club and bars, gambled in her casino, took in the art gallery, viewed movies in her 491-seat theater, exercised in her gymnasium, treated themselves in the beauty salon, worshipped in the synagogue on the Sabbath or at the interdenominational service in the theater on Sunday, avoided the ship's thirteen-bed hospital and, if they actually had time to read, visited the ship's library. Leather upholstery, marble floors, walls hung with commissioned oil paintings and tapestries, music from her bands and grand piano, the finest services that might be provided on land were all brought to the ship for an extravagant experience at sea.

One hundred and sixteen years earlier, the *William and Mary*, on its maiden westbound voyage, could offer few options for its 208 paying passengers. Its sixteen crew members were there to sail the ship, not serve its passengers. If the weather was good, passengers could walk the length of her 125-foot deck. Since most of the Frisians spoke little English, opportunities to converse with the other passengers were limited. Men might stand at the rail for hours, scanning the empty horizon—flat for 360°—searching for another sail, an ice flow, some creature from the deep breaking the surface, anything to break the monotony. In writing of his voyage to the Bahamas several years later, Charles Ives commented, "One cannot understand the phrase 'a wilderness of water' until he actually sails day after day with nothing in view but the deep below and the deep above."[11] "Melancholia oceana," is what J. H. Ingraham called it, "the same unbroken horizon, forming the periphery of a circle, of which his vessel seems to be immovable, the everlasting center."[12]

Meals on board the *William and Mary* were not served by white-jacketed wait staff in a finely appointed dining room but were prepared either by oneself or the designated passenger cook at a common on-deck stove or camboose and then eaten wherever one might find a place to sit. Lying in the dark steerage berth was another option, but considering the odor of unwashed bodies, the stench of sickness and death, and the smell of tobacco, urine, and bilge water coming up from below, this was the choice of very few.

[11]   Ives, *The Isles of Summer; or Nassau and the Bahamas* (New Haven, CN: Ives, 1880), 29.
[12]   Ingraham, *The South-West* (New York: Harper & Bros., 1835), 1:15.

For most, week five at sea passed slowly and uneventfully. Members of the Tjalsma family and the Kooistra family would have been happy with an uneventful week. On Monday, April 18, nineteen-year-old Lyckle Tjalsma died. She was the oldest of the Tjalsmas' seven children. Sjoukje Tjalsma, now pregnant with the couple's eighth child, grieved as if Lyckle were her only child. The same day, Jacob and Antje Kooistra lost their one-year-old Marinus, just one week after the death of their toddler Bauke. Every parent on board became fearful and wondered if their child would be the next. Mercifully, the rest of the week passed without another death. The Frisian group was now down to seventy-seven.

The surface of the sea was broken by a glittering swarm of
small, bright-colored fish that skipped over the water
or sailed for many yards on their wing-like fins.
Stephen W. Meader, *Whaler 'round the Horn*

Week Six: New Optimism

Sunday, April 24: Captain Stinson let it be known that the ship was at latitude 41½° N and longitude 52½° W. If his computations were correct on April 7, and if his current readings were accurate, they had traveled 1,641 miles in seventeen days, an average of 96 miles per day or an underwhelming rate of 3.5 knots per hour. Food supplies and drinking water were fast becoming dangerously low; on the previous day, passengers had eaten the last of the salted meat.

The weather on Sunday was still and warm. Some on board wished they could jump over the rail for a swim. Izaak Roorda wrote in his account, "Quite a number of large fish could be seen playing around our ship as the water was very clear. On the 24th of April, we found a flying fish on the deck."[13] Sjoerd Bekius was also intrigued by the fish and wrote:

[13] *Roorda Family History*, 23.

73

We saw . . . mostly porpoises, which at times appeared above and at times disappeared under the water. One morning when awoke, we saw a large number of tunny [sic], or according [to] the . . . sailors, they were the "farmer with his pigs." These fish swam extraordinarily fast; the young ones we saw were about eight feet long, the full grown ones were from fifteen to twenty feet.[14]

Bekius was happy to be on deck once again, having spent a full two weeks sick and confined to his bunk. By the twenty-eighth of April, he commented that eleven persons had died since leaving Liverpool. On the following day, three-year-old Maaike Sikkema became the twelfth. In three weeks' time, the Sikkemas had lost both of their children.

By the end of the week, despite sickness and dwindling food supplies, there was reason to be encouraged. A course change to the southwest allowed the sails to pick up more wind, so much so, that they were able to realize almost two hundred miles a day. They also began seeing birds—seagulls—an indication that the American coast was finally within reach.

A very rare evening followed, a celebration of sorts, in which they entertained themselves with music. At the captain's request, one of the Frisian girls came out on deck dressed in the traditional provincial costume from head to toe, complete with lace bonnet and gold *oorijzers* at her temples to the wooden clogs on her feet. The captain and his mates were delighted at the sight, and there was the appearance that the tensions that had surfaced previously were perhaps now a thing of the past.

Haagsma records that the evening was "divinely beautiful."[15] Roorda wrote of the sunset, "Never had my eyes seen anything so

---

[14]   *Bekins Blue Book, Centennial Celebration: The Family of Sjoerd Bekius, Known as Bekins in America* (n.p.: Bekins, 1947), 26.

[15]   Haagsma, *Lotgevallen*, 15.

beautiful. It is impossible to describe the gorgeous coloring found in the clouds."[16] Our travelers went to their bunks that night with a new optimism and the vision that perhaps things would turn out well after all. Soon they would be in America.

[16] *Roorda Family History*, 23.

The lighthouse on the Bahamas for which I was instructed to ask has not yet been granted. I have, from time to time, urged it upon the [British] government, in interviews, and I think they will decide to erect it.[17]

Abbott Lawrence, US Minister to Great Britain

Week Seven: Channel Fever

Sunday, May 1: Captain Stinson announced to the passengers that, sometime the following day, they would reach the Bahamian Islands and that New Orleans would then be reached in another four or five days. Some cheered with the news; others, like Sjoerd Bekius, were disappointed, probably remembering what Broer Haagsma had mentioned about it being a six-week trip. But unknown to either Bekius or Haagsma, and certainly not voiced by the captain, the average time for sailing ships from Liverpool to New Orleans in the spring of 1853 was slightly over

[17] Letter written to secretary of state, Daniel Webster, September 30, 1852, as Lawrence was closing his post in London; Hamilton Andrews Hill, *Memoir of Abbott Lawrence*, 2nd ed. (Boston: Little, Brown, 1884), 242-43. In 1852, a 151-foot-tall, cast-iron lighthouse was constructed in England for exhibition purposes; it was this lighthouse that was disassembled and finally reinstalled on Great Isaac Rock, but not until in 1859. It remains there today, although rusted and in poor condition.

"Channel Fever" depicted in an engraving by Matthew
White Ridley (*as it appears in* Harper's Weekly
in the collection of the Library of Congress)

seven weeks, and the *William and Mary* was tracking at just about
that time.

Early Monday morning, passengers lined the railings for the
first sight of land. Bekius wrote, "Filled with a burning desire to
see land, we were craning our necks to catch a glimpse of it."[18] In
nautical parlance this is called "channel fever." All day long, they
searched the horizon but saw nothing.

Below deck, in the nearly empty Frisian steerage
compartment, Arijen and Jeltje Westerhuis watched their four
year old, Rinske, pass into eternity. With land just hours away,
another small bundle was dropped into the sea.

Later that night, near midnight, Captain Stinson found he
had mistakenly sailed farther west than he had intended. Since the
north-flowing Gulf Stream between Florida and Grand Bahama
Island moves at the rate of 3.5 knots, southbound ships sail to the

[18]   *Bekins Blue Book*, 26.

east of Grand Bahama and Abaco Islands. Haagsma recorded that, while sailing westward with a strong north wind, they suddenly found themselves just three or four ship lengths from striking Matanilla Reef, north of the islands. At the last second, the helm was turned to port, and certain shipwreck was avoided. Coming about, they changed course to the east and began skirting the coast of Little Abaco Island.

Izaak Roorda wrote that he was awakened at two o'clock in the morning with the news that land was in sight. Abaco was one of the most isolated islands of the Bahamas. In 1853 it still had no government-operated mail connection to the rest of the world. A sparse but gentle mix of blacks and whites resided on Abaco: the blacks, remnants of the African slave trade; the whites, British loyalists who had fled the Southern states during the American Revolution. Included in the number of refugees in 1785 was Wyannie Malone, a widow from Charleston, South Carolina, along with her children. Now, some sixty-eight years later, many in Hope Town, Abaco, found a blood connection to the widow Malone.

As remote as the Abaconians were, they did have one connection to the outside world. The men of Abaco discovered that, although they had no success with farming and had only a slim market in fishing or sponging, they did have one natural resource in their favor: shallow reefs surrounded their island. *Bahama* comes from the Spanish term *baha mar* and means "low sea." The Abaconians learned that with so many foreign vessels passing through their waterways, they could turn a profit salvaging the contents of those that went aground. In time the government regulated the wrecking trade, and wreckers were required to be licensed. All goods recovered from a ship were brought to Nassau, where they were to be sold at auction. In the final distribution, a wrecker could realize up to 60 percent of the sale price. It is no wonder then that those in the wrecking business would thwart efforts to construct lighthouses or place-marker buoys to warn navigators of the unseen dangers. Unmarked Elbow Cay was conveniently at their very front door.

Before dawn, Roorda wrote, "We were only a stone's throw away from the coast, but we were in great danger because of the many reefs near the shore."[19] Haagsma was also up early on Tuesday morning and wrote that he "saw a few islands, including the coast of Elbow Key."[20]

By seven o'clock that morning, they had reached Hole-in-the-Wall, an unusual opening in the face of the cliff at the southernmost point of Abaco. Subsequently the helmsman turned to starboard and set on a west-northwest course through the Northwest Providence Channel, precisely the course direction given by Blunt.

> The best course is, when up with the Hole-in-the-Wall, to steer W. ¾ N., 95 miles, which will carry you to the west edge of the Bank, and about 4 miles from the Little Isaac, taking care to keep in twelve or sixteen fathoms, in which you ought to pass two miles from the Great Isaac.[21]

At noon they passed Stirrup Cay, a small island that is part of the Berry Islands. Stinson wrote, "Stirrup Key bore S 10 miles distant, after which the weather became thicker and wind increased, with a heavy sea."[22] Keeping well north of Stirrup was the right course. Waters around Stirrup Cay are extremely shallow and strewn with hundreds of shipwrecks. Another ten years would pass before a lighthouse was constructed on the island.

Crew member Stephen Purington had another concern. He wanted to pass the Great Isaac Rocks while there was enough

19   *Roorda Family History*, 24.
20   Haagsma, *Lotgevallen*, 18.
21   Blunt, *American Coast Pilot*, 254.
22   "Another terrible catastrophe," *Weekly Herald*, New York (May 21, 1853), 1.

daylight to see the rocks. He wrote, "The wind was blowing fresh from east-southeast and the weather partially cloudy. I found it necessary to carry a heavy press of sail in order to make the Isaacs before dark."[23]

Proceeding on their northwest course throughout the afternoon, the skies became cloudier, making it impossible to read the sun's altitude and determine the ship's position. By seven o'clock, the sun began setting, and a wind from the southeast began forming squalls. Stinson gave the order to shorten sail. An hour later, the captain appeared on deck and mentioned to passenger Joseph Brooks that due to the dangerous reefs, he intended to stay up through the night. Brooks found him to be visibly agitated.[24] Seaman Purington noted that when the daylight was lost, they believed they were north and west of the Isaacs and that the course could be changed to the southwest. Again from Blunt:

> He who has no experience in this place ought not to pass beyond the Great Isaac by night but may anchor to the NE of the center of the island, in from seven to ten fathoms, on sand, and wait for daylight.[25]

Rather than heeding this point of caution, Captain Stinson decided to continue on. Blunt continues:

> On the edge of soundings, although you do not feel the general current, yet there is a set of tide, which may either run a vessel off the edge or upon the keys; but this cannot happen if the lead, which ought to be kept *constantly* going,

23 Ibid.
24 Joseph Brooks wrote a descriptive account of the event and sent it to British consul William Mure. Mure in turn had it published in the *Daily Picayune*, New Orleans (June 25, 1853), 5. It was republished in the *New York Daily Times* (July 4, 1853), 1.
25 Blunt, *American Coast Pilot*, 255.

is properly attended to, as it will warn whether to keep to starboard or larboard, in order to preserve the proper depth.[26]

Stinson did run the lead, but not constantly. At 8:00 p.m. they played out twenty fathoms (120 feet) of line and found no bottom. At 8:15 p.m., they did so again; still no bottom. They sailed on.

[26] Ibid.

A decent man would not have behaved like this
to a full cargo of old rags in bales.
Joseph Conrad, *Lord Jim: A Tale*

Great Isaac Rocks

No one knows the precise moment the ship went aground—some say as early as 8:00 p.m.; others say it was 8:20 p.m.; some claim it was 9:00 p.m.—but this much is certain, the second it happened, everyone on board knew something calamitous had occurred. Roorda wrote:

> We heard a terrific rumble. The ship stopped, then seemed to leap six feet into the air. Then for a moment we lay still. Then two waves seemed to lift the stern and set it upon a rock. A deathlike fright seemed to grip us. In our excitement we rushed to the lower part of the ship, then back again to the deck among the screaming and crowding passengers.[27]

Passenger Ebenezer Miller later reported:

[27] *Roorda Family History*, 24.

The ship kept rolling from side to side with the greatest violence, sometime appearing as if she would have gone on her beam ends altogether, which renders standing or walking on deck without falling a thing of almost impossibility.[28]

Haagsma also wrote of a loud crackling sound and immediately noticed the damaged hull. "Everyone expected to perish at once . . . the cries and scramble were terrible."[29] In Bekius's letter to his family, he likewise mentioned the expectation of imminent death.

We suddenly heard what sounded like a thunderclap. This was followed by a severe shock, and we were stranded on a rock. The wind rose, so that frequently the ship began to roll. Our only thought was that in a few moments, we would find our grave in the waves.[30]

Tiete Koolstra many years later told of passengers being "thrown from one side of the craft to the other and not one [of us] remained standing after the crash. Trunks had been fastened to the ceiling rafters and when the boat struck a rock, all were torn loose and thrown about, injuring many."[31]

The jolly boat, hanging over the stern in its davits, immediately filled with women and children, so many in fact, that the davits began to bend and twist. Suddenly the stern line let loose, and the boat dropped, held now only by the line to the bow. Partly in the water, its occupants clung to the boat and scrambled the best they could to reenter the ship.

A few noticed that shortly after the original impact, Captain Stinson had his crew lower one of the four boats into the sea.

[28] Miller's letter was written on behalf of eight *William and Mary* passengers. "Wreck of the William and Mary," *Liverpool Mercury* (June 7, 1853), 5.
[29] Haagsma, *Lotgevallen*, 18.
[30] *Bekins Blue Book*, 27.
[31] "Man recalls wreck," *La Crosse Tribune and Leader Press*, October 5, 1924.

Immediately the waves caught it and smashed it into the side of the ship. He ordered the crew to lower a second, which was then kept tethered to the prow and occupied by four of the crew.

Around 11:30 p.m., the captain told some of the men that he expected that the tide would raise the ship off the rocks, and, if manning the pumps through the night could keep the ship afloat, he would try to run the ship ashore in the morning. Roorda, Brooks, and several of the other male passengers at once went into the hold and began working the two hand pumps. Just after midnight, the ship moved off the rocks and drifted westward into deeper water.

Efforts were made to locate the ship's signaling ammunition and rockets but with no success. Some found cotton quilts, cut them up, and used portions to slow down the entering sea. Others, less practical in thinking, in desperation began climbing the masts. Some passengers fell to their knees, pleading for God's help, yet still others cursed their condition.

Sometime through the night, the crew rounded up food and water, surreptitiously moving it first to one of the cabins and then to the waiting lifeboat. Once completely loaded, the boat was moved away to keep it safe from the rocking ship.

Roorda, Brooks, and their companions continued to pump, despite sore hands and backs, standing in water knee deep and the color of brown beer. Stinson had told them, "If you pump, you will live; if you do not pump, I will leave you to your fate."[32] At two o'clock in the morning, the first mate reported the water in the hold to be down to three feet, words that were a great encouragement to those pumping.

At five o'clock in the morning, passenger Brooks walked toward the stern and noticed that, in addition to the four crew members sitting in the lifeboat, now the first and second mates

---

[32] Haagsma, *Lotgevallen*, 19.

were there as well. Brooks at once confronted the captain and accused him of preparing to abandon the ship. Roorda was grateful to overhear Stinson's assurances to Brooks and to Bonnema that he would not leave the ship until all others were safely off.

But within the hour, the captain had a change of heart. Standing by the rail, he told those on deck to be quiet. He pointed toward the east to land now visible in the distance—the western tip of Grand Bahama Island—and momentarily diverted everyone's attention. With his other hand, he signaled to the crew in the lifeboat to come close to the ship to allow him to make his escape.[33]

Attention now shifted to the ship's longboat being removed from where it had been stowed over the after house. Once lowered into the sea, there was a sudden rush of those on deck to enter it. In the words of Ebenezer Miller, "No sooner [was the boat] in the water than all regulation and order were lost."[34] Frisians Ulbe Bergsma, Oene Wagenaar, and Izaak Roorda noticed it as well and made a fast leap over the rail and into the boat. Someone else jumped and missed the boat but was helped out of the water. Four others jumped, two men and two women, but they could not reach the now separating long boat. An elderly man jumped, missed the boat, and made a desperate attempt to hold on, hoping someone would pull him on board. Instead, a crew member with an ax in hand brought it down, severing the old man's fingers, leaving him to sink into the sea. His daughter, already in the longboat, cried in horror, refusing to be silent. She next found herself picked up by the crew and thrown into the sea with her dying father.

Those on deck looked down, screaming in shock at what they were seeing. One woman, catching sight of her husband in

---

[33] Crew member Stephen Purington, a Bowdoinham neighbor and relative of the captain, saw things differently. In a written statement, he claimed the captain "had to be urged very strongly before he would consent to leave the vessel." "Another terrible catastrophe," *Weekly Herald*, New York (May 21, 1853), 1.

Woodcut illustration of the *William and Mary* from the *Illustrated News*. Incorrectly drawn and identified as a "bark," it was corrected in pencil by Seaman John D. Best (*courtesy Kari Best Stiegelmar*)

the longboat, took off her wedding band and threw it into the waves—hurling curses toward her husband. Bekius later wrote, "I stood speechless and nearly fell down unconscious and prayed God that then and there He might cut off the thread of my life so I might not witness the catastrophe which was at hand."[35] Siebren Wesselius expressed to his children, "I cannot begin to write you the cry of anguish and horror which then ascended. But I entreated the Lord could still send deliverance, and in that way, we spent the day. I thought of the words, 'Call upon me in the day of distress and I will help you, and thou shalt honor Me.'"[36]

Even seaman Purington, now secure in the lifeboat, admitted, "I never saw anything in my life so fearful. Some were

[34] Miller, "Wreck of the William and Mary," *Liverpool Mercury* (June 7, 1853), 5.

[35] *Bekins Blue Book*, 27.

[36] Wesselius in a letter to his children that was published in *De Nieuwsbode* (Sheboygan), July 12, 1853. The scripture he paraphrased was Psalm 91:15, "He will call upon me, and I will answer him; I will be with him in trouble, I will deliver him and honor him."

upon their knees praying for the Lord to have mercy on them—some were crying, others were running, catching hold of the officers and crew, telling them that they were unfit to die, that they were unprepared to meet their God."[37]

Though the order defied common sense, Stinson obdurately yelled back to the three crew members remaining on deck, "I go to the mates in the boat; you immediately save the others.[38]

---

[37] "Another terrible catastrophe," *Weekly Herald*, New York (May 21, 1853), 1.
[38] *Middelburgsche Courant*, Middelburg, Zeeland (June 23, 1853), 1.

The sea was incessantly ploughed by the ships that ply between New York or Boston and the Gulf of Mexico, and overrun day and night by the little schooners coasting about the several parts of the American coast. We could hope to be picked up.
Jules Verne, *Twenty Thousand Leagues Under the Sea*

Abandoned

Nineteenth-century maritime writer Matthew Fontaine Maury, in his classic, *Geography of the Sea*, begins:

> There is a river in the ocean. In the severest droughts it never fails, and in the mightiest floods it never overflows. Its banks and its bottoms are of cold water, while its current is of warm. The Gulf of Mexico is its fountain, and its mouth is in the Arctic Seas. It is the Gulf Stream. There is in the world no other such majestic flow of waters. Its current is more rapid than the Mississippi or the Amazon, and its volume more than a thousand times greater.[39]

Captain Stinson, his officers, and his boyish crew were eager to put distance between them and the doomed ship. Raising the

[39] Matthew Fontaine Maury, *The Physical Geography of the Sea* (New York: Harper and Brothers, 1855), 25.

lugsail on the lifeboat's short mast, they sailed westward toward the Gulf Stream. With normal shipping traffic moving on the swift northward moving current, they were certain to be picked up by a coastal schooner or perhaps a ship bound for New York.

In contrast to the chaos, confusion, and clamor on the ship, the small boat moved along in near silence—an early morning outing. Though ankle deep in seawater, they had a compass and a sufficient amount of bread and drinking water, and they were safe and at home on the waves. But it was not their security that brought the silence; it was their guilt. Even the young Maine sailors, John Best of Bath, Nicholas Card of Bowdoinham, Edward Weeks of Portland, and Loami Ross of Litchfield, knew it was not right to abandon a ship of men, women, and children totally unskilled in survival on the sea. Avoiding each other's eyes, they scanned the horizon for a moving sail. Occasionally there would be a glance over the shoulder toward where they had last seen the *William and Mary*. They consoled themselves with thinking that surely the passengers were skillful enough to dismantle the masts and spars and create rafts for their survival. And had they not seen a bark nearby? Certainly it would stop and rescue any who remained on the ship.

It was a few minutes after eight o'clock in the morning when the longboat and its twenty-seven occupants drifted away from the ship and the cries of its stranded passengers. In addition to the three Frisians, there were four crew members: Isaac Ridley, twenty-one, and Lemuel Prebble, thirty-seven, both of Maine; Thomas Allen, twenty-seven, of Baltimore; and Portuguese-born Joseph Roe, twenty-one, recently of New York; plus twenty Irish and English. Although Ulbe Bergsma, Oene Wagenaar, and Izaak Roorda could not understand word for word the exchanges among the Irish in the boat, they fully sensed their intent—to overpower the Frisians and lighten the boat by three persons. One of the Irish lunged at Bergsma, hitting him over the head. Immediately Roorda and Wagenaar drew out their pocket knives and threatened to slash anyone who came toward them. Hastily repaired during the night, but still leaking badly, the boat required constant baling, handful after handful. Roorda wrote, "We continuously dipped water to save our lives, while holding our knives in one hand."[40]

It was not long past noon when the officers and crew in the lifeboat observed a sail to the south. Driven along by the 3.5-knot Gulf Stream, they were well north of the western tip of Grand Bahama Island. By 1:00 p.m., they were alongside the brig *Reuben Carver* of Rockland, Maine. The *Reuben Carver*, under the command of Captain Edward Cobb, had left Sagua la Grande, Cuba, and was en route to New York, when she spotted the small boat. Once on board and at Captain Cobb's suggestion, Stinson began preparing his written report on the loss of his ship—a statement that would in two weeks appear in the *New York Daily Times*. Claiming the ship had filled with water and was fast sinking, he reported as fact: "At 8 a.m., left her, and in a few minutes, she went down."[41]

In the longboat, Bergsma, Roorda, and Wagenaar continued to be on the alert. The hope of the sailors was to row across the Gulf Stream and, if possible, reach the Florida coast by evening. At noon, they spotted a ship, although still some distance off. The rowers changed direction in hopes of getting the attention of the ship. Fortunately for those in the longboat, seamen high in

---

[40]   *Roorda Family History*, 25.
[41]   "Disaster at Sea," *New York Daily Times* (May 17, 1853), 3.

the rigging noticed the small craft, alerted the ship's captain, and within the hour, they were brought on board the ship *Pollux*. A packet ship like the *William and Mary*, the *Pollux* was en route from New Orleans to Liverpool. As happy as the twenty-seven refugees were to be rescued, it must have been a great disappointment to realize that after seven weeks at sea and so very close to the American coast, they were now turned around and headed back to where they had started. When another ship was seen on a course for New York, a signal was sent requesting the acceptance of twenty-seven passengers. The signal was ignored. Captain McIntyre provided the famished group with food and water, their having had nothing since the evening meal the night before.

Roorda made an appeal to Captain McIntyre to change direction and attempt to rescue others on the *William and Mary*, although some feared she had already sunk. At first McIntyre agreed with his plea, but with the approach of nightfall, and the fear of his ship hitting a reef in the darkness, McIntyre resumed his course up the Gulf Stream. Roorda concludes, "Now all we could do was ask God to send help to them."[42]

For the 165 or so souls left standing on the deck of the *William and Mary* as the lifeboat and longboat moved ever farther away, there was a feeling of total abandonment. If the captain and officers—those knowledgeable in the workings of the ship—had given up any hope for their survival on the *William and Mary*, then what hope remained for them? Although some immediately looked to the three remaining crew members—William Busby, the British steward; Patrick Ward of Philadelphia; and Samuel Harris of Rhode Island—for direction, it failed to materialize. Haagsma noticed they had discovered a bottle of liquor and "had lost their common sense."[43]

[42]   *Roorda Family History*, 25.
[43]   Haagsma, *Lotgevallen*, 20.

Some moved to despair, believing their lives soon to end. The invention of the life jacket was still a device of the future; death by drowning seemed inevitable. Even worse was the fear of being torn apart by sharks. Nineteenth-century author G. J. H. Northcroft noted six or seven species of sharks inhabiting the waters of the Bahamas, and although some were regarded as relatively harmless, the villainous reputation of the yellow shark and the black shark certainly struck fear into the hearts of those about to be forced into the water.[44]

Others on board made every effort possible to prolong the time remaining. Several men cut the anchor chains to allow the ship to drift into the current. A distress flag was sent up one mast. At five in the afternoon, they saw a three-mast vessel—possibly the *Pollux*—but as Brooks aptly commented, "Like the Levite, she only looked on and passed by."[45] A few men attempted to make two large rafts from the spars and other parts of the ship, hoping that when the ship sank, rafts might provide a means of survival for a least a few souls. Others continued to pump water out of the ship throughout the day. And some continued to pray.

By nightfall, the weather had turned stormy, slamming the immigrants with strong winds, pelting rain, and fierce lightning and thunder. In the middle of the storm, a young English woman prematurely gave birth to a child, her husband having left her earlier that morning in the longboat.

If any sleep was to be found that night, like the previous night, it was fitful and insufficient. In the back of everyone's mind was the realization that tomorrow could be either the day of rescue or the day of sudden demise to the sea.

---

44 See Northcroft's *Sketches of Summerland: Giving Some Account of Nassau and the Bahama Islands* (Nassau: Nassau Guardian, 1900), 131.
45 *New York Daily Times* (July 4, 1853), 1.

PART III

Rescue and Healing

Jesus, lover of my soul, let me to thy bosom fly,
while the nearer waters roll, while the tempest still is high;
hide me, O my Savior, hide, till the storm of life is past,
safe into the haven guide, O receive my soul at last.

Charles Wesley

Ascension Day

It was a new day; dawn arrived once again for the famished, exhausted passengers. Haagsma remembered that it was Ascension Day, May 5, the fortieth day after Easter. "It was on that day," he wrote, "that we experienced His wise, invisible hand extended in a wonderful way."[1]

People began moving about, grateful the ship was still afloat. In the early morning haze, they could make out the low profile of a long island, evidence that they had drifted northward through the night. At somewhere between five and ten miles to the east and beyond reach, the island nevertheless provided a faint hope; perhaps someone from the island would see them and come to their rescue.

Considering the volume of northbound marine traffic known to be riding the Gulf Stream through the Straits of Florida,

[1]   Haagsma, *Lotgevallen*, 21.

it is a mystery that no vessel came to the aid of the sinking ship. On May 23, the day the British bark *Pollux* left New Orleans en route to Liverpool, two other British vessels did likewise, the *Rankin* and the *Royal Sovereign*. The same day, the bark, *Asa Fish*, and the schooners, *Grace* and *E. S. Jane*, all set off on the same route on their way to Philadelphia. The following day, ten vessels left New Orleans on the same course: three for Boston; three for New York; three for Liverpool; and one, the brig *Oneco*, for Baltimore. And the next day, another seven vessels left. Despite the likely presence of twenty-three sailing vessels in the vicinity of the *William and Mary* on May 4 and 5, apparently not a single one saw her, or if they did, they did not alter their course and come to offer aid.

"In the afternoon about 12 o'clock," wrote Sjoerd Bekius, "we spied a ship in the distance. Then the fathers and their children dropped to their knees praying to God that this might prove to be their deliverer, and this prayer was answered."[2]

While still a long ways off, "It appeared like two tiny sticks floating on the seas," said Tiete Kooistra.[3] It was not a large ship, a coastal schooner. Immediately the flag of the *William and Mary* was lowered to half-mast. What happened next brought tears to the eyes of the now hopeful immigrants. The schooner made a very intentional course change and headed directly toward them. Their rescuers were on the way.

⁓

Today there is BASRA—the Bahamas Air Sea Rescue Association—an all-volunteer service to those in distress on the sea. But Robert Sands, captain of the schooner *Oracle*, was not a coast guard volunteer; he was not in the business of rescuing people shipwrecked on Bahamian reefs. At age thirty-four, he and two of his younger brothers, William and Richardson, worked as

---

2   *Bekins Blue Book*, 28.
3   "Man recalls wreck," *La Crosse Tribune and Leader-Press*, October 5, 1924.

salvagers, "wreckers" as they were known on the islands. Robert "Amphibian" Sands was a man equally at home on the sea as he was on his native Abaco Island. Married for thirteen years, he was the father of two sons and two daughters, ages ranging from twelve down to two.

Sands, like many on Abaco, had roots in the American Revolution. His maternal grandfather was Ephraim Malone, the oldest son of the widow and island matriarch Wyannie Malone. Ephraim was said to have been wounded at Bunker Hill and, between 1781 and 1783, had fought in the revolution in South Carolina as a loyalist. For his service to the Crown, he had received a sizable land grant in Hope Town on Elbow Cay, Abaco, in 1807.

Ephraim had four children, three of whom remained in the Bahamas, marrying and integrating with the islanders. Daughter Eliza, at sixteen, married Charles Sands of Cherokee Sound, Abaco. The couple eventually had nine children, of whom Robert was the first.

Young Robert grew up in a tropical paradise. His playground as described today by *Fodor's* consisted of "clear, shallow waters . . . teeming with triggerfish, grouper, parrot fish, green moray eels, angelfish, jacks, damselfish, sergeant majors, stingrays, sea turtles, dolphins, and even the occasional reef or nurse shark."[4] He could comb miles of white sandy beaches, searching for objects the surf would wash onto the shore. Or he could climb the limestone bluffs with his brothers and venture into the pine forests to hunt for wild pigs. But no paradise is without its serpent, and Abaco had its share. Late summer and early fall brought repeated storm damage from tropical depressions and hurricanes. When disease hit the island, as it did in 1852 with a cholera outbreak, there was no defense. In a period of just weeks, nearly one hundred residents fell victim and were buried in a mass grave near the beach. Far less

4   *Fodor's 2011 Bahamas* (New York: Fodor's Travel Publications, 2010), 146.

sudden or shocking was the impact that the island's isolation had on its residents, especially the young people; their education was understandably primitive and limited, providing them with few vocational opportunities.

⌒

The first thing those on the deck of the *William and Mary* noticed about their rescuers was that there were seven of them and that all were very dark skinned. To the light-complected, northern Europeans unaccustomed to exposing their backs to the sun, Sands and his crew were seen as black men. Some must have wondered if the islanders' hearts were as dark as their skin. Would they harm them further, rob them, get them on board their schooner, and then overtake them and throw them overboard? Would they try to separate them, to kill the men and ravish the women? Could their plight become even worse? Or were these creatures capable of showing human compassion?

The wreckers spoke English and quickly moved over the ship to assess its damage and determine the value of her contents. Having been abandoned by her officers, everything on board was now theirs for the taking. The railroad iron could not be moved; much of the crockery was broken; the fine textile goods were now wet, soiled rags. They were left with parts of the ship—sails, cordage, instruments—and the valued possessions of the passengers—family heirlooms, silver spoons, and prized items that the immigrants would never have left behind in Friesland. For some, the notion of leaving one's personal possessions on the ship was extremely difficult. Trijntje Tuininga remembered that the final advice she had received from her grandmother when leaving Friesland was that she guard her treasured items at all cost. So she tightly held a small bag containing her headdress, several silver spoons, some lace, and, most precious of all, an article of clothing from each of her deceased children. As she prepared to leave the ship, one of the sailors grabbed her bag, never to be seen by Trijntje again.[5] Broer Haagsma was less sentimental. "We were obliged to abandon all of our baggage, " he wrote, "but that was a matter of minor concern. Our only aim and desire was to save our lives, and to that end, Providence granted evident aid."[6]

Tiete Kooistra was of the opinion that Sands and his crew "were not overly anxious to rescue the Hollanders."[7] Eventually Sands explained that he was sure he could move the women and the children to the beach of the nearest island, but in doing so, they must take only the clothing they were wearing; there would be no room for anything else. Once deposited on the beach, the *Oracle* would return for the men, until all were safe again on land. After quick embraces, some forty-four women and an equal number of children passed over the rail of the *William and Mary* and jumped down to the deck of the *Oracle*. It was not a large boat; some wondered if they would all fit. Nor was it a clean boat; it was a workboat that frequently carried whatever the wreckers thought would draw a good price at auction in Nassau. The sails were raised, the wind caught, and the schooner moved away toward the island in the east.

Landing the women and children safely on the beach was another challenge. The western coast of Grand Bahama Island, from Settlement Point on the north to Freeport on the south,

[5]   Northcroft concurs that generally the interest of the wreckers was not altruistic and comments, "Through the [wreckers'] timely intervention, many lives were saved, no doubt, and a certain amount of property recovered; but robbery, and many nefarious practices were encouraged by the system," "Sketches," 296-97. Bahamian circuit magistrate Inglis reported, "The wrecking system every day develops its sad depravity and indicates the urgent necessity of more prompt and effective measures; if not for prevention of enormous plunder, for at least the recovery of some portion of the articles stolen." Craton and Saunders, *Islanders in the Stream: A History of the Bahamian People* (Athens, GA: University of Georgia Press, 1992), 142.

[6]   Haagsma, *Lotgevallen*, 21.

[7]   "Man recalls wreck," *La Crosse Tribune and Leader-Press*, October 5, 1924.

is prone to shoaling; charts today warn mariners to come no closer than four miles. The only safe way for the schooner to land its refugees was to anchor the *Oracle* off shore and then make repeated trips with the schooner's boat, first through the breakers and then up onto the beach. Once all were transported, the anchor was drawn, sails were raised again, and the *Oracle* was turned in the direction of the *William and Mary* and its seventy anxiously waiting men. Still, a few of the group chose to remain with the ship to continue pumping and assist with the salvage efforts.

That night, somewhere between Settlement Point and Mosquito Point, there was an emotional reunion of passengers on the beach. They were alive, and after forty-five days of tossing about on the ocean, they were once again on firm ground. Yet all their material possessions were lost. They were without food, water, and shelter. They had no idea how long they could survive on the island, whether or not the island was inhabited, and if it was, whether the islanders would provide help or present hostility.

One of the most discouraged Frisians took his pewter fork from his pocket, stuck it in the sand, and said. "There, I'll never need that again. All is over, and we are left here to die." To this, Johannes Tuininga, who had lost two of his children on the ship, replied, "Not so, I still think there is hope and as an emblem of my faith, I'll take this fork."[8] Tuininga's granddaughter wrote years later that Johannes used that fork for the rest of his life, until the tines were finally worn off.

"As a silent usher to night, the short twilight of the northern Bahamas is dominated by some of the most magnificent sunsets seen anywhere in the world," wrote P. J. H. Barratt in his book on Grand Bahama Island. "At night the Southern Cross can be seen

---

[8]   Brown, "Anna Brown's life story of John Tuininga," in *Dutch Immigrant Memoirs and Related Writings*, selected and arranged by Henry S. Lucas, rev. ed. (Grand Rapids, MI: Eerdmans, 1967), 189.

low on the horizon, while overhead meteorites enter the earth's atmosphere making a shooting gallery out of the heavens."[9]

While a few stood watch over their beach encampment, most wanted nothing more than sleep, something many had not had for three nights. But as Haagsma next reveals in his account, "Soon we were surrounded by enemies. Unashamed they attacked our camp from all sides, and, regardless of how we defended ourselves, still several were wounded."[10] Fortunately, their attackers were entomological; whether the large and plentiful mosquitos or the ubiquitous sand fleas, we cannot tell. Bred in the low-lying mangroves and swamps across the island, they abound twelve months of the year, although seldom mentioned today by the Bahamian tourist industry. Despite the irritation brought by their attackers, the gnawing emptiness of their stomachs, and the continuing uncertainty of what morning would bring, one by one, they drifted into sleep.

---

[9] P. J. H. Barratt, *Grand Bahama* (Harrisburg, PA: Stackpole Books, 1972), 28.
[10] Haagsma, *Lotgevallen*, 22.

I think the Bahamas the best place I have ever found.[11]
Winslow Homer

In the Bahamas

Of the twenty-one islands in the Bahamian archipelago, Grand Bahama Island is the fourth largest, some seventy miles long and nine miles wide at its greatest point. In pre-Columbian times, the Lucayans occupied it, but it was the Spanish explorers who later named the island Gran Bajamar—the great low sea. In 1513 Juan Ponce de León visited the western-most portion of the island in search of his legendary Fountain of Youth. Having no success, he went on to Florida but left behind on the island two members of his crew to search more diligently.

"After its discovery by the Spanish," wrote Barratt, "the island—or more correctly, the reefs off the island—has been a graveyard of galleons, men-of-war, merchantmen, and passenger

---

[11] Homer, in a letter to lithographer Louis Prang, October 18, 1905, collection of the Goodrich/Whitney Museum of American Art, Philadelphia, PA.

ships. It is easy to understand why the island had never attracted visitors—it was a good place to avoid."[12]

On Friday morning, a party of the castaways was sent out to explore the island and find food and water and, hopefully, to make contacts leading to their removal. Sjoerd Bekius mentioned finding some young oxen, a clue that the island was inhabited. Dense undergrowth kept them close to the rocky shore, and there they encountered a friendly islander representing the government and the island's estimated nine hundred residents, almost all of whom were black. Despite their remoteness, they had years of experience in dealing with the needs of those left on their beaches. The official directed them first to a well and later brought sea biscuits and fish. Although the refugees were grateful, the quantities were hardly sufficient to assuage the hunger of all.

Back in the encampment, the children played at water's edge, fascinated by tiny sand and ghost crabs and the much slower hermit crabs, none of which would have been seen on Friesland's coast. It is likely they chased many of the harmless lizards sunning themselves on the coral and limestone rocks. Sand dollars and large conch shells were everywhere along the beach.

During the afternoon, the reconnoitering team set off again along the beach, this time finding several homes. Although none of the islanders appeared wealthy, they lavishly extended hospitality, sharing with the group their corn bread, fish, and roast pork. Haagsma was amused at seeing a woman in her rocking chair, keeping herself in motion with one foot, and keeping her child's cradle in motion with the other.

By the end of the day, the *Oracle* and another boat, the *Contest*, had brought the last of the passengers and the news that the *William and Mary* had finally slipped beneath the waves,

[12]   Barratt, *Grand Bahama*, 16.

and almost with the loss of another Frisian. Those who had remained on the ship to work the pumps, stayed until the final moment, jumping into the schooner's boat just as the ship sank below the surface. One was not so fortunate. Apparently caught in the sinking ship, he was grabbed and pulled out of the water unconscious onto the deck of the *Oracle*.

Early the next morning, Saturday, Sands and his crew returned, picked up some of the castaways, and began what would be a five-day sail to Nassau, the capitol of the Bahamas. Curiously, Sands did not take the most direct route but instead first sailed northward around Settlement Point, across the shallow waters north of Grand Bahama Island and eastward to Abaco Island. Here he stopped at Elbow Key, his home port, perhaps to release several of his crew, most certainly to pick up food supplies for themselves and their passengers, and possibly to unload a portion of their wrecking haul (see map, p. 138).

Both Bekius and Kooistra commented that for those left behind, there was nothing to eat that day. Some walked along the beach and found shellfish; Bekius called them "oysters," which they cooked and ate with great delight.

By Sunday evening, two more boats had arrived, and the remainder of the immigrants began their sail for Nassau. These were able to follow the southern coast of Grand Bahama Island, with stops along the beach when necessary. Haagsma noted in his journal being fed buckwheat cakes, bacon, fish, and turtle soup en route. It was on one of their shore stops that they learned of the March 17 wreck of the *Osborne*, a ship from Kennebunk, Maine, traveling from Liverpool to New Orleans with 215 immigrant passengers. Haagsma wrote that on the *Osborne*, "The captain was not the first but the *last* to leave the ship."[13]

[13]   Haagsma, *Lotgevallen*, 24. The *Osborne* and the *William and Mary* were not the only vessels to sink in the Bahamas that season. Between January 10 and June 30 of that year, five ships, two barks, three brigs, and three schooners

All along the way, the immigrants looked out across the water's surface. Back home the water was sometimes blue-gray or green-gray, but always gray. Here it was turquoise and emerald green. On the Waddenzee, little could be seen below the surface; here the water was crystal clear, and one could see coral and myriads of fish far below. Occasionally they would see a turtle rise for a breath of air. In shallow places, they saw stingrays, leopard rays, and manta rays, some of which would skim the surface. But it was the sharks following the boats for a meal opportunity that frightened them the most.

En route they experienced still another fatality. Pieter van der Tol, one of the single men, died off the lower coast of Abaco Island. It is very possible that he was the person pulled from the sinking ship six days earlier.

"Nassau is a sailors' town," wrote J. Linton Rigg "It has been . . . for more than 250 years and has a history as exciting and violent as can be found anywhere, a history of naval warfare, piracy, pillaging, buccaneering, slave running, wrecking, blockade running, and bootlegging."[14] Although it was a British colony in 1853, during the seventeenth century, it had passed between the British and Spanish several times. During the Revolutionary War, Nassau was briefly held by the Americans, then by the Spanish in 1782, before returning to the British again the following year.

On Thursday, May 12, the two schooners crossed the Northwest Providence Channel on their approach to the Nassau bar. Mariners were warned in Blunt's directions to look for signal flags on Hog Island, just east of the harbor entrance, as to the

were lost. Report of Timothy Darling, consul, to William L. Marcy, secretary of state, July 1, 1853, Record Group 84, Nassau Bahamas Consular Posts, UD Entry 608, 27; National Archives of College Park, MD (NACP).

[14] J. Linton Rigg, *Bahama Islands: A Boatman's Guide to the Land and the Water*, 4th ed. (New York: Scribner's, 1973), 97.

advisability of crossing the bar. The Admiralty blueback charts note good anchorage just past where a fixed marker known as Tony Beacon lines up with a cocoa-nut tree on Norths Cay. For the small boats bringing in the refugees, there was sufficient water, and the seas were calm.

What amazed all was the clarity of the bay. William Drysdale, on his entrance to Nassau harbor a few years later wrote, "[We] discovered that we were floating in water as transparent as air and leaned over the schooner's rail and watched the bottom, thirty feet below us."[15]

Haagsma was impressed with how beautiful the city looked, especially in the late afternoon sun. High on the hill and easily seen from the harbor was the impressive home of the governor. To the right of it, toward the west, lay Fort Charlotte, a fortification built in the eighteenth century. Scattered throughout the city were spires of several churches, congregations that would soon be used to bless the lives of the destitute travelers.

On Friday morning, the two schooners moved from their harbor moorings to the wharf at the bottom of George Street. Here their passengers climbed a series of coral limestone steps, entering a city unlike any they had ever seen. In Drysdale's words, "Everything about us was either dazzling white or rich cream color—streets, houses, stone walls, even the soil in such gardens as we passed. The fragrance of flowers filled the air."[16]

Leaving the water's edge, they walked passed the Vendue House, once the city's slave market, and onto Bay Street, Nassau's main thoroughfare. After weeks on the water, suddenly there was so much to take in. The streets were shaded with rows of almond

---

[15] William Drysdale, *In Sunny Lands: Outdoor Life in Nassau and Cuba* (New York: Harper & Bros., 1885), 5.
[16] Ibid., 6.

Nassau Harbor (*courtesy Yale University*)

trees and filled with black vendors, many carrying their wares in baskets on their heads. Walking westward along Bay Street, they passed the British Naval Yard and eventually were led to several large buildings: former military barracks near the fort they had seen from the boat. Here they were given accommodations—food, water, and lodging—for the duration of their time in Nassau. While in no way comparable to a hotel, the large, three-story buildings, with their wide, wrap-around porches and magnificent views of the harbor, were the only facilities in Nassau that could accommodate such a large number of travelers lacking means. Those in the group who were ill or injured from the journey were brought to the hospital on nearby West Street.

With the arrival of the *William and Mary*'s passengers that morning, word spread quickly among the colonial offices. One of the first to respond was the office of John Thomson, Nassau's agent to Lloyds. All business, he immediately communicated to the secretary of the Liverpool Association of Underwriters a report on the loss of the ship and her cargo. With greater interest in the survivors that morning, Charles T. Malassez, in his office on Frederick Street, rushed to meet the deadline for Saturday's edition of the *Bahama Herald*. As the assistant commissary general of the uniformed personnel in the British Army, Malassez wasted no time in his effort to move the abandoned travelers on to their destination. The next morning, the *Herald's* readers found three items relating to the *William and Mary*. The first was a call for transportation bids:

> Wanted: Transportation for New Orleans
> Tenders in duplicate will be received at the Office until Monday, the 23rd, instant noon for the hire of a vessel or vessels to convey about 150 shipwrecked emigrants, their stores, etc. from Nassau to New Orleans.
> A sample of good wholesome water, fuel for cooking, proper cooking apparatus, and the necessary fittings, must be provided by the party whose tender may be accepted.
> The vessel tendered will be inspected immediately after the opening of the tenders by the Emigration Officer, and if approved of will be required to sail not later than fifteen days from the date of approval.
> C. Malassez, A.C.G.[17]

Malassez was not the only one in Nassau to move into action. With lightning speed, the Committee for the Relief of the Emigrants per the *William and Mary* was formed and made its appeal for assistance.

> Loss of the *William and Mary* Emigrant Ship
> The attention of the Christian Public of New Providence is earnestly solicited to the dreadful calamity

---

[17]   *Bahama Herald* (May 14, 1853), 2.

which has befallen the above named Ship in the almost total loss of the property of 164 Passengers, the majority of whom are of the poorer classes.

Through the noble exertion, chiefly of Mr. Sands, master of the wrecking schooner *Oracle*, the lives of these emigrants have been brought to Nassau so destitute of clothing, as to furnish a strong ground of appeal to the compassion of the community.

To aid this benevolent object, sermons will be preached and collections afterward made (D.V.) in the Episcopal Churches and Chapels of New Providence . . . on Sunday morning, the 22nd, instant.[18]

The third item in the paper was an account of the wreck and subsequent rescue, drawn heavily from seamen William Ward and Samuel Harris. Both were highly critical of Stinson's actions, asserting that "Had not the captain and crew deserted the ship, . . . [it] might have been run ashore."[19]

On the same day, the city's other newspaper, the *Nassau Guardian*, also carried an account of the shipwreck, concluding with the statement that the immigrants were "taken to the Western Barracks, where rations have been issued from H. M. Commissariat Department and every attention paid to them by the United States Consul."[20]

In reality the United States consul had no obligation to care for the 164 travelers. Their only responsibility was to the American citizens that had arrived on the schooners—the three *William and Mary* crew members. It is certain that as soon as their boat entered Nassau harbor, William Busby, William Ward, and Samuel Harris would have walked eastward along Bay Street in

[18]   Ibid.
[19]   Ibid.
[20]   *Nassau Guardian*, May 14, 1853.

the direction of the American flag and the consul office at the foot of East Street. Here they met American consul Timothy Darling. A native of New Brunswick, Canada, Darling grew up in Maine before coming to the Bahamas. Now forty-two, Darling was married to Lucy Sargent—reportedly a cousin of artist John Singer Sargent—and the father of five children. Known as a man of strictest integrity, he was well respected throughout the West Indies. Before the end of his career, Queen Victoria would knight him for his service to the colony. Now under his direction, the seamen would be provided with food, lodging, and laundry service while they remained in Nassau—all at the expense of the American government. Curiously, also registering with the three sailors was Peter McDonald, the passenger-designated cook.

On any given Sunday morning in 1853, the atmosphere in Nassau would have been very different from the other six days. The harbor would be quiet, the markets and shops closed, and the streets—otherwise filled with those doing business—would be pathways to the island's seven churches. Although we have no record of which church the Frisians visited, the most likely would have been St. Andrews Presbyterian Kirk on Princes Street.[21] Founded in 1798 by Scottish settlers, the congregation would have warmly welcomed the refugees. There they would have met elder and Sunday school superintendent Timothy Darling. Although he was limited in his role as American consul, as a believer and leader in the church, he showed great benevolence. Haagsma recorded that on Sunday, May 15, "We visited one of the churches, and on Pentecost we were able, with the congregation, to offer our silent prayers to Him who so remarkably saved us when our souls were oppressed by the fear of death."[22]

---

[21]   This church would have been more like the churches in Friesland, even to the point of being called a *kerk*.

[22]   Haagsma, *Lotgevallen*, 25.

It is no wonder the sick fly hither for relief,
being sure to find a cure here.

Peter Henry Bruce

Nassau Town

Throughout the eighteenth and nineteenth centuries, writers have praised the Bahamas, and Nassau in particular, as the ideal location for healing and restoration. British surgeon Major J. T. W. Bacot wrote convincingly of the benefits to those suffering from arthritis and asthma.[23] American doctor Lewis F. Cleveland, in a book addressed specifically to "invalids and travelers," touted the location's physical and mental benefits in such a manner as to leave one wondering if the island's commercial interests financed his publication.[24] An anonymous writer targeted "those who desire health, long life, and pleasure," directing them to Nassau, "the sanitarium of the western hemisphere."[25] But the genial,

---

[23] J. T. W. Bacot, *The Bahamas: A Sketch* (London: Longmans, 1868), 52-57.
[24] Lewis F. Cleveland, *General Description of the City of Nassau and the Island of the New Providence, Bahamas, West Indies* (New York: W. Baldwin, 1871), 1.
[25] Anon., as quoted in *Nassau, Island of New Providence, Bahamas: A Guide to the Sanitarium of the Western Hemisphere, its Attractions, and How to Get There* (New York: Murray, Ferris & Co., 1877), 3.

115

Street in Nassau, New Providence Island
(*courtesy Library of Congress*)

healthful, life-giving atmosphere that the writer spoke of was not assured. A century earlier, nineteen-year-old George Washington accompanied his ailing half brother, Lawrence, to Nassau for healing. Although the future first president greatly enjoyed his visit and supposedly called the Bahamas, "the isles of perpetual June," his brother failed to find renewal and died the following year. In the fall of 1852, a cholera epidemic passed through New Providence Island, believed to have come from a ship entering the harbor. In six months' time, 696 people died on New Providence. Unbeknownst to the Frisian travelers, within weeks of their departure from the island, there would be an outbreak of cholera that would take many lives, including that of the governor John Gregory.

In 1853 Nassau lay quietly in the sun, still several years away from the advent of tourism and the establishment of grand hotels. For many in the Frisian party, the stopover in Nassau was

The west end of Bay Street, the road the Frisians would have
taken from their barracks to the town market. The tall obelisk
in the distance was located near the barracks
(out of view) (*courtesy Yale University*)

restorative, a respite in their hard journey. Food, while lacking
in variety, was certainly in abundance—unlike their final weeks
on board the *William and Mary*. The daily allotment per person
included one pound of bread, one pound of beef or pork,
three ounces of rice, one ounce of sugar, and one-half ounce of
coffee—all initially funded by the colonial government, with the
expectation of reimbursement by the *William and Mary*'s owners.
Many of their number took daily walks from the barracks to the
market to take in the local culture. Still dressed in their Dutch
garb, they were as much an attraction for the locals as the locals
were for them. Others were content to sit in the shade and idle the
hours away watching the boats enter and leave the harbor. We can
be certain that many of the children would be found playing on
the beach near the barracks.

There were others who were anxious to move on as quickly as possible—to get under way to New Orleans, up the Mississippi River, and to their new home wherever that might be. There was land to purchase, houses to build, and crops to sow before the onset of winter. Each day spent sitting around Nassau was a day lost from their work.

The days in Nassau, although restorative for most, were difficult for Antje Kooistra and her three sons. She had lost her two youngest children while at sea, and on Monday, May 16, her husband, Jacob, died. In an interview many years later, son Tiete said, "Here again is a test of men. One will always find those who could live without nourishment for a week, while others become seriously sick in but a day."[26] Antje's only consolation was that, although the bodies of her children were dropped into the sea, Jacob would have a Christian burial in Nassau's potter's field.

Accommodations on board the *William and Mary* had been austere, but they were even worse on the *Pollux*. This bark was not prepared in the least to care for the needs of twenty-seven additional passengers. Without the availability of interior space, they were forced to remain on deck for the duration of their return voyage to Liverpool. Exposed to the sun's heat by day and the cold winds each night, their only protection from the elements was a tattered, discarded sail. Food and water supplies were stretched to the limit. Izaak Roorda was particularly uncomfortable. When he had jumped from the rail of the *William and Mary* into the longboat, he broke both of his wooden shoes. And his socks, which had become wet in the daily cleaning of the deck, soon had to be patched with sailcloth. In his account of the return voyage, he wrote, "On the morning of the ninth [of May] and the night of

---

[26]   "Man recalls wreck," *La Crosse Tribune and Leader-Press*, October 5, 1924.

the twenty-third, we had heavy rains. A large quantity of water was caught and used for drinking. After this, everyone felt better."[27]

On board the brig, *Reuben Carver*, conditions were no better; Captain Cobb did not have food available for his nine famished passengers. After six days of making their way along the coast of Florida, Georgia, and South Carolina, they overcame the slower-moving brig *Oneco*. The *Oneco* had left New Orleans on April 25, heavily burdened with 525 hides, 232 bales of cotton, 68 hogsheads of sugar, 2 barrels of molasses, 150 barrels of pork, and 4 barrels of beef—all destined for the port of Baltimore. In a rendezvous off the coast of North Carolina, Captain Emery turned over to Captain Cobb what he felt he could provide for the next six days.

Word of the arrival of the immigrants spread quickly over New Providence Island, and islanders immediately began responding to the need. On Wednesday, May 18, another notice appeared in the *Nassau Guardian*.

> The Wrecked Emigrants
>
> We have much pleasure in recording the benevolent acts of a committee of ladies of our town who have been administering to the necessities of the unfortunate emigrants wrecked in the Am. Ship *William and Mary* by superintending the making up of articles of clothing for the most destitute at the Public Buildings. Collections will also be made in their behalf at the various places of worship on Sunday next.[28]

The "Public Buildings" were in a cluster of three buildings on Bay Street, situated diagonally across the street from the office of the American consul. They housed the court, the post office,

---

[27] *Roorda Family History*, 25.
[28] *Nassau Guardian*, May 18, 1853.

and most of the other official government functions and served as a natural collection place for items that could benefit the stranded passengers.

Throughout the week, visits would be made to the barracks to check on the welfare of their temporary occupants. Committee representatives brought in much-needed articles of clothing and food items. Malassez came to secure verbal statements and affidavits from several of the passengers and update Bonnema on progress made to move the group, and Darling came from time to time to check on needs. Dr. H. N. Chipman, who very soon would be kept exceptionally busy with the city's approaching epidemic, came to determine the state of their health. A young, single military officer, Lt. William John Chamberlayne, of the First West India Regiment, took a special interest in the travelers. Chamberlayne was a kind and gentle man who was known for spending his spare time, of which he had much, making fine pencil drawings and watercolor sketches of the places in which he was stationed.

Broer Haagsma, by nature a curious person, spent his first week exploring the city of Nassau, just as he had done in Liverpool. One of the first things to catch his eye when he arrived at the wharf on Friday morning and looked up George Street in the direction of the governor's mansion was a white statue.

Returning to the Vendue House at the bottom of the street, Haagsma could see a huge church and a clock tower to the left. This was the Anglican Church of Christ, a twelve-hundred-seat sanctuary and the largest church in the city. Beyond it, at the end of the street, was a long stairway that went up to the governor's front door. And midway up the steps—the statue.

On its six-foot-high base, Haagsma found the simple inscription "Columbus 1492." Lady Brassey, who had visited

George Street with the governor's mansion or government house on
the high ridge. Note the statue on the steps to the mansion
(*courtesy Yale University*)

the governor in 1885, described it as "Columbus in curious
costume."[29] Fifty years later, Alpheus Hyatt Verrill thought the
nine-foot-tall figure was "swaggering" and "piratical-looking."[30]
Whether realistic or romantic, the statue was commissioned by
colonial governor Sir James Carmichael Smyth and completed by
British sculptor William Groggon in his studio at Jesus College
in Oxford, England. Working under the direction of Washington
Irving, who was in England preparing his biography on Columbus,
Groggon is believed to have made the statue out of an artificial
stone known as Coade stone. It was installed on the steps in 1832
and has remained at its sentinel post ever since.

Also of interest to Haagsma, and no doubt to the others,
was Fort Charlotte, the limestone fortress that loomed over their
barracks. Named after Saharia Charlotte, wife of King George III,
it was entirely hand carved out of the stone ridge. Below grade
were dungeons and a maze of rooms and tunnels; above were

---

[29]   Annie Brassey, *In the Trades, the Tropics & the Roaring Forties* (New York: H.
      Holt, 1885), 321.
[30]   Verrill, *West Indies of Today* (New York: Dodd, Mead, 1931), 236.

the ramparts outfitted with forty-two cannon and, around the structure, a waterless moat with a drawbridge. In the fort's entire history, it had never been necessary to fire a single charge. To Haagsma, it was a "masterpiece of fortress architecture."[31]

On Sunday morning, May 22, as announced the previous week, the city's pastors preached messages of Christian charity, and a collective offering was received to benefit the 164 refugees. It would be several days before it was known if the collected amounts would have any impact.

The effort in arranging transportation for the castaways was not going as assistant commissary general Charles Malassez had hoped. By the announced deadline of May 23, offers had come from the owners of two schooners, the ninety-two-ton *Time* and the eighty-four-ton *Rover*. Together they could not move the entire group to New Orleans.

On Tuesday, May 24, 1853, the city of London was poised to begin a grand birthday celebration for its sovereign. Her Majesty's birthday event began promptly at 6:45 a.m. with a musical program presented by the band of the Royal Marines. This was followed by a parade through St. James Park and featured bands and drums of the Royal Foot Guard, 250 in number.

Throughout the entire day, bells in the church towers rang in celebration. At dusk, hundreds of brilliantly lit gaslights were ignited on buildings all around the city. Some illuminations spelled out in lights, "God save the Queen and Prince"; others displayed either the royal arms, a simple crown, or the Brunswick star. Most illuminated the royal initials, "V. R."—Victoria Regina. The evening's pleasant weather brought all London into the streets to view the light displays.[32]

[31] Haagsma, *Lotgevallen*, 25.
[32] The extraordinary events commemorating the queen's birthday were reported to the same degree in the London dailies the following day. The

That evening, various members of the administration—the Duke of Norfolk, the Earl of Aberdeen, the Viscount of Palmerston, the Chancellor of the Exchequer, to name just a few—presented fourteen balls or state dinners in public offices and private residences around the city. The Royal Bodyguard held its full-dress dinner, and the Archbishop of York held a dinner just for bishops. But by far, the most lavish event that evening was presented by the Marquis and Marchioness of Breadalbane at their mansion in Park Lane. The full London *corps diplomatique* was present, including the American envoy and minister plenipotentiary Joseph R. Ingersoll. The guest list was resplendent with dukes and duchesses, lords and ladies, marquises and marchionesses, counts and countesses, viscounts and vicountesses, and even a few misters and misses—a guest list reported by the *Morning Chronicle* to number upward of eleven thousand persons.

In every event, glasses were raised to salute the thirty-four-year-old monarch's health, which was not robust one month after giving birth to her eighth child. Other than an afternoon carriage ride with her mother, the Duchess of Kent, and her husband, Prince Albert, and three of their children, it does not appear that Queen Victoria was seen in public on her birthday.

In a quiet colonial Nassau town, some 4,342 miles from London, the governor, John Gregory, held a celebration to honor the queen in his residence. Aside from the obligated military officers stationed in the colonial city, the event was reportedly attended by fewer than a dozen persons and bore no resemblance to the events that day in London. From their location in the western barracks that night, the Frisians were startled by an unexplained rocket and fireworks salute off the nearby battery.

Times and the *Morning Chronicle* on May 25 appeared to cover every detail of the celebration, both in London and in cities throughout Great Britain.

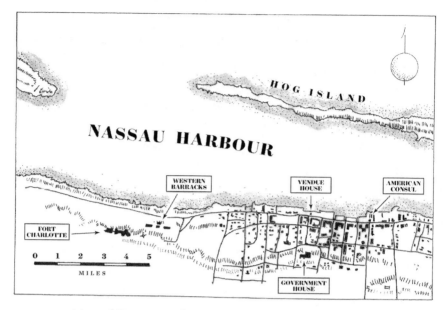

Map of Nassau Harbor. What was Hog Island in 1853
is today the resort area of Paradise Island
(*map by Kenneth A. Schuuf und Jun Schuuf*)

Bruinsma: *You would renounce the glory of martyrdom?*

Kuiper: *Gladly.*

Bruinsma: *And for what would you exchange it?*

Kuiper: *For home. My wife knitting in the lamplight, and my children and I at a game*

Jan de Hartog, Skipper next to God

The Runaway Captain

On Tuesday morning, May 16, the brig *Reuben Carver*, of Rockland, Maine, entered New York harbor and made her way past Governor's Island on the East River and into the large basin of the Atlantic Dock Company. In just one decade, the Brooklyn facility, with its easy-access, deep-water slips, an hydraulic lift, and rows of warehouses was an attractive alternative to the much older and congested bulkheads on the Manhattan side of the river. The *Reuben Carver* had left Sagua la Grande, Cuba, thirteen days earlier with a sweet cargo of sugar and molasses, consigned to sugar importers Robert & Williams. But in addition to her payload, she also delivered the captain of the *William and Mary*, her two mates, and six of her crew. Captain Stinson's report, written soon after they were picked up by the *Reuben Carver*, was ferried across the East River and filed with the New York Associated Press Telegraph Service. That same afternoon, it was received over the wire in Boston and published by the *Daily Evening Transcript* under the caption "Terrible Shipwreck—200 Lives Lost." The following morning, the story appeared in the *New York Daily Times*. In Stinson's own words:

> At 8:30 struck on sunken rock . . . at 12 o'clock midnight found four feet of water in hold . . . at 4 o'clock a.m., weather black and squally, with heavy seas, eight feet water in the hold . . . 7 a.m. ten feet water and the ship going down; mates and crew in boats together with as many passengers as could be stowed in the longboat and lifeboat, the two other lifeboats having been stove after launching; at 8 a.m. left her, and in a few minutes she went down . . . After leaving the ship some hours, saw a bark, apparently bound to Europe, hove too in the direction of the longboat and lifeboat, and suppose she was engaged in picking them up.[33]

On the editorial page of the same paper was the publisher's more passionate statement:

> We have supped on horrors of late and are filled. But here is still another! Yesterday morning, arrived at this port, a vessel bringing the Captain, Mate, and six of the crew of the *William and Mary*, a ship belonging to Maine; which, on her way from Liverpool to New Orleans, laden with railroad iron, struck on a ledge off the Bermuda [*sic*] Islands, on the 3rd of May, drifted off, and went down, carrying more than 200 passengers with her. Except those above mentioned, as brought into New York yesterday, only three of the crew and a few passengers were saved.[34]

The same day, the *Hartford Daily Courant*, under the caption, "Awful Shipwreck—Two Hundred Lives Lost," reported, "The

[33] *New York Daily Times* (May 17, 1853), 3.
[34] Ibid., 4.

names of the unfortunate passengers are unknown—the list having been left behind or lost in the general consternation."[35]

The reader might conclude that either the ship sank so rapidly that the retrieval of this all-important record was not possible, or the ship's officers were grossly incompetent in leaving behind such a vital document.

That afternoon, Stinson left New York City for his home in Maine. If there is any record of his mode of transportation used, it has yet to be found. Two schooners, the *Ophir* and the *Bengal*, left New York that day for Portland, and the transport of either is possibile, although both would have meant a slow, four- or five-day sail. In his haste to return home, it is more likely that Stinson, along with his first mate Welsh, would have taken a train to Boston. In May of 1853, there was an express that left every evening at five o'clock. With stops in New Haven, Hartford, Springfield, and Worcester, they would have arrived in Boston at 12:30 a.m. on Wednesday. From there, it is believed that Stinson took the 7:00 a.m. train to Portland and the afternoon Portland-Kennebec train into Bowdoinham. In so doing, it is very possible that he was home by Wednesday evening. From the Bowdoinham station, it was a short, three-minute walk up the hill to his home, but in all probability, it was the most difficult leg of his journey home.

Stinson returned in shame. In Liverpool he had permitted the overloading of his cargo hold and his steerage compartment and then left port with insufficient food supplies and inadequate safety precautions. On his approach to the Bahamas, he had veered far off course, delaying passage through the Northwest Providence Channel. Once there, he failed to use due caution in an area known to be especially treacherous. Following their collision on the Great Isaac Rock, in panic, he abandoned his passengers,

[35]   *Hartford Daily Courant* (May 17, 1853), 2.

several of his crew, his vessel and its cargo. His uniform, once worn in pride, was now an embarrassment.

On Thursday morning, May 18, news coverage of the sinking of the *William and Mary* was moved to the front page of the *New York Daily Times,* in the lead column position. The full 189-line column reported a somewhat different account and the admission that the previous day's report was given "very briefly and imperfectly." What followed was the first hint of the guilt of the captain and his officers.

> Captain Stinson has since vouchsafed the public no further explanations, and the narrative of the terrible scene . . . can only be gathered second-hand. Careful inquiry, based mainly upon the recollections of one or two survivors of the wreck, has placed us in possession of the principal facts of the case; yet, in the absence of all information from the officers of the vessel, any narration of the disaster must necessarily remain incomplete.[36]

Receiving such a statement would never happen. With Captain Stinson back in Maine, First Mate Welsh in Boston, and Second Mate Ross immediately shipped out on another voyage, there would be no further explanation. Two of the crew remained behind on board the *Reuben Carver* in Brooklyn; the remaining four are unaccounted for, although there is evidence that seaman John Best remained in New York through the end of the month.

In the lengthy *Times* report was still the belief that the ship sank soon after the abandonment of her officers and crew but that the loss of life was less than originally believed. Both the *Times* and the *Brooklyn Daily Eagle* reported confirmation of the captain's belief in a partial rescue. A Captain Nickerson of the coastal schooner *Smith Tuttle,* arriving in New York on Sunday,

---

[36] *New York Daily Times* (May 18, 1853), 1.

May 15, with a load of lumber from the Chassahowitzka River in Florida, stated that he had passed an English bark, name unknown, on May 12, some one hundred miles north of the Bahamas. In a brief exchange between vessels, he learned that the eastbound bark had picked up twenty-five passengers from a boat of an American vessel that had sunk some days earlier. A separate article inside the *New York Daily Times* made a new assertion.

> The silence of the captain of the vessel is not a little remarkable. His sudden disappearance from the city is not less so. There must be reasons for this conduct, and what they are, the community would be glad to know. A statement duly authenticated by the survivors should have been prepared and published by the Master before he found it convenient to leave New York for his home in Bowdoinham.[37]

The *New York Tribune*, in its edition the following day, asked the question that was on everyone's mind.

> How is it that the captain, officers, and crew could be saved, but so few passengers? We simply ask for information, for our idea of a captain's duty has been that he should think most of his passengers and least of himself.[38]

That Thursday, the day the *Bangor Daily Whig & Courier* reported the loss of the *William and Mary*, Stinson faced a certain interrogation on the details from John Harward. Two days later and still closer to home, Bath's *Weekly Mirror* declared to its Kennebec readers, "Loss of Bath Ship, and Nearly 200 Lives."

On Stinson's arrival in Bowdoinham, the guilt of having lost his ship, its entire cargo, the lives of almost two hundred passengers, and three of his crew weighed heavy on him. Perhaps

[37] Ibid., 4.
[38] *New York Tribune* (May 19, 1853), 4.

he thought about how his father and mother had gone into exile when war threatened the Kennebec Valley before he was born. Or he may have remembered stories of his great uncle James and how he retreated to Canada during the Revolutionary War. Knowing nothing of the rescue of the passengers and crew and their transfer to Nassau, Stinson's entire focus turned to retrieving his wife, Thankful, and their five-year-old son, Charles, and moving to where they would not be found.

Foreign news in 1853 traveled remarkably slowly, and word of the dramatic rescue off Grand Bahama Island, although only forty miles distant from American soil, was still foreign news. Three weeks after the rescue, American papers continued to report a large loss of life. On May 25, the New Orleans *Daily Picayune* sympathetically commented on the report that "175 souls suddenly perish[ed]" and five days later specifically called attention to the "German Colony Drowned." (Repeatedly, the Frisians were referred to as Germans.) At the same time, the *Boston Journal* refuted Captain Stinson's published explanation and called on him "to give account for the loss of nearly two hundred lives." The *Illustrated News*, a New York weekly, in its May 28 edition, reported that, of the 208 passengers on board the *William and Mary*, "nearly all went down with the vessel." Significantly, the publication featured a fine wood engraving captioned "Wreck of the Bark *William and Mary*." While creating a rather sensational visual image of the horror of the event, it included several subtle details in conflict with personal accounts. Seaman John Best, watching the New York papers, purchased a copy, and with his pencil, crossed out "Bark" and changed it to "Ship."[39]

---

[39] A copy of the newspaper and the only known illustration depicting the *William and Mary* remains in the possession of the Best family in Denver, Colorado.

I cannot bid adieu to Nassau without attesting the spontaneous,
hearty kindness evinced by her people universally.

Horace Greeley

Leaving Nassau

Shortly past noon on Thursday, May 26, several of the Frisians would have seen the British mail steamship *Conway* enter Nassau harbor, drop anchor, and deposit for an afternoon excursion a dozen passengers. Under the command of Captain Thomas Sawyer, the British steamer made monthly trips between Navy Bay, Panama, and Savannah, Georgia, with brief stops at Kingston, Jamaica, and Nassau. While in Nassau, it was customary for Edward Weale, the ship's purser, to pick up mail destined for the United States, as well as copies of the city's two newspapers from the previous weeks. By eight o'clock that evening, the ship was underway again and expected to arrive in Savannah on Sunday evening. There Purser Weale would deliver the Nassau papers—with their accounts of the rescue of the *William and Mary* passengers—to the offices of the *Savannah Daily*

Georgian and the *Daily Morning News*. By the next morning, the news would be telegraphed to newspapers up and down the East Coast. By Tuesday morning, a similarly worded rescue account would appear in Boston and New York papers.

> Savannah, Monday, May 30. We learned from the officers of the British mail steamer *Conway* from Jamaica, & c., that all but two of the passengers on board the ship *William and Mary*, recently wrecked off the Great Isaacs have been saved. They were rescued by a wrecking schooner while the ship was drifting, just before she sunk [*sic*].[40]

"It is like life from the dead, . . . startling and gratifying," announced the *New York Daily Times* in its editorial comment.[41]

The *Burlington Free Press*, in an article captioned "The Consequences of Neglect," held the British government responsible for the loss of the ship. In a carefully stated charge, the editor of the *Free Press* drew attention to previous requests urgently calling for the construction of a lighthouse on the Isaacs. The article concludes with the transcription of a letter from the president of the board of underwriters in New York City, written a year and a half before the shipwreck to Daniel Webster, secretary of state. The board understood that the American ambassador in London had communicated the need for a lighthouse and was now requesting the Department of State to press the matter with Her Majesty's ministers.

⌒

Following discussions between Charles Malassez and Oepke Bonnema, it was decided that the Frisians, now a group of seventy, would remain together and leave on the *Time*, the larger of the two vessels. Sixty-two others would leave the same day on the smaller

[40] *Savannah Daily Georgian* (May 30, 1853), 2.
[41] *New York Daily Times* (May 31, 1853), 4.

Rover. The remaining twenty-two—mostly single Irish—would wait in Nassau until a third vessel could be identified, approved, and made ready. This arrangement was particularly pleasing to the Frisians, eager to get underway again and especially happy to travel with their own. Departure for the *Time* and the *Rover* was set for Wednesday, June 1.

Under normal circumstances, people might need some time to prepare and to pack up. With the castaways, aside from what had been given to them by the people of Nassau, a change of clothing and one dollar in their pocket, there was nothing to pack. It was just a matter of making one last walk down Bay Street to the quay steps and the waiting schooner.

Captain Kemp drew up his passenger list. Whether he received a list from A. C. G. Malassez and then transcribed it

Detail of the passenger list of the schooner *Time*. Frisian names were a challenge, and every name is incorrectly recorded (*courtesy National Archives and Records Administration*)

to the manifest form, or whether he wrote down the names as they were spoken to him, we do not know. But we are certain that of the names recorded, not one is correct. First to appear are Rients Sikkema and his wife, Ymkje, of Barradeel; on Kemp's list they are Rems and Turke Sebbera. Next was Hendrik Jans Kas of Franekeradeel; on Kemp's list he is Hendrik Sanstam. Not knowing the language, every man, woman, and child is listed as a farmer from Germany. Similarly, all those on board the *Rover* are listed as Irish farmers. We have no explanation why Kemp's list includes the names of three persons who had died and excludes the name of at least one person who was on board.

It was three days after the departure of the *Time* and the *Rover* that the city papers acknowledged the contributions given on behalf of the stranded travelers.[42]

> His Excellency, Governor John Gregory, provided £20
> Dr. Chipman and the Committee of St. Andrews Benevolent Society, raised £25
> The Pastors and their churches, a total of £25, 13 shillings, 4 pence
> Timothy Darling and the congregation of St. Andrews Presbyterian Kirk, £14, 11 shillings, 4 pence
> Timothy Darling and the Sabbath School at St. Andrews, £3, 16 shillings, 6 pence
> Samuel Cunningham and the members of Mr. Romer's Baptist Church, £1, 10 shillings[43]
> Lt. W. J. Chamberlayne, 1st West India Regt., the balance of

---

[42] *Nassau Guardian*, June 4, 1853.
[43] Thomas "Poppy" Romer was a slave until the Emancipation in 1834. Despite being illiterate, he established four churches on New Providence Island. Although the £1, 10 shillings was a relatively small contribution, like the widow's mite, it represented a generous spirit from a group that had little to offer.

Early morning bustle of the Nassau market place
(*courtesy Yale University*)

a fund for which he was responsible, £4, 8 shillings

In addition, three Nassau businesses and five individuals were acknowledged for their donations of goods and clothing. Finally, the ladies of Nassau were thanked for their time and success in providing clothing, especially women's apparel. Their committee had collected and distributed 69 gowns, 124 undergarments, 72 shirts, 60 trousers, 60 blouses, 78 pairs of shoes, 72 hats, 24 bonnets, 57 rags, 30 beds, 20 towels, and 3 boxes of soap.

In writing to his family, Sjoerd Bekius praised the generosity of the people of Nassau and expressed the conviction that the Dutch were not nearly so Christian in that regard. "Most of the people were colored," he wrote, and "very sympathetic. Wherever we moved along the streets, they offered us bread. They planned a collection for us. They gave us clothing and shoes for our feet."[44]

Hendrik Kas wrote a similar letter to his family in Friesland,

---

[44] *Bekins Blue Book*, 28.

noting the sacrifice made for them. "We met several black people on that island," wrote Kas. "They are the best people of all. They would give the clothes off their backs for poor seaman. Each [of us was given] an English testament, for the people are very religious everywhere. They sell nothing on Sunday and worship faithfully in the churches and in the homes."[45]

The heart attitude and serving spirit of the Bahamian people also moved Haagsma. "Everyone [in Nassau] seems to take pride in doing something for others," he wrote, "and their deeds have the mark of a Christian religion which they profess."[46]

---

[45] Kas, transcribed and translated letter, undated, in the collections of Heritage Hall, Calvin College and Seminary, Grand Rapids, MI, 2-3.
[46] Haagsma, *Lotgevallen*, 25.

A faintly delineated gray bank lining the western horizon marked the "land of flowers" of the romantic Ponce de León. Can that be Florida! The Pasqua de Flores of the Spaniards—the country of blossoms and living fountains, welling with perpetual youth!

Joseph Holt Ingraham

To New Orleans

By Wednesday morning, June 1, the *Time* was fully stocked with water, food, and cooking supplies, sufficient to make the trip to New Orleans. Dr. Chipman visited everyone on board and officially declared all to be in sound health. With a strong northwest wind, the *Time* sailed close-hauled out of Nassau harbor and onto the sea. Despite being only one-fifth the size of the *William and Mary* and having only one deck, there were no complaints from her passengers. For the duration of the voyage, all would be fully exposed to whatever weather was presented to them. Haagsma described the environment as *vredig*—peaceful. Below deck, the hold was filled with seventy casks and one hundred cases of wine, cargo that would make the trip profitable for the owners. Kemp also carried with him the most recent newspapers from Nassau for the papers in New Orleans.

That day, and on into the night, the schooner *Time* sailed northward around the Berry Islands, with the *Rover* never

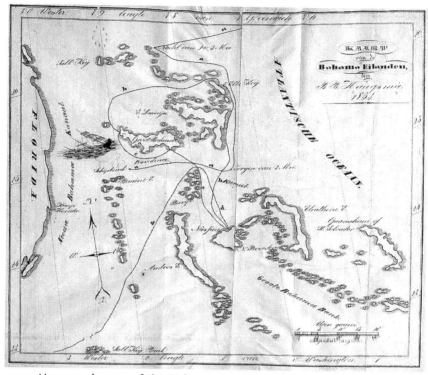

Haagsma's map of the Bahamas as it appeared in his account
of the shipwreck (*courtesy of Tresoar*)

Line a. The course of the *William and Mary* to the point of contact
on Isaac Rocks

Line b. The path of the *Oracle* from Grand Bahama Island to
Nassau

Line c. The route of the second and third schooners to Nassau

Line d. The course of the schooners *Time* and *Rover* as they left
Nassau for New Orleans

far behind. Rather than sailing on the Northwest Providence
Channel, the course was set to the southwest, something that
never would have been done with the larger ships. Even with the
Time and *Rover's* drafts of ten feet and nine feet respectively, the
shallow seas demanded continuous vigilance between the Berry
Islands and Andros Island.

The *Time* was built on Abaco Island in 1847 and, over the
next six years, was a frequent visitor to American ports. In April

Captain Kemp had delivered to New Orleans the mate and crew of the *Osborne*, the ship that had experienced the same fate off the coast of Grand Bahama Island as the *William and Mary*. An irony entirely lost to everyone on board the *Time* was that this small schooner, now conveying its destitute passengers on the fifth leg of their journey, had a previous engagement with the *William and Mary*. Less than six months earlier, this schooner had delivered a load of fruit to South Carolina and was tied up for several days in Charleston harbor, right next to the *William and Mary*, prior to the ship's Atlantic crossing. No one ever knew.

All day Thursday the convoy of two continued on their southwest course, that evening skirting the Cay Sal Banks or, as it was then called, Salt Cay Banks. This low atoll is the western-most part of the Bahamas and is actually closer geographically to Cuba than any of the large Bahamian islands. A light beacon on the northwest side of the bank gave clear warning to the *Time* and the *Rover* to keep their distance. The following day, with a course change to west-southwest, they sailed directly into the Gulf Stream. By Saturday evening, the two schooners passed Key West, then Garden Key, and finally Loggerhead Key, the very end of the chain of islands on Florida's southwestern tip. The course was set to 315° in the direction of the mouth of the Mississippi River, five hundred miles to the northwest. With the prevailing wind from the east, and no obstructions between Loggerhead Key and the Mississippi Delta, the *Time* and the *Rover* could expect good sailing. All was going well; spirits were high.

While the schooners slowly carried their passengers along, news of the remarkable rescue off Grand Bahama Island moved up the East Coast with telegraphic speed. And as quickly as that word found itself in print, editors directed their focus on what one paper called the "Runaway Captain."[47] Although several were

[47] *New York Daily Times*, editorial (June 4, 1853), 4.

suspicious of the captain's account right from the start, now with the news of the rescue, editors used all their power to openly rebuke Stinson for his actions.

The *New York Commercial Advertiser* is believed to be one of the first to severely condemn Stinson for the abandonment of his human cargo and falsely report the event. Editor Francis Hall concluded:

> If Captain Stinson can bear his self-imposed, life-long burden, we have neither envy nor pity to spare him; but we suppose the man who could do as it now appears he has done, has long since become indifferent to human sympathies and impervious to human scorn and contempt.[48]

On Friday, June 3, the *Boston Daily Evening Transcript* published the *Commercial Advertiser*'s remarks to its Boston readership, with copies to other papers. The fire was lit, and it spread quickly. The next day, June 4, both the *New York Daily Times* and the *Weekly Herald* published a report which had originally appeared in the *Savannah Republican*, one that praised the efforts of the few seamen who had remained with the ship and those of Captain Sands, in contrast "to the cowardly and reprehensible conduct of Capt. Stinson and his officers."[49]

An editorial comment that day in the *New York Daily Times* concluded that the fault of this tragedy "lies at a single door, and there can be no apology for neglect of duty so palpable and so cruel."[50]

The same day, and within reading reach of Captain Stinson, owner John Harward, and the entire Bath community, the *Bath Weekly Mirror* announced that it had found Stinson's report to be "unsatisfactory." In the opinion of the editor, the ship was lost

---

[48] Hall, *New York Commercial Advertiser*, June 2, 1853.
[49] *New York Daily Times* (June 4, 1853), 8.
[50] Ibid., 4.

due to the "cowardly inefficiency and great lack of seamanship on the part of the captain and absence of discipline (probably resulting from the captain's incapacity) among the crew . . . every part of the affair is marked by panic."[51]

The *New York Morning Courier and Enquirer*, continuing the theme of condemnation, asserted, "If this is human nature, humanity has sunk low indeed. Deeds such as these are fit to make every true man hide his face for shame."[52]

Even in the Bahamas, though out of range of the magnetic telegraph and unaware of what was being expressed in the United States, the *Nassau Guardian* voiced a similar remark. They saw the captain's report as in indication of his "cowardness and inhumanity" and that his fears "caused him to entertain a very exaggerated and unjustifiable view of the vessel's situation."[53]

We will never know how many of the newspapers were seen by Captain Stinson, if any. But there is no question that word of his abandonment of the ship and its passengers spread quickly through Bath, Bowdoinham, and the Kennebec Valley and would soon influence his decisions.

On Sunday, June 5, the *Time* continued its northwest journey through the Gulf of Mexico toward the mouth of the Mississippi. From Haagsma's journal for that day, we receive a glimpse of a somewhat cynical Captain Kemp and the young journalist. Having a sense that his Frisian passengers were, for the most part, people of faith, the salty captain remarked to Haagsma, "It surprises me that your people are not reading the Bible today." Haagsma, somewhat embarrassed, makes no mention of his response to the captain. He does, however, address the reader of

---

[51]   *Bath Weekly Mirror*, June 4, 1853.
[52]   *New York Morning Courier and Enquirer*, June 5, 1853.
[53]   *Nassau Guardian*, June 4, 1853.

his account with, "You probably wonder what our people were really doing. Well, they were lying on the deck practically all day, like cattle in a pasture. In the case of only a few did a sense of religion have sufficient power to move them to take the best of all books, the faithful guide on the often difficult pathway of life, in hand."[54] In both Liverpool and Nassau, Haagsma was impressed with how the people there honored God by respecting the fourth commandment and disappointed that this was not the case with some of his fellow travelers after coming so close to death.

---

[54]   Haagsma, *Lotgevallen*, 27. Considering the likelihood that their Dutch *Bijbels* would have been lost with their other possessions and the fact that few if any could read the English Bibles they were given in Nassau, this should not have come as a surprise.

PART IV

Finding a New Home

The sun shines down hotly upon your head—the water in the gutter
waxes green, or dries up—gaunt dogs prowl at large through the streets . . .
During the oppressive nights, thousands of mosquitoes swarm about your
ears, which the fitful sea breeze strives in vain to dispose.
You cannot sleep.
George Wharton, *The New Orleans Sketch Book*

New Orleans

There were signs that they were getting closer to the mouth
of the Mississippi. First they noticed ships sailing in the opposite
direction, almost all heavy and low in the water. Then there was
the change in the color of the sea. What had been blue became
green, and as they drew closer to the delta, it became brown. The
water's surface was alarming and turbulent as the river downflow
mingled with the heavier seawater. Finally, on June 7, in the low
morning sun, they saw off in the distance their first American
landmark—a lighthouse.

Fifty years earlier, at the completion of the Louisiana
Purchase, Thomas Jefferson proposed that a monumental
lighthouse be built at the entrance of the Mississippi River,
symbolic of the huge acquisition and practical in its location.
Designed by architect Benjamin Latrobe, and constructed
by Winslow Lewis, the elaborate, temple-like structure was

unfortunately built on a foundation of soft clay. Even before its completion, its columns began to topple, its walls crack, and soon, the entire lighthouse listed under its massive weight. Builder Lewis, however, was convinced he could build another lighthouse, one that would last, if it was placed on a firm foundation. With a congressional appropriation and recycled materials, Lewis began building a simple, eighty-foot-high, brick structure on a secure foundation. Completed in March of 1823, this would be the lighthouse that directed Captain Kemp on his approach to the Northeast Channel that June morning.

In early June, the press gave full coverage to the case *United States vs. Daniel Maloney*, a trial being heard in the US Circuit Court in Manhattan. Daniel Maloney, captain of the ship, *Roscius*, was charged in the brutal beating death of one of his crew. At a time when the public was particularly sensitive regarding the actions of another captain and his conduct at sea, those reading the papers in late May and early June certainly would have made a connection between the captains. If Maloney could be charged with the murder of a sailor known only by his first name, could not a court of inquiry lead to a charge against Timothy Stinson for the lives lost due to his actions?

We believe Stinson spent early June visiting his six sisters and two brothers, all living in Maine, all accessible, although some at a distance. Ruth was the oldest and lived in Richmond, an eight-mile train ride from Bowdoinham. At age forty-six, she was married to a blacksmith and had three young children. Next in line was Stinson's brother, John, forty-four, also a sea captain. When in port, he lived with his wife and two children in Arrowsic, a twenty-mile trip down the Kennebec River. Stinson's sister, Mary, forty-three, lived twenty miles up the Kennebec. She and her farmer husband lived near the village of Farmingdale with their six, and soon-to-be seven, children. Also in Farmingdale were Stinson's sister, Eliza Jane, forty, and her husband, a sea captain, with their two children.

Stinson's other four siblings all lived in Bowdoinham and were within walking distance. Sarah, thirty-eight, and her farmer husband had a three-year-old son and an infant daughter who was born while Stinson was on the *William and Mary*. Another sister, Caroline, was four years older than Stinson and still single. His younger siblings, Henry Clay and Hannah Hunter, twenty-nine and twenty-seven, respectively, were also unmarried in 1853 and living with their widowed mother, Mehitable Stinson, sixty-eight. One by one, each would have been told by Stinson that he was leaving the sea and that he, with his wife and son, would be moving away from Maine.

Leaving was hardest for Thankful Stinson. Although her husband was accustomed to being away from his extended family, Thankful, at age thirty-four, had never been far from home. When she married the captain, she knew they would have long periods of separation. But she always had her father, Nathaniel Purington, and stepmother, Jane, within steps of her door; she saw her younger sisters, Minerva and Mary, and brothers, Albert and Charles, almost daily. As a child, Thankful had lost a brother, a sister, and her mother within seven years. Saying good-bye to her family now, under the present circumstances, was no less harsh; it would be their final farewell.

⌒

"The Father of Waters—the torturous and elastic Mississippi River—" wrote A. Oakey Hall in 1851, "possesses a most unpoetic mouth."[1] Similarly, Robert Russell wrote four years later, "The Mississippi, near its mouth, does not strike one with its majesty

[1] Hall, *The Manhattaner in New Orleans, or, Phases of Crescent City Life* (Baton Rouge: Louisiana State University Press, 1976), 2.

or grandeur."[2] If viewed from high overhead, the shape of the mouth would resemble a huge bird's claw. Some fifteen miles from the Gulf, the singular main stream divides and flows out through multiple passes. With hurricanes moving across the Gulf every summer, and the Midwest's broad watershed sending down its seasonal floods, both the depth and the course of the passes changed constantly. Considering the narrowness of the passes, the shallowness of their bars, the constant strong downflow, and the unpredictable winds, it was clear to most captains that the only safe and reliable way to move from the Gulf to the wharves of New Orleans, 110 miles upriver, was with the services of a steam-powered towboat and the trained eye of a river pilot. An 1852 government chart of the delta advises mariners not to attempt to sail through the mouth of the Mississippi on their own and adds that "vessels are rarely detained for want of tow-boats, as there is considerable competition, and they keep a good look out for the offing."[3]

Sometime on Wednesday, June 8, the steam towboat *Porpoise*, under master Brown, tied lines to both the *Time* and the *Rover* and began a slow pull up through the Northeast Pass. The *Porpoise* was indeed an old workhorse, built in Cincinnati, Ohio, and in service for twenty-five years, she would last another two years, a remarkably long career for a wooden-hull steamboat. On the right, they passed the northeast lighthouse and on the left, what remained of Balize, a former French fort and river marker. After three hours, the schooners were instructed to drop their anchors and release their towlines, allowing the *Porpoise* to return to the Gulf for another vessel. Later that day, the *Porpoise* returned, now pulling the three-mast ship, *Jonathan Cummings*, in from Liverpool.

---

[2]   Russell, *Extract from Journal of a Tour to America* (Edinburgh: W. Blackwood, 1857), 1.

[3]   *Reconnoissance of the Passes of the Delta of the Mississippi* (n.p.: US Coast Survey, 1852).

The *Cummings* had begun its journey on April 13, carrying forty immigrant passengers, a cargo of crated merchandise, and 3,437 bars of railroad iron. Once again both the *Time* and the *Rover* were taken in tow, and all four vessels resumed their slow journey upriver.

From Haagsma's pen: "We stared about at the beautiful river banks, which were decked in a luxurious green and lovely woods, presenting a beautiful scene."[4] A New Orleans writer, known only as "a resident," gives this picture: "The whole [river bank] is now occupied by the sugar planter, and for eight months of the year, the eye of the traveler sees nothing before him but the waving sugar cane, presenting one unbroken living landscape of the most beautiful green ever beheld upon the lap of nature."[5]

From time to time, the vessels would collide with large, submerged tree trunks, some of which had begun their journey to the sea from forests three thousand miles upstream. With each collision, "The women would moan . . . thinking that the rocks of the Bahama Bank were also found in the Mississippi."[6] On one of these encounters, the *Time* became so entangled in the branches of a large willow that axes had to be brought out to cut away some of the branches and allow the schooner to once again float free.

The use of steam power on the river began just prior to the War of 1812 and over the next three decades turned the Mississippi into a commercial highway. But high-pressure steam was temperamental and dangerous. Eight years before the arrival of the *Time* and the *Rover*, when Captain Brown was the master of the towboat *Pilot*, the boiler exploded, throwing him into the river and killing four of his crew. Now the steam boiler on the *Porpoise* began to fail and, sometime during the night, stopped running entirely. Immediately it became necessary to keep the

---

[4]   Haagsma, *Lotgevallen*, 28.
[5]   *New Orleans as it is* (New Orleans: Printed for the publisher, 1850), 20.
[6]   Haagsma, *Lotgevallen*, 29.

four boats from drifting downstream and from colliding into each other. Each vessel had two options: to drop anchor and hope it held sufficiently in the river mud and would not get caught in floating timber or to send out a boat to tie off at a tree on the bank—providing there was a tree, and it could be seen in the dark. Imray's sailing directions for this portion of the Mississippi advised "Every vessel, while on the river, should have its boat alongside with a good hawser in it, according to the size of the ship, ready to run out to a tree."[7] We do not know what action the four crews took, but Haagsma tells us the problem was repaired, and the four continued on through the night.

Thursday morning, June 9, brought a curious piece of news to the deck of the *Time*. Sometime over the last day, in an exchange between Captain Kemp and Captain Brown, the Nassau captain must have mentioned that his passengers were those who four weeks earlier had been rescued from the *William and Mary*. At that point, the New Orleans captain reported that he had read in the *Picayune* just three or four days earlier that the officers and crew of the *William and Mary* had arrived in New York and that, according to her captain, their ship had gone down with a loss of some two hundred lives. Although we do not know where along the river this conversation took place, Haagsma mentions that Captain Kemp was able to stop and send a telegraph message on ahead to New Orleans that the "lost passengers were coming up the river."[8]

All day Thursday the Frisians continued their slow northwest journey up the river through Plaquemine Parish— their second full day in America. So far they had seen only this brown waterway before and behind and mile after mile of green

---

[7]   *A Sailing directory for the West India Islands: containing instructions for navigation among the islands of Porto Rico, Hayti, Jamaica, Cuba, & c., and for the various ports in the Bay of Honduras and the Gulf of Mexico*, 6th ed. (London: James Imray, 1851), 246.

[8]   Haagsma, *Lotgevallen*, 29.

riverbank, interrupted by occasional small communities with names like Fort St. Philip, St. Sophia, and Jesuits Bend.

Early Friday morning, just before dawn, their course suddenly turned to the east and then made an acute turn to the west. And there at last, on the northwest bank, lay New Orleans, the "Crescent City," the "Queen of the South." All along the right bank was the city levee, the unloading and loading stage for hundreds of vessels arriving and leaving this inland port. As far as the eye could see were stacked bales of cotton, hogsheads of sugar, and casks of molasses. Piled high were bags of corn, sacks of oats, and bales of hemp. There were rows of wooden containers of all sizes—boxes, crates, pails, barrels, and hogsheads—all filled with merchandise that within twenty-four hours would be moved off the levee and sent in other directions.

Tethered all along the bank were vessels of every description, all bow to levee, stern to river—sloops, schooners, flatboats, three-mast ships, brigs and barks, and the tall, white river steamers—an unbroken line of commerce sure to impress the provincial Frisian worker. Haagsma wrote, "In the golden rays of the morning sun, the scene was beautiful. Those colossal, mostly white buildings, those hundreds of gigantic steamboats, and those luxurious banks on each side of the winding river, presented an unsurpassable scene."[9]

The *Time* and the *Rover* were towed as far as District 1, where they were released from the *Porpoise*; the *Time* to dock 9, at the foot of Julia Street, and the *Rover* to dock 10. There both were turned over to A & J Dennistoun & Company, merchandising agents in the city.

Owing in part to the advanced notice sent by Captain Kemp the previous day, several in the city were prepared for their arrival. First to arrive at the *Time* was Mr. J. B. Schroeder of the

---

[9]   Ibid., 30.

Deutsche Gesellschaft, the German Society. As an immigrant from Oldenburg, Germany, a city not one hundred miles from Friesland, he was well aware of the difficulties that awaited new arrivals and especially young families. Schroeder was an energetic forty-three year old, a husband and father of three girls, and a tireless advocate for German-speaking people. His routine each day was to leave his home in the city's Garden District and walk down to the levee. There he would greet each arriving ship, determine if there were Germans on board, and then assist them in processing through the customs office. For those making New Orleans their destination, he would help in finding work, a place to stay, medical care, if necessary, even financial assistance when needed. For those like the Frisians, whose intent was to travel farther upriver, Schroeder would help in making steamboat connections. Because of the yellow fever epidemic, which had broken out every summer since 1847, Schroeder knew the importance of moving immigrants out of the city as quickly as possible.

Schroeder's work was demanding, and his contribution to the well being of those passing his doorstep cannot be overstated. On several occasions, he took personal responsibility for small children orphaned on their voyage to the United States. Sometimes his efforts were met with resistance and opposition, as was the case just one week before the arrival of the *Time*. That day he had boarded the ship *Statesman* and was assaulted and threatened by two of the ship's mates. Not to be intimidated, Schroeder had both men charged and brought to court on the day the *Time* arrived.

In his June 13 report to the Deutsche Gesellschaft, Schroeder wrote:

> I made my way on board [the *Time*] in order to offer the assistance of the German Society to any Germans among them. I found there to be no Germans, . . . however, there

were 70 Dutch, many [of whom were] German speakers. I brought the agent of these Dutch, a Mr. Bonnamar [*sic*], to Mr. Ferd. Kennett & Co., which immediately declared itself ready to deliver the 70 to St. Louis, and also agreed, in the end, to supply them with sustenance for the trip to St. Louis. Mr. Ferd. Kennett & Co. entreated me to see to, at their cost, the embarkment of the 70 people on the steamboat *Grand Turk*, as well as their provisioning. I went to work directly.[10]

Schroeder was not alone in his assistance. At the British Consulate at 118 Common Street, William Mure quickly drafted an appeal for support from the citizens of the city. At age forty, Mure had spent the past ten years in the position of Her Britannic Majesty's consul in New Orleans and demonstrated a particular sensitivity toward the plight of immigrants coming up the river. A widower and the father of four young girls and an infant son, Mure was also an astute businessman and, aside from his consular duties, made a profit from the cotton that went down the river, as well as from other commodities coming up the river. A transcription of the manifests from both the *Time* and the *Rover* were also forwarded to the office of the New Orleans *Daily Picayune* for its Friday evening edition.

Bonnema and Haagsma immediately completed plans to book passage for the group on the next steamboat to Saint Louis, one leaving at 5:00 p.m. the next day. Schroeder then walked with them from the levee to 93 Magazine Street, Ferdinand Kennett & Company, grocers in the city. There they placed an order for the entire group for delivery to the boat.

After what had been a cramped, five-day voyage, all were eager to step once again onto land and take their very first steps in America. They were routinely processed through the customs

---

[10] Schroeder, Deutsches Haus Collection, 2008.0113, item 4, Proceedings of the Deutsche Gesellschaft von New Orleans, 1847-54, Williams Research Center, the Historic New Orleans Collection.

office—despite having brought virtually nothing with them—and then spent the remaining day on the levee. Schroeder's report mentions his securing lodging for those not leaving on Saturday but makes no reference of his doing so for those who arrived on the *Time*. The assumption must be that they remained on the deck of the schooner on Friday evening.

By day, the levee was alive with commercial activity, sailors, stevedores, deck hands, merchandising agents, clerks, planters, and slave traders with their human wares. On Friday afternoon, a thunderstorm passed through the crescent city, dampening everyone unable to find cover. Along the levee, three ships were struck by lightning, leaving their masts severely damaged.

The city's newspapers reported more nefarious activites on the levee after dark. A body was found floating in the water; upon examination, it appeared the person was robbed, strangled, and tossed into the canal. A man was arrested for harboring and concealing a runaway slave. Two young boys were apprehended for stealing a bottle of wine, valued at thirty cents. Twenty-five "fair damsels" were arrested for being lewd and abandoned. A man was arrested for buying stolen tobacco from a slave, another for drunkenness and indecent exposure, and yet another for being drunk and carrying a concealed weapon. And a young boy was brought to the police office and charged with juvenile vagrancy, being found "wandering the streets without a home."[11]

Captain R. G. A. Levinge, a British visitor to New Orleans wrote that, in his opinion, the city was "the most demoralised [sic] place in the world; there are whole streets of houses of more than doubtful reputation, alternating with hells and billiard rooms. They are open to the street, a crimson curtain being the only separation from it."[12] It is unlikely the Frisians saw any of this.

---

[11] *Daily Picayune* (June 11, 1853), 4.
[12] Levinge, *Echoes from the Backwoods; or Sketches of Transatlantic Life* (London: H. Colburn, 1846), 2:57.

On Saturday morning, readers of the *Daily Picayune* found the following:

> An Appeal—The destitute condition of the unfortunate passengers saved from the wreck of the ship *William and Mary* demands the sympathy and immediate aid of the citizens of New Orleans. The particulars of this sad shipwreck are too well known to require comment. . . . They arrived here yesterday, 139 in number, of whom forty-five are children, and almost all of them are poor, destitute, and without means of leaving the city.[13]

Although the writer misidentified the national origins as German and Danish, he concluded his appeal:

> In such distressing circumstances, charity knows no geographical limits, and the undersigned, therefore, feels assured that he will not appeal in vain to the generosity of the citizens of New Orleans to relieve these unfortunate people. Contributions will be received at this office until Tuesday evening. William Mure, British Consulate, 118 Common St.

Two other newspapers on Saturday, the *Deutsche Zeitung* and the *Louisiana Staats Zeitung*, announced to the city's large German community the arrival of the "miserable and poor" and the need for collective assistance. That very morning, gifts began arriving.

It is not at all surprising to find young Haagsma walking about the city Saturday morning, making the most of his very brief stay, just as he had done in Liverpool and Nassau. Although he makes no mention of visiting a book store, it is apparent that before leaving New Orleans, he purchased an 1853 edition of

---

[13] Mure, *Daily Picayune* (June 11, 1853), 2.

Conclin's New River Guide, or A Gazetteer of all the Towns on the Western Waters; containing Sketches of the Cities, Towns, and Countries Bordering on the Ohio and Mississippi Rivers, and Their Principal Tributaries. This small, 128-page guidebook provided Haagsma a concise source of information, pieces of which would find their way into his travel account.[14]

Travelers usually see what they want to see, and what Haagsma found were beautiful buildings on clean streets. He was particularly impressed with the stock exchange and the customs house, both under construction. He also saw portions of the city that were not pleasant, but he avoided their description. As alert and sensitive as he was to the issue of slavery, he makes no mention of the city's open slave market, the largest in the South. Had he picked up the *Picayune* for the two days he was in New Orleans, he would have found the following notices:[15]

> Auction Sales this Day Wm. D_____ sells negro girl, Suzana, belonging to estate of the late Charles B_____, at 12 o'clock, at Bank's Arcade.
>
> Negroes for sale—a first rate blacksmith, 1 carpenter, 1 tanner and butcher, cooks, washers, and ironers, and house servants; also a number of field hands, both men and women. Persons wishing to buy would do well to call as they will be sold at reasonable prices and satisfactory guarantees given. Apply to _____
>
> Slave Depot, 195 Gravier St. The undersigned has always on hand a well-assorted lot of slaves for sale, consisting of field hands, mechanics, and house servants. He will receive and sell or purchase for his friends on commission and has orders for 20-25 slaves, for which the highest cash prices will be paid.

---

[14]   *Conclin's* (Cincinnati: J. A. & U. P. James, 1853).
[15]   *Daily Picayune*, June 10-11, 1853.

For every advertisement offering the sale of slaves, there were three promising rewards for runaways.

> Run away June 4th a negro man, ADAM, black color about 35 years of age, 5' 10", thin body and sharp features, looks down and sullen, will try to make his way up the river.
>
> Fifty dollars reward – Ran away from wood yard of the subscriber about the 1st of March one mile above Hurricane Plantation & 30 miles below Vicksburg, a bright mulatto man ED or NED, 26 years, 5' 10", straight hair and badly marked by the whip.
>
> Twenty dollars reward – Run away from Steamer *Prince* in N.O. A dark griffe negro boy named BEN, from 25 to 30 years, about 5' 8" or 5' 9", has one finger cut off below the first joint.
>
> Ten dollars reward – Run away from the subscriber on Wed. night, the 8th, the boy HACHEN, aged 25 years, 5 ft 8 inches high, very black complex., a scar between the eyebrows in the shape of the letter B. Speaks English broken but French perfectly.

The anonymous writer of *New Orleans as it is*, summarizes, "It is here before you in unmistakable character, how completely unfeeling, inhuman and brutalized a man may become, and yet be a 'gentleman and respectable.'"[16] Very likely it was here that the seed of Abraham Lincoln's Emancipation Proclamation was planted in his mind. In 1860 Lincoln wrote, "When a boy, I went to New Orleans on a flat boat and there saw slavery and slave markets as I have never seen them in Kentucky."[17]

Throughout the day, the Frisians heard the blast of steamboat whistles as boats left for upriver destinations. The first

[16] *New Orleans as it is*, 73.
[17] Lincoln to Alexander Stephens, January 19, 1860, as quoted in Richard Campanella, *Lincoln in New Orleans: The 1828-1831 Flatboat Voyages and Their Place in History* (Lafayette: University of Louisiana at Lafayette Press, 2010), 217.

left at 8:00 a.m., four left at 9:00 a.m., another four left at noon, two at 4:00 p.m., and nine were scheduled to leave at 5:00 p.m. But only one was to leave for Saint Louis.

English-born architect and New Orleans resident Thomas Kelah Wharton described in his journal the "stifling pernicious air" that summer.[18] "Lord help the unacclimated stranger," recorded Wharton, knowing of the thousands of immigrants passing through the city. For several weeks, doctors were fearful that Yellow Jack had returned early. There were ten cases in New Orleans in late May and early June in which it appeared that yellow fever was back. Since the symptoms in each case were slightly different, there was no agreement among city doctors on the diagnosis—not until June 10, the day the Frisians arrived in the city. Dr. Erasmus Darwin Fenner, in his report on the epidemic wrote:

> Case 11—Margaret R_____, an Irish girl, age 22, had lived in New Orleans six months, entered Charity Hospital, Ward 36 (Dr. Robertson) June 10th—then sick six days and died on the 11th, after turning yellow.

> Case 12—June 10, Dr. Sunderland was called to see a young man, James M_____, at Mrs. Conroy's boarding house on Race Street. When he got there, he found the patient dead but a few minutes . . . the body was yellow.[19]

Both cases were unmistakable. Dr. Fenner tried to make a connection to the ships that were arriving from Europe, but in subsequent investigations, his theory was shown to have too many exceptions. Jo Ann Carrigan, in an article on the 1853 epidemic, wrote,

---

[18]   Samuel Wilson Jr., Patricia Brady, and Lynn D. Adams, eds., *Queen of the South: New Orleans, 1853-1862: The Journal of Thomas K. Wharton* (New Orleans: Historic New Orleans Collection, 1999), xxv, 38.

[19]   Fenner, *History of the Epidemic Yellow Fever at New Orleans, La. in 1853* (New York: Hall, Clayton, 1854), 25-26.

From mid-July until the last of August, the pestilence raged through New Orleans in full fury. The mortality reached almost incredible heights: 200 one week, 400 the next, then up to 500, 900, 1,200 and 1,300 per week. Yellow fever deaths for the week ending August 27 amounted to the staggering total of 1,365.[20]

No one could determine the cause. Someone conjectured it was the work of an oppressive foreign government; a New York City newspaper theorized it was the result of slavery; others believed the Church of Rome was to blame. Closer to home, it was thought to have something to do with filth and poor sanitation or perhaps the heat and humidity. Someone went so far as to suggest a relationship to insects, maybe mosquitos. Swamps surrounded the city.

Not knowing the cause, it was hard to come up with preventative measures. The board of health thought it could change the atmosphere by firing cannon in the city and burning large pots of tar. Carrigan noted that the cannon fire ceased after two days but that the burning of tar pots continued for some time. As leader of the German Society during the epidemic, J. B. Schroeder established four offices of the society around the city to assist sick Germans; soon all the agents became ill. Only four persons, compared to two hundred of the previous year, attended the annual meeting of the society.

During the summer of 1853, almost eight thousand persons died in New Orleans of yellow fever. It would take another forty-seven summers before army surgeon Walter Reed made the connection between mosquitos and yellow fever. Our travelers, by God's grace, were able to leave the city thirty-two hours after their

---

[20] Carrigan, "Yellow fever in New Orleans, 1853: Abstractions and Realities," *Journal of Southern History* 25 (Baton Rouge: Southern Historical Association, 1959), 346.

arrival. If space had not been available to them on the steamboat leaving Saturday night, they would have had to remain in the city another seven days.

The weather very hot, mosquitoes penetrating into every crack and crevice of the boat, mud and slime on everything; nothing pleasant in its aspect, but the harmless lightning which flickers every night upon the dark horizon.
Charles Dickens, *American Notes*

Steamboat to Saint Louis

Compared with the five previous vessels used by our travelers, the 688-ton *Grand Turk* was the largest and finest. From bow to stern, she stretched 241 feet, more than 100 feet longer than the *William and Mary*, and almost 31 feet from side to side. Her main deck appeared to be no higher than two feet above the river. The ceiling was exceptionally high to accommodate the many cords of wood fuel, tons of freight, and multiple furnaces. The forward half of the boat—the business end—was entirely open and free of guardrails to maximize its load capacity. The second deck—the boiler deck—was much lower in ceiling height, open only for a small portion forward of the smoke stacks, and otherwise outfitted on either side with rows of private cabins. Above it was the hurricane deck, a broad deck entirely open to the weather, a promenade for river viewing. Slightly forward of the midline and rising another twenty feet above this deck was

Steamboat *Grand Turk* (*courtesy New Orleans Public Library*)

the pilothouse or Texas, the quarters for the pilot on duty. Just behind the Texas were two steam vent stacks; just forward of the Texas, and towering over all, were the boat's fluted smoke stacks, and, suspended between them on wires, were the letters "G. T." There were two flag poles, the tall jack staff at the bow, essentially a navigation site aid for the pilot, and a much shorter staff on the stern, flying the stars and stripes. Perhaps the most prominent feature of all were the paddle boxes on either side of the boat, each painted with "Grand Turk" in black, capital letters on white, not to be mistaken for any other boat. Compared with many of the other steamboats lavishly festooned in their carpentry, the *Grand Turk* was dignified in her no-nonsense simplicity and practicality.

Judging from a notice that appeared in the *Daily Missouri Republican* that month, the *Grand Turk* certainly had the endorsement of that journal. "We can commend this boat to the traveling public in her accommodations, table, berths, the civility and gentlemanly deportment of her officers, as well as their skill and carefulness in managing their craft," wrote the editor. "They have no superiors."[21]

---

[21]   *Missouri Republican* (June 25, 1853), 2.

When the *Grand Turk* arrived from her homeport of Saint Louis and tied up at the New Orleans levee on June 8, immediately her gangplanks were lowered to the main deck, and swarms of stevedores began to unburden her freight load. Containers of flour, barrels of whiskey, and kegs of butter were rolled off and placed on the levee. Carts were used for the more cumbersome bales of hay and bales of hemp. Heaviest of all were some 269 hogsheads of tobacco, soon to be turned over to four of the city's tobacco dealers. Last, there were hundreds of packages, too numerous to itemize by contents, noted in the manifest only as "sundries."

Once the main deck was cleared, the process was reversed. Taken on board were 175 hogsheads, 153 barrels, and 94 boxes, all filled with sugar for two dealers in Saint Louis. Some 238 kegs of nails were loaded for a hardware merchant. Destined for grocers throughout the Midwest were 54 sacks of coffee beans, 51 sacks of rice, and 3,000 sacks of salt. Altogether, shipments were taken on board consigned to fifty-seven Saint Louis merchants.[22]

Once all shipments were secure, clerk H. S. Philips was ready to receive his passengers. On riverboats, there were two classes, cabin passengers and deck passengers. Cabin passengers were affluent tourists and business travelers. For about $15, they were given private accommodations on the boiler deck, salon dining, and promenade access to the hurricane deck. Deck passengers, on the other hand, had a roof over their heads, mattresses spread out across the floor, a common toilet, and little more. Their movement was restricted to the main deck. Deck passengers usually brought their own food for the trip, although meals with the crew could be purchased for about $.25. Those willing to assist in loading wood each day could reduce their passage cost to $2.25; children between three and fourteen would pay half that amount, and

[22] *Missouri Republican* (June 22, 1853), 3.

any children under three would travel for free. While we have yet to uncover a passenger manifest, considering their prior accommodations, and knowing they carried food provisions with them, we can assume our Frisian travelers were among the large class of deck passengers.

First in line to board on Saturday afternoon were group leader Oepke Bonnema and his bookkeeper-journalist, Broer Haagsma. Behind them were Tjipke Algera; Jan and Anna Balkstra; Sjoerd Bekius and his cousin, Maartje Schaaf; Hendrikus and Anna de Boer; Herke and Anna de Jong and their two children; Jelle Gersema; Bauke and Klaaske Graafsma and their remaining child; Sytske Heemstra; Bertus Hofstra; Pietje Hollander; Jan Jansen; friends Grietje Jansonius and Hendrik Kas; widow Antje Kooistra and her surviving three children; Dirk Kuiken; Gerrit Molenaar; Cornelis Ploegsma; Beinze Rienks; Hendrik Rienks; Peter Salverda; Rients and Ymkje Sikkema, now without children; Johannes and Riemke Stienstra and their three children—one of the few families untouched by death; Sjoerd Tjalsma, his very pregnant wife, Sjoukje, and their five remaining children; Johannes and Trijntje Tuininga and their surviving three; the van der Ploegs—Jan, Baukje, Marten, and Metje; J. K. van der Veer; Siebren and Marijke Wesselius and their three children; the Westerhuis family, Arijen and Jeltje and their now four children; and Dirk Zwicht.[23]

Once again, they were not alone; the *Grand Turk* would be packed with a varied lot of immigrants. From Saturday, June 4, through Saturday, June 11, eleven vessels had arrived in New Orleans—from Le Havre, Barcelona, Malta, Aspinwall, and Liverpool—each bringing those desiring a new start in America. Three ships, the *Statesman*, the *National Eagle*, and the *Charles*

---

[23] While we have no known passenger list for what was a crowded steamboat, we can say with a high degree of certainty that those listed here were on board the Grand Turk.

Crocker, brought a total of 1,007 passengers. During the same period of time, seven steamboats had left New Orleans for Saint Louis, the stepping-off point for many of the new arrivals.

Herman Melville, in his final novel, *The Confidence-Man,* describes Mississippi steamboat travelers as:

> English, Irish, German, Scotch, Danes; Sante Fe traders in striped blankets, and Broadway bucks in cravats of cloth of gold; fine-looking Kentucky boatmen, and Japanese-looking Mississippi cotton-planters; Quakers in full drab, and United States soldiers in full regimentals; slaves, black, mulatto, quadroon; modish young Spanish and Creoles, and old fashioned French Jews; Mormons and Papists . . . jester and mourner, teetotalers and convivialists.[24]

John James Audubon described a similar assortment on his Mississippi experience in 1843:

> Our *compagnons de voyage,* about one hundred and fifty, were composed of Buckeyes, Wolverines, Suckers, Hoosiers, and gamblers, with drunkards of each and every denomination, their ladies and babies of the same nature, and specifically the dirtiest of the dirty.[25]

It was the gambler and his associates that added a netherworld element to river travel, particularly on the lower Mississippi. Wherever people congregated, wherever a dollar was to be found, the river gambler and his criminal cousins were bound to be active. Totally unbias in whom they duped, they worked equally among the cabin class and deck passengers.

---

[24] Melville, *Confidence-Man: His Masquerade: An Authoritative Text, Contemporary Reviews, Biographical Overviews, Sources, Backgrounds, and Criticism,* ed. Hershel Parker and Mark Niemeyer, 2nd ed. (New York: W. W. Norton, 2006), 16.

[25] Maria R. Audubon, *Audubon and His Journals* (Freeport, NY: Books for Libraries Press, 1972), 451.

One hour before sailing, pitch pine was tossed into the steamer's furnaces, producing a dark smoke, the signal to those on the levee that the time of departure was at hand. Although the *Grand Turk* was expected to leave at five o'clock in the afternoon, it was not until six o'clock that the ship's bell was rung, the steam whistle blown, and the boat finally backed into the stream for its 1,218-mile run to Saint Louis. Captain W. R. Claytor was not competitive in moving up the river. There were steamboats that intentionally raced up the river and set speed records in doing so. Four records were set in 1853 on the 268-mile leg between New Orleans and Natchez, the fastest time being nineteen hours and forty-seven minutes, set by the *Eclipse*. But present river conditions called for cautious piloting. The *Picayune's* column, "River Intelligence," each day reported falling river depths with some portions of the river and its tributaries being so low that they were closed to navigation.

All Saturday evening and into Sunday, the *Grand Turk* moved through turn after turn on her serpentine upriver journey. By Sunday morning, they had reached Baton Rouge, a city sitting high on a bluff on the right bank of the river. Because of its position over the water, the residents of Baton Rouge had been protected over the years from floods and hurricanes. This was not the case with the village of Waterloo, two hours north of Baton Rouge. Although the town prospered as a cotton and sugar exporting community in 1853, a flood in 1884 washed out the levees, and, within a decade, there was no trace of the town. But here on June 12, 1853, the Frisian passengers on board the *Grand Turk* observed a curious pageant. The boat had stopped to take on wood, a refueling task that had to be done usually twice a day—normally a fifteen-minute operation. One of the black men loading wood that morning was being urged by some of the travelers to shake off his slave chains, remain on the steamboat, and make a run for freedom. An irony sure to escape everyone that morning was that the *Grand Turk* had been built five years earlier in Freedom, Pennsylvania, a town established by abolitionists. It was their practice to place signs along the Ohio River with the single word "Freedom," letting runaway slaves know they had reached freedom in Pennsylvania. That Sunday morning, a slave in Waterloo, Louisiana, made his break for freedom.

On Monday, their third day on the river, the *Grand Turk* stopped in Natchez, Mississippi. Originally established by the French as Fort Rosalie, in 1830 it was renamed for its earlier Native American inhabitants. Haagsma took opportunity to purchase some refreshments, and in so doing, he noticed that the town appeared to be profitable from a business point of view. Or perhaps he read in *Conclin's* guide that the village had fifteen hundred houses, three churches, a courthouse, four banks, two bookstores, three printing offices, and several stores, foundries, and factories, and a population of eight thousand. In *Conclin's*, "The city is romantically situated on a very high bluff . . . 300 feet above the level of the river."[26] Mimicking *Conclin's*, Haagsma would later describe Vicksburg as "romantically situated on a hill 300 feet high."[27]

Rainfall in Mississippi's broad watershed was scarce in the spring of 1853. By mid-June, most steamboats with deep drafts were taken out of service. A few pilots chose to risk the loss of perishable cargoes by remaining on the river, trusting in their skill to avoid sandbars, while hoping for rain. On this trip, the *Grand Turk* had several advantages: her cargo for the most part was not perishable; she had a relatively shallow draft of seven feet, seven inches; and she was on an upriver course. Vessels heading into the current had a better chance of freeing themselves if they

[26]   *Conclin's*, 106.
[27]   Haagsma, *Lotgevallen*, 32.

became grounded than those moved by the current and heading downstream.

But on Tuesday morning, the fourth day, it happened. Several miles south of Vicksburg, Mississippi, the *Grand Turk* found herself stuck on a sandbar. When this happened, a pilot might try several maneuvers. He might send out a boat and a lead line to determine where deeper water might be found. He might use some mechanical means to free the boat, perhaps a cargo shift, or he might employ another steamboat. In drought conditions, when the river was falling, it could be days before a boat was freed. Eventually the paddle wheels would be reversed, and the vessel would be able to move toward deeper water. Haagsma offers no information as to how the boat was released but says encouragingly that the delay was not long.

All day Tuesday, the heat continued to build. The *Daily Missouri Republican* reported that day the weather to be remarkably warm and dry. From his law office farther upstream, in Springfield, Illinois, forty-four-year-old Abraham Lincoln commented that business had slacked off on account of the heat. "Owing to the excessively warm weather," wrote Lincoln, "there is no disposition on part of the members of the bar to crowd [the docket] forward. We are not surprised at this for ever we who are working men find it difficult to bear up under the high temperature."[28]

That Tuesday was Timothy Stinson's thirty-third birthday. How and where he celebrated is unknown. Earlier in the month, John Harward had given Stinson a letter received from a merchant in Boston. The letter was a simple request for further information concerning the loss of the *William and Mary*, a letter which Harward had intended for Stinson to reply to directly. The merchant, however, never received a response. It was about the

---

[28] As recorded in *The Lincoln Log: A Daily Chronology of the Life of Abraham Lincoln*, comp. by Lincoln Sesquicentennial Commission (Washington, DC: Government Printing Office, 1960).

time of his birthday that Stinson, his wife, Thankful, and their son, Charles, disappeared from Bowdoinham.

On Tuesday, back in New Orleans, readers of the *Daily Orleanian* found the following notice:

> To the Shipwrecked Passengers—Those passengers remaining at different boarding houses who are able to leave the city are requested to call at 118 Common Street on Tuesday, between the hours of 10 and 11 a.m. so that arrangements may be made for their passages to their different destinations. Wm. Mure[29]

And on Tuesday, but much farther east, residents in Friesland were devastated to read a lengthy account of the shipwreck in the *Leeuwarder Courant*. One line, "*Ik zag nooit in mijn leven iets zoo vreeselijks*,"[30] Stephen Purington's translated remark of never having seen anything so shocking in his life, was certain to leave them horrified. The article was a rewrite of the item that had appeared in the *New York Weekly Herald* on May 21, a copy of which had finally made its way to Europe. On the next page of the June 14 *Courant*, there appeared a brief report from Liverpool, that three Frisians—Ulbe Bergsma, Isaak Roorda, and Oene Wagenaar—were saved and had made it back to that city with a small number of non-Frisians. Several days earlier, the *Courant* broke the news of the shipwreck in three short paragraphs, noting the rescue of the captain and his crew. Neither article held out any hope for the others.

Twenty-nine-year-old Pieter Runia, a tailor in Kimswerd and friend of Broer Haagsma wrote, "This news spread like a thunderclap over the entire province, tears of pity ran down the faces of everyone."[31]

[29] Mure, *Daily Orleanian* (June 14, 1853), 1.
[30] Purington, *Leeuwarder Courant* (June 14, 1853), 2-3.
[31] Runia, as published later in *De Hollander*, November 9, 1853.

It would be another three days before Frieslanders would read an account of the rescue in the *Leeuwarder Courant*; the story that originated in the *Nassau Guardian* on May 13 was delivered by ship to Savannah, then by telegraph to New York, by ship to London, and finally by telegraph to Leeuwarden some thirty-five days later.

All through the rest of Tuesday and into Wednesday, the *Grand Turk* continued her twisting, ever-turning journey upriver, around one bend after another. By noon on Wednesday, they had left Louisiana behind and continued on, with Arkansas on the left bank and Mississippi on the right. That evening they reached what Haagsma termed "the prosperous little cities of Napoleon and Victoria."[32] *Conclin's* lists Napoleon as a "flourishing little place" but gives no description of Victoria.[33]

Maps of Arkansas today show no town with the name of Napoleon. Could Haagsma have been confused with what he saw? Or could Napoleon have suffered the same fate as Waterloo—a victim of the river's ever-eroding banks?

Mark Twain, in his account, *Life on the Mississippi*, tells the story of his going downriver and asking the steamboat captain to drop him off at Napoleon. The conversation continues:

> "Go ashore where?"
>
> "Napoleon."
>
> The captain laughed; but seeing that I was not in a jovial mood, stopped that and said,
>
> "But are you serious?"
>
> "Serious? I certainly am."
>
> "Why, hang it, don't you know? There is n't any Napoleon any more. Has n't been for years and years. The

---

[32] Haagsma, *Lotgevallen*, 32.
[33] *Conclin's*, 96.

Arkansas River burst through it, tore it all to rags, and emptied it into the Mississippi!"

"Carried the whole town away?—banks, churches, jails, newspaper offices, court-house, theatre, fire department, livery stable—everything?"

"Everything. Just a fifteen-minute job, or such a matter."[34]

Napoleon, Arkansas, was a town with prosperous ambitions. Established by a former French soldier and named after his commander, in 1853 the town was a relatively young, twenty-three years old. On the riverbank was a large storage building for processing freight. Not far from it and still under construction was a federal hospital for those injured on the river. There were churches, a school, a hotel, and stores; Napoleon was the seat of government for Desha County. Included in the town's population of six hundred persons were merchants, several doctors, a few carpenters, a couple of painters, and slaves. But the town also had a dark reputation, and those who visited had little good to say about it. While levee construction efforts were made over the years to hold back the river, none were sufficient in checking the stream. During the Civil War, the river was intentionally diverted toward Napoleon, and the city was virtually abandoned.

In 1863 mapmakers Charles Magnus and F. W. Boell published a map in two colors (pink land, blue water) of the lower Mississippi showing the location of every town from the Gulf of Mexico to the city of Saint Louis. There, on the west bank, just at the confluence of the Arkansas River, was the city of Napoleon. (Several miles upstream, on the Mississippi side, was the town of Victoria.) A decade later, a flood washed Napoleon from subsequent maps; today, all that remains on the riverbank are a few tombstones of the former town's residents.

[34] Twain, *Life on the Mississippi* (New York: Harper & Bros., 1899), 251.

On Thursday morning, June 16, the *Grand Turk* reached Helena, Arkansas. Between it and Saint Louis there remained 525 miles of river. Daytime temperatures all week rose into the nineties. Cabin passengers lingered over meals in the salon, napped in their private quarters, took cool drinks from the bar, got a trim from the boat's barber, and spent hours at the card table. Every morning, the deck passengers would first clear their mattresses from the floor, wait in line for the use of the toilet, prepare their meals, and hope something on the boat or along the bank would capture their attention. For Thursday, that did not come until sometime in the evening, when passengers began drifting off to sleep. Wishing to take advantage of a sleeping passenger, a pickpocket on board was able to reach into a man's pants pocket and remove his wallet. Although completely unnoticed by the sleeper, the theft did not miss the vigilant eye of the *Grand Turk*'s mate. The thief was immediately apprehended, restrained with a rope, and sternly lectured on the error of his ways. At this point, the person appeared contrite, was released by the mate, and told to not attempt to leave the boat. But the next morning, as the boat approached Memphis, the thief took opportunity to jump overboard and swim for the nearest bank.

On Friday, June 17, Captain Claytor was obligated to interrupt the journey upriver and address necessary repairs. There were unidentified problems with the high-pressure boilers, a matter that could not be ignored. Steamboat boilers were fed by river water, and as a result of the high level of sediment, it was necessary to keep them from choking. Of all the threats to steamboat navigation—collisions with other vessels, fires, snags with river debris, and storms—boiler explosions were the most common and almost always deadly. On the Mississippi River alone, during the period from 1843 to 1852, between 650 and 700 lives were lost as a result of boiler explosions. But the *Grand Turk* had also sustained considerable damage to her paddle wheels.

Unavoidable collisions with tree trunks floating down the river—
some completely submerged—so damaged the blades, that the
boat's progress up the river was greatly impeded. As the boat's
engineer worked on the boilers, the boat's carpenter set about
replacing the broken blades, an effort that went on all through
the night.

By Saturday morning, repairs were finished, and the *Grand
Turk* resumed her trip up the river. That evening, after a full
week on the lower Mississippi, they finally reached New Madrid,
Missouri.

New Madrid: few travelers on board the *Grand Turk* that day
had ever heard of that town. Unless they had a copy of *Conclin's
New River Guide*, it is unlikely they would have known anything of
what had occurred at this point forty-two years earlier, believed
by some to be the most significant geological phenomena ever
experienced in the United States. On December 16, 1811, a massive
earthquake, estimated with a surface-wave magnitude of between
8.1 and 8.6, rocked the Mississippi River Valley, ripples of which
were felt by President Madison in the White House, tremors that
reportedly caused church bells to ring in Boston. New Madrid, at
the quake's epicenter, was demolished. One eyewitness reported:

> The earth on the shores opened in wide fissures, and, closing
> again, threw the water, sand, and mud, in huge jets, higher
> than the tops of the trees. The atmosphere was filled with
> a thick vapor or gas, to which the light imparted a purple
> tinge. The sulphurated gasses that discharged during the
> shocks tainted the air with their noxious effluvia and so
> strongly impregnated the water of the river, to the distance
> of one hundred and fifty miles below, that it could hardly be
> used for any purpose for several days.[35]

---

[35] *Conclin's*, quoting a Dr. Hildreth of Marietta, OH, 88-90.

After five weeks of tremors, on January 23, 1812, a 7.8 quake again shook the Mississippi Valley, and then, two weeks later, an 8.8 quake was felt in twenty-three states. Over a period of five months, there were more than two thousand quakes in the New Madrid area.

Summarizing *Conclin's* three-page description of New Madrid, Haagsma boils it down to being, "formerly located high on a rock, but in an earthquake in 1800 [*sic*] it sank down."[36]

Sunday, day eight on the river, brought our travelers past the rusty banks of Kentucky and by early afternoon to the confluence of the Ohio River. Briefly ascending the eastern tributary, the *Grand Turk* made a stop at Cairo, a sleepy hamlet on the southernmost tip of Illinois. *Conclin's*, frequently lavish in praise of the river towns visited, calls attention to the town's failure to establish itself as a major port city. A kinder Broer Haagsma declines comment. Back on the river, the *Grand Turk* began her last leg of the trip to Saint Louis, a 191 mile long section of relatively straight river.

To many cabin passengers, traveling by riverboat on the Mississippi was hardly a pleasant experience. English writer Francis Milton Trollope was not happy with her fellow travelers or her accommodations. "I would infinitely prefer sharing the apartment of a party of well-conditioned pigs to the being confined to its cabin." Understandably, she was repulsed by the habit of spitting on the floor. Over all, she found riverboat travel boring. "We began to wish that we could sleep more hours away."[37]

From high up on the hurricane deck of his steamboat, cabin passenger Walt Whitman looked out over the landscape in agreement with Mrs. Trollope. "The shores of this great river are very monotonous and dull," he wrote, "one continuous and rank flat, with the exception of a meager stretch of bluff, about the neighborhood of Natchez, Memphis, etc."[38]

---

[36]   Haagsma, *Lotgevallen*, 33.
[37]   Trollope, *Domestic Manners of the Americans* (New York: H. W. Bell, 1904), 16.
[38]   Whitman, from "November boughs" in *The Complete Writings of Walt Whitman* (New York: G. P. Putnam's Sons, 1902), 6:212.

Sleep was also what New Yorker Juliette Starr Dana wanted on board the *Minnesota*. "We found the beds so full of bed bugs," she wrote in her diary, "that it was impossible to sleep, and after killing one cockroach also, I did not attempt it."[39]

Charles Dickens also had trouble sleeping in his cabin. His complaint was the ringing of the bell by the bow lookout, the man whose job it was to warn of submerged timber. "Always in the night this bell has work to do," vents Dickens, "and after every ring, there comes a blow which renders it no easy matter to remain in bed." Dickens was on the Mississippi for just two days but complained that the Father of Rivers was nothing but "an enormous ditch," a "foul stream."[40]

Naturalist John James Audubon, in a letter to his uncle, reported the steamboat *Gallant* to be the "filthiest of all filthy old rat traps." Water for washing was drawn from the river, and a single bar of soap and a solitary towel had to be shared by 150 fellow travelers. "My bed had two sheets, of course, measuring seven-eighths of a yard wide; my pillow was filled with corn-shucks."[41]

Of the various letters known to exist from the Frisian deck passengers, not one expresses a complaint on their base accommodations up the river. Perhaps their memories were still fresh with the occurrences of the past months, experiences that would remain with them the rest of their lives. A positive Haagsma wrote in his journal, "I did not tire of that river voyage; those thousand turns each presented something of interest every minute."[42]

[39]   Dana, *Fashionable Tour through the Great Lakes and Upper Mississippi: The 1852 Journal of Juliette Starr Dana*, ed. David T. Dana III, foreword by Brian Leigh Dunnigan (Detroit: Wayne State University Press, 2004), 93.
[40]   Dickens, *American Notes*, 110-11.
[41]   Audubon, *His Journals*, 450-51.
[42]   Haagsma, *Lotgevallen*, 31.

The city lies at your feet, with its busy and industrious population;
the river, with its dark bosom dotted by palatial steamers, flows
by on the east; the long trains of cars as they thunder along the
American Bottom; the hills which rear their brows against the sky
in the west—all combine to render the scene lovely and picturesque.
Jacob Taylor, *Sketch Book of St. Louis*

Saint Louis, Missouri

Early Tuesday morning, June 21, after nine-and-a-half days on the river, the *Grand Turk* reached the city of Saint Louis, Missouri. Established as a French trading post only eighty-nine years earlier by fur trader Pierre Laclede Leguest and named in honor of King Louis XV and his patron, Saint Louis IX, the outpost was conveyed to the United States as part of the massive land purchase from France in 1803. With the arrival of the first steamboat fifteen years later, its growth was explosive. Water access to the port of New Orleans to the south, the Great Lakes cities to the north, the eastern manufacturing points via the Ohio River, and the western frontier by way of the Missouri River positioned the city as the hub of the nation—the Queen City. According to *Conclin's*, "Miners, trappers, hunters, emigrants, and people of all character and languages meet here and disperse in pursuit of their various objects in every direction, some beyond the remotest points of civilization."[43]

When Dickens visited Saint Louis in 1842, he saw "wharfs and warehouses and new buildings in all directions; and . . . a great many vast plans which are still progressing."[44] Five years later, when Alexander MacKay visited Saint Louis, he reported that "Within its precincts, particularly about the quays, and in Front and First Streets, it presents a picture of bustle, enterprise, and activity; whilst on every hand, the indications of rapid progress are as numerous as they are striking."[45] By 1853 the population was estimated to be over ninety thousand, in a city that stretched out along a five-mile curve on the west bank of the Mississippi. Remarkably, by the time of the arrival of the Frisians, there was no visible trace of the catastrophic fire that four years earlier had destroyed 640 homes in the city and twenty-eight steamboats tied along the levee.

In the city's grid was a picture of order. In 1853 numbered streets generally ran parallel to the river, from First Street, nearest to the water, to Eighteenth Street, on the far west. Perpendicular to these were streets named after prominent Americans or men associated with the city—Washington, Franklin, Biddle, Carr, and so forth—and then streets named for a variety of trees—Locust, Olive, Pine, Chestnut, Walnut, Spruce, and the like.

Unlike the open-armed welcome and embrace the Frisians received in Nassau and in New Orleans, their entrance into Saint Louis went entirely unnoticed. Other than the routine listing of steamboat arrivals in the *Daily Missouri Republican*—the *Grand Turk* was one of ten arrivals on June 21—no other announcement

---

[43]   *Conclin's*, 81.

[44]   Dickens, *American Notes: For General Circulation* (London: Chapman and Hall, 1942), 117.

[45]   MacKay, *The Western World, or Travels in the United States in 1846-47* (Philadelphia: Lea and Blanchard, 1849), 2:129.

appeared in the Saint Louis press. Several of the Frisian leaders sought out the direction of the Netherlands consul in the city but found a disappointing response. Dutch-born tobacco merchant Frederick R. Toewater represented the Dutch government in matters relating to immigration. Certainly he would have read in the Missouri papers some word on the loss of the *William and Mary* and how his countrymen had escaped the tragedy with only the clothes they were wearing. But rather than responding with assistance to the travelers' simple requests, he dismissed them. Then, quoting a portion of international law related to shipwrecked passengers, he offered his help in seeing them back to Friesland. It may have been that Toewater's business interests limited his consular activity. The annual premium tobacco sale at the state tobacco warehouse would be held in two days, an event that could engage him for the entire day. Or perhaps he was not kindly disposed toward Frisians. One thing the Frisians were certain of, there would be no help from the Dutch consul.

On Tuesday afternoon, the rebuffed party hoped to find accommodations at a German-owned inn. Haagsma notes, "We were not treated cordially."[46] When the manager insisted on full payment in advance, the Frisians moved on to a French hotel, where they found better treatment.

Siebren Wesselius took advantage of the stop to write to his children in Grand Rapids, Michigan, and relieve them of their concerns. "God has not only saved our lives," he began, "but we all have unblemished health." Wesselius then went on to describe the terror they had encountered in the shipwreck and their gratitude in their rescue, concluding with the news that they would remain in Saint Louis for five days before proceeding to their destination in Iowa.[47]

---

[46] Haagsma, *Lotgevallen*, 34.
[47] *De Nieuwsbode*, Sheboygan, WI (July 12, 1853), 2.

It seems surprising that the Frisians remained in Saint Louis for five days, especially knowing of their eagerness to move farther up the river, purchase land, and begin building homes. Then we learn of the latest heartbreak for the Tjalsma family. When on the Atlantic, they lost their oldest child. Now Sjoukje Tjalsma, after carrying her baby through multiple episodes of seasickness, a shipwreck, near starvation, and the stress of constant movement, gave birth to a stillborn child. Perhaps it was out of consideration for her health that the group passed on the opportunity to book passage on either of two boats leaving for Galena, Illinois, on Thursday afternoon—the brand new *Brunette* and the *Minnesota*. The next boat to leave was scheduled for Saturday afternoon. It is also possible that both steamboats were so heavily booked that they could not accommodate the group, even though the original ninety-two was now down to sixty-seven. Jan and Anna Balkstra decided they could go no farther; they would remain in Saint Louis for the present. Several others, sensing a release of their original commitment by virtue of the shipwreck and subsequent experiences, were now looking for the opportunity to separate likewise, some to the Dutch settlements in Michigan and others to the West.

A few days before the arrival of the Frisians, another traveler had stepped onto the Saint Louis levee from a Mississippi steamboat. Like many of the young men in Bonnema's party, he too had reached the decision that it was time to leave home and see where he might establish his mark. He was seventeen and had already demonstrated a quick wit and giftedness with words. Since neighbors were frequently the targets of his pen, he wrote under an ever-changing index of pen names—W. Epaminondas Adrastus Perkins, Son of Adam, John Snooks, Peter Pencilcase's Son, Thomas Jefferson Snodgrass, and half-a-dozen others. But on arrival in Saint Louis, he presented himself as Samuel Clemens and made his way to the home of his sister, Pamela, and her husband, William A. Moffett.

Clemens liked the city from the start. "The first time I ever saw Saint Louis," he wrote some years later, "I could have bought it for six million dollars, and it was the mistake of my life that I did not do it."[48] He arrived with thirty-five dollars in his pocket and immediately found work in the composing room of the *Evening News,* but within months, he moved on to New York, then Philadelphia, Washington, DC, and wherever else his heart led him.

Broer Haagsma also liked Saint Louis from the start. For the benefit of those in Friesland who would later read his account, he compared it to Leeuwarden, the largest city in the province, although only one-fourth the size of Saint Louis. He appreciated the city plan and found the buildings "colossal and exceptionally beautiful."[49] He could see himself living in Saint Louis.

On Thursday, June 23, the *Eastern Times* announced to its Kennebec Valley readers, "Capt. Stinson, who so cruelly deserted the *William & Mary,* with her two hundred passengers, has gone to Australia."[50] Over the next week, other papers around the country would repeat the rumor.

In 1855 lithographer Leopold Gast and his brother created an expansive panoramic view of the Saint Louis waterfront, showing a continuous flotilla of riverboats tied along the western bank, a row of forty-seven pairs of tall black stacks.[51] Haagsma noticed many of those same boats, and during his five-day stay in the city, the newspaper record places some sixty vessels at the levee. The saints were there—*St. Ange, St. Louis, New St. Paul,* and *St. Nicholas.* All four boats would meet a martyr's end. The fancy ladies

[48] Twain, *Life,* 168. The name Mark Twain did not come into use until 1863.
[49] Haagsma, *Lotgevallen,* 35.
[50] *Eastern Times,* Bath, ME (June 23, 1853), 3.
[51] Gast, in Leopold Gast and Brother, *Saint Louis, MO in 1855 (graphic), engr. on stone.*

were also there—*Kate Kearney*, *Clara*, *Isabel*, *Martha Jewett*, and *New Lucy*. The *New Lucy* had the reputation of being the fastest lady on the river. And then there were the gentlemen—*Jesiah Lawrence*, *Geo. Collier*, *Ben Campbell*, *Patrick Henry*, and *John Simonds*. The *John Simonds* was prominently featured in Leopold Gast's view of Saint Louis and was prominent when the Frisians passed through as well; at almost three hundred feet in length and rated at 1,024 tons, she was one of the largest vessels on the levee. She would have a relatively long career on the river; her final chapter would be serving in the approaching war, first as a Confederate weapons supplier and later as a Union hospital boat.

One steamboat missing for most of the week was the very boat the Frisians would have taken to Galena, Illinois—the *Michigan*. The 482-ton *Michigan* was a new boat, just recently placed in service and originally scheduled to leave on Saturday for the Upper Mississippi. But on Tuesday afternoon, on her return run from Galena, the *Michigan* was slammed by a mile wide tornado, toppling both of her tall chimney stacks and pushing her onto an island on the Illinois shore. In the melee, two of her crew drowned. Despite her damage, she made it back to Saint Louis and was immediately taken out of service. Until repairs could be completed, the little steamer *Ben West* would fill in for the stricken boat.

The 241-ton *Ben West* was built in 1849 and, by river standards, was growing old; the average lifetime for a wooden-hulled riverboat was only four years. When the boat was less than a year old, one passenger wrote of her being "a miserable boat," with "no room to breathe," and "scarcely fit for passengers."[52] But during the winter of 1852-53, the *Ben West* was overhauled, renovated, and returned to service much improved.

---

[52] Tony Martini, "Willden Family—English Preacher and Mormon Pioneer," *Graveyard Gossip* (blog), March 31, 2010, http://graveyardgossip.blogspot. com/2010/03/willden-family-english-preacher-and.html. Britisher Charles Willden had nothing good to say about the boat. He and his family were on the *Ben West* only six days when his two-year-old daughter died.

Detail of Leopold Gast's lithograph of the Saint Louis waterfront,
showing the large steamboat *John Simonds*. The full two-panel
illustration depicts forty-seven steamboats
(*courtesy Library of Congress*)

Bonnema secured passage for all through agent R. F. Sass,
with departure set for four o'clock on Saturday afternoon. Once
again, groceries were purchased for what would likely be a three-
or four-day journey. Each issue of the *Daily Missouri Republican*
carried a long list of grocers located near the levee. Our travelers
were now within days of reaching their new home.

There were graceful curves, reflected images,
woody heights, soft distances; and over the whole scene,
far and near, the dissolving lights drifted steadily, enriching it,
every passing moment, with new marvels of coloring.
Mark Twain, *Life on the Mississippi*

Saint Louis to Galena, Illinois

Saturday, June 25. Late that afternoon, the *Ben West's* pilot backed away from the levee and its long row of riverboats, eased out into midstream, and pointed the bow upriver. Fifteen miles upstream, the boat passed the mouth of the Missouri River and, for the first time in more than thirteen hundred miles, the Frisian passengers saw a river that was not dark and muddy.

Four months had passed since the group had left home. No one ever expected the journey would take so long or that they would encounter so many hardships. And it was not over. Sometime on Sunday, only five days after the delivery of their stillborn child, Sjoerd and Sjoukje Tjalsma lost their three-year-old son, Sjoerd. No information was recorded as to where or when or why. The custom on the river was to make burial at the next wood stop along the riverbank. Two years earlier, when the *Grand Turk* was making her way to Saint Louis, she lost thirty emigrant passengers to cholera. It was noted in the newspaper that two or three burials were made at each wood stop upriver. The graves would be left unmarked, and in time, most would be lost to the river's ever-changing course. Sjoukje Tjalsma, however, would have no part of leaving the body of her small child in the mud of the riverbank, insisting on hiding the corpse until they reached their destination.[53]

On Sunday afternoon, our travelers passed Hannibal, Missouri, on the left bank, the boyhood home of Mark Twain, and later that day, Quincy, Illinois, on the right. Sometime during the night, they skirted the darkened city of Nauvoo, high on the Illinois bank. After his expulsion from Missouri, Mormon leader Joseph Smith moved here to established a new community, a theocracy of sorts, that he named Nauvoo, derived from Hebrew, meaning "to be beautiful." Its centerpiece was an elaborate, three-thousand-seat temple, to be seen by all passing up or down the river. But the years at Nauvoo were turbulent, and in 1844, Joseph Smith and his brother, Hyrum, were jailed in nearby Carthage and eventually murdered by an armed mob. Four years later, the temple was destroyed, and the Mormon community moved on to Salt Lake City, Utah. In 1853 Nauvoo was occupied by Icaria, a utopian socialist commune, but its days, too, were short lived.

By Monday morning, June 27, the *Ben West* stopped in Burlington, Iowa, former capital of the Iowa Territory. On the same day, in now distant Nassau, Bahama, governor John Gregory composed a six-page letter to His Grace, the Duke of Newcastle. Previously Gregory had informed the duke of how Nassau had provided for the refugees from the *William and Mary*. Now he was declaring his expenditures and respectfully requesting reimbursement. By his accounting, the cost of hiring and outfitting three schooners to move 166 castaways from Nassau

---

[53] Pearl Coster, interview by Kenneth A. Schaaf, March 10, 2013.

to New Orleans was £ 996.[54] He further called to the attention of His Grace a claim of £ 131 received from Robert Sands, reported to be his expense in rescuing the abandoned passengers. Gregory conveys his being "painfully impressed with the magnitude of the expenditures—the more so, as I entertain considerable fear that the Law Officer of the Crown will fail in recovering the amount from the owner, charterer, or master of the late ship *William and Mary*, my belief being, that they are all Americans residing out of Great Britain and beyond the reach of our law."[55] Finally, the governor recommends to the Duke of Newcastle that the Crown consider an amendment to the Passengers Act of 1852 which would require foreign-owned ships passing through colonial waters to post a bond of £ 1000. We have no indication that reimbursements for these amounts were ever realized.

The following day, Governor Gregory sent Newcastle what is believed to be his last letter on the *William and Mary* affair, a rambling four-page cover letter to a report from emigration officer Pinder. In it, Gregory draws attention to what he believes were the "deplorable conditions in which the emigrants are allowed to embark in British ports with regard to clothing."[56] Both Pinder and Gregory appear oblivious to what the passengers of the *William and Mary* lost, first in the shipwreck and second to the plunder of their rescuers. He notes the efforts taken via private charity and contributions by the shopkeepers of Nassau to see that every man, woman, and child from the *William and Mary* left Nassau for New Orleans with a change of clothes, something that, in the future, he thought could better be supplied out of the "wealth and abundance of Liverpool and Dublin." One month later, the fifty-seven-year-old governor succumbed to the cholera epidemic that swept through Nassau.

[54] In US currency, this was equivalent to $4,887, or in today's value, $111,000.
[55] Gregory, Colonial Office 23/143, no. 7805, Department of Archives, Nassau, Bahamas.
[56] Ibid., no. 7806.

On Tuesday morning, June 28, those on the *Ben West* received an unexpected greeting. As the boat glided by the dock at Davenport, Iowa, a man on the bank yelled out in Frisian, "Wer komme jimme wei?" Immediately Haagsma responded that he was from Wonseradeel, to which the gregarious Frieslander replied, "Ik bin fan Wolvegea." Haagsma comments that this was the first Frisian they had met in America, yet no one seems to have caught his name.[57]

From Davenport, the boat crossed the river and stopped at Rock Island, Illinois, site of a federal arsenal. In 1853 Rock Island was the focus of a heated debate. Railroad interests proposed the construction of a bridge across the Mississippi, from Rock Island to Davenport, the first ever to span the river. The city of Saint Louis saw the proposed bridge as a menace to their trade monopoly and fiercely opposed its construction. Riverboat owners also saw a railroad bridge as a threat to their industry, virtually claiming ownership of the river and its use. But just two weeks after the Frisians made their brief stop in Rock Island, bridge construction was begun on the eastern bank.[58]

Early on June 29, while it was still dark, the *Ben West* entered the narrow, winding Fever River, followed it upstream for seven miles, and tied up at the wharf in Galena, Illinois. By 1853 Galena had grown to some thirteen thousand souls. The lifeblood of the city was in the rich veins of lead lying in the hills surrounding the town. Native Americans were the first to mine it, followed by the

---

[57] Haagsma, *Lotgevallen*, 36.

[58] The rivermen did not give up without a fight. Three years later, and within days of the bridge's opening, the steamboat *Effie Afton* collided with the bridge, igniting to flame both the boat and the bridge. When the owners of the steamboat filed a suit for damages against the railroad, lawyer Abraham Lincoln was engaged on the defense team. In his argument, Lincoln recognized the position of Saint Louis and the rivermen to keep the river open to trade, but he stressed that the need to travel east to west was just as great as their desire to travel north to south. The jury could not be persuaded to one position over the other and was dismissed. It was not until 1862 when the Supreme Court ruled in favor of the bridge.

French. But it was in the 1820s and 1830s that the industry began to boom, and as lead was smelted and sent down the river in the form of pigs, Saint Louis became the primary beneficiary. Were it not for the shipments of lead, it is doubtful any of the riverboats would have ventured a stop so far off the Mississippi.

Although the lead boom had begun to wane, the town still had the appearance of a thriving community. Galena's newspaper, the *Weekly Northwestern Gazette*, just the day before the Frisians' arrival, announced:

> Galena's Main Street is a miniature Broadway. The street is filled with people and teams from early dawn till late at night; every store and shop that lines its sides is crowded with merchandise. Her docks and wharves are alive with business. Three or four steamboats, crowded with passengers arrive and depart daily.[59]

Elizabeth Fries Ellet, visiting Galena the previous summer, wrote,

> It was a novel amusement in the evenings to sit by the window and see rushing almost under it, with the noise made by the western high-pressure boats, steamers so large as apparently to fill up the little river that skirts the city, and is now shrunken by the drought into half its accustomed limits. At night the appearance of these boats, lighted up and filled with lively passengers, is very picturesque. All that ascend or descend the Mississippi stop at Galena.[60]

On disembarking the *Ben West*, the Frisians were met by Hermanus De Jager, thirty-six, a Netherlander and former teacher who arrived four years earlier and was working in Galena as a merchant. De Jager was known in Galena as having a better-than-

---

[59]   *Weekly Northwestern Gazette*, Galena, IL (June 28, 1853), 2.
[60]   Ellet, *Summer Rambles in the West* (New York: J. C. Riker, 1853), 47-48.

average education, a fondness for books, and a willingness to share his large personal library with his neighbors. He was also known to boast of his patrician Huguenot heritage, and he claimed to have descended from Henry IV of France, also known as Henry of Navarre.[61] It is very possible that De Jager had read the brief note in the Galena newspaper the previous day that the shipwrecked travelers had made it through New Orleans and concluded they would soon be coming up the river. It was his intention to help the Frisians with their baggage, totally unaware of the paucity of their belongings.

Immediately De Jager was surrounded by his countrymen, each of them eager to tell of their experience on the *William and Mary*. De Jager was just as quick to pick up their cause, to tell their story, and to solicit help in bringing Stinson to justice. Unfortunately, in the multitude of voices, portions of the story became garbled. People saw things differently; stories conflicted. De Jager quickly wrote what he had heard and sent it off to the editor of *De Hollander*, a Dutch-language, weekly newspaper in Holland, Michigan. It would be the first of five submissions on the journey of his new friends.

On Thursday, June 30, Bonnema, Haagsma, and most of the men—a party of about thirty—left Galena on the steamboat *Levee* and headed northward on the Mississippi in search of land opportunities. Under De Jager's watchful eye, the women and children remained behind in Galena. Once a suitable site was found for the settlement and shelters constructed, someone would return for them.

---

[61]   Obituary for Herman De Jager, *Galena Daily Gazette*, Galena, IL, December 6, 1889.

Passed a prairie called Le Cross [sic] (from a game of ball played
frequently on it by Sioux Indians). It is a very handsome prairie, with a
small square hill on its summit, . . . bounded in the rear by hills.
Zebulon Montgomery Pike, Journal

The Final Ascent

Back on the broad Mississippi, the party soon reached
Dubuque, Iowa, Bonnema's original settlement goal. But a quick
glance at the hilly terrain was all it took to keep the party moving
upriver to land more like what they had left behind in Friesland.
Hour after hour they looked out over the bow of the *Levee*,
scanning the Wisconsin bank on the east and the Iowa shore to
the west. Eventually they passed the northeast corner of Iowa and
began looking out over Minnesota.

By noon on Friday, July 1, the party of men reached what was
then called Prairie La Crosse, Wisconsin, a small town established
only seven years earlier. It was time to step off the *Levee* and begin
looking at options in earnest. Flags were seen on several buildings in
town, displayed for the upcoming Independence Day celebration.
Wasting no time, the men spent that afternoon walking around
the area, concluding that it was too sandy for their purposes. That

night, Bonnema fell ill, and the search for the site of their colony was postponed. It was not until Tuesday of the following week that Bonnema felt well enough to continue the search. It appeared that the best possibilities in Wisconsin were sandwiched between the Mississippi River and a high bluff ten miles to the east. On Wednesday they ferried across the river to consider land in Minnesota but quickly concluded that transportation conditions there were not suitable to their enterprise. The following day, they returned to Wisconsin, this time exploring land south of La Crosse but again had transportation concerns. On Saturday, July 9, Bonnema and several of the men were back in Minnesota. Eager to make a purchase, they acquired a house and eighty acres of land from a German settler some three miles off the river.

No longer the focus of attention in the national press, the plight of the Frisians was now the subject of De Jager's pen. Through his efforts, word of their ordeal was now being distributed among the Dutch communities in western Michigan, Wisconsin, and even back to Friesland. On July 13, *De Hollander* (Holland, MI) published De Jager's list of the families and singles that had reached Galena, Illinois, two weeks earlier. Also disclosed for the first time was the misperception that, since Bergsma, Wagenaar, and Roorda had separated from the main company of travelers, they had thrown in their lot with the *William and Mary* crew.

During the second week of July, Bonnema's advance team turned its attention to a flat area north of La Crosse and Onalaska. Finally, on the fifteenth, the decision was made to stake a claim on 640 acres—one section or one square mile of land—about eight miles northwest of Onalaska, four miles east of the Mississippi on the Black River. Immediately a messenger was dispatched to call for those waiting downstream.

Several days later, De Jager wrote that a Frisian by the name of Schaafsma arrived with the message to advance. Certainly he was mistaken; it was Schaafsma who had left the group while still in Liverpool. Nor was there anyone else on either side of the river with that name. Perhaps he meant Graafsma, or Gersema, or perhaps even Haagsma. Regardless of the identity of the messenger, arrangements were made on the next boat to La Crosse. Rients and Ymkje Sikkema, the couple that had lost their three year old and their three month old at sea, made the decision to go no farther; they would remain in Galena. Siebren and Marijke Wesselius and their three children also chose to stay put in Galena, in anticipation of the arrival of their son, Tjalling, and son-in-law, Pieter Bijlsma. Both young men had immigrated to the United States in 1849 with their wives and established themselves in Grand Rapids, Michigan. Once they arrived in Galena, they would take the new arrivals back with them to western Michigan. This news would certainly not please Oepke Bonnema, but it was something he could do little about. Since Siebren Wesselius had a tie with Vrouwen Parochie in Het Bildt, he very likely would have discussed his plan with Maartje Schaaf and Sjoerd Bekius. If not, Bekius was certainly resourceful enough to make his way from Galena to the home of his uncle, Maartje's father, in another Frisian colony, this one prospering under the name of Vriesland, in western Michigan.

The best route to reach western Michigan for the Wesselius family and the Schaaf-Bekius cousins was via the Galena and Chicago Union Railroad. In July of 1853, however, the rail line had not yet completed its track bed as far west as Galena. The first leg of the journey would require an arduous, sixty-mile stage ride from Galena to Nora, Nora to Freeport, and Freeport to Rockford. Once in Rockford, trains would leave each morning at 7:30 and each afternoon at 3:00 for a relatively smooth four-hour-and-forty-five-minute trip to Chicago.[62] In Chicago, the travelers would board a train of the Michigan Central Railroad to Kalamazoo, and from that point northward, it was a slow forty-mile-plus wagon trek. Certainly, anticipation grew with every passing mile.

In an effort to promote justice, in his July 20 report, De Jager drew attention to the derelict efforts of the *William and Mary* crew and Captain Stinson in particular, or as referenced by De Jager, "the rascal of a captain, Spinson or Spenson," and the deception that was employed in the escape plan.[63] Absent the verification of Haagsma or Bonnema, the story now included unidentified Hollanders making a run with the captain and his officers. Surfacing once again was the shocking story of the elderly Irishman, who, in an attempt to enter the longboat, had his hands severed by an ax wielding crew member and the tossing overboard of his protesting daughter, both left to drown within view of their horrified family.[64] De Jager concludes with an indictment of the three *William and Mary* crew members left behind on deck, on the charges of theft, drunkenness, and abandonment of their duty.

Having made their claim to a section of land, it was now necessary for Bonnema and company to hire a surveyor to identify and mark their purchase. Haagsma recorded that on Wednesday,

---

[62] In a letter to his family, Bekius mentions passing through Columbus. He most likely meant Chicago. *Bekins Blue Book*, 29.

[63] De Jager, *De Hollander*, July 20, 1853.

[64] Although accounts of death on board the *William and Mary* impacted the ship's Dutch passengers to a much greater degree than the Irish, English, or Germans, no single family felt the horror of unjust loss as did the Diamond family. John Diamond left his family in the long boat; Mrs. Diamond reportedly died in Nassau, and their baby died on the *William and Mary*. It is believed to be Mrs. Diamond's father and sister who drown trying to escape the ship. Regrettably, little is known of this family.

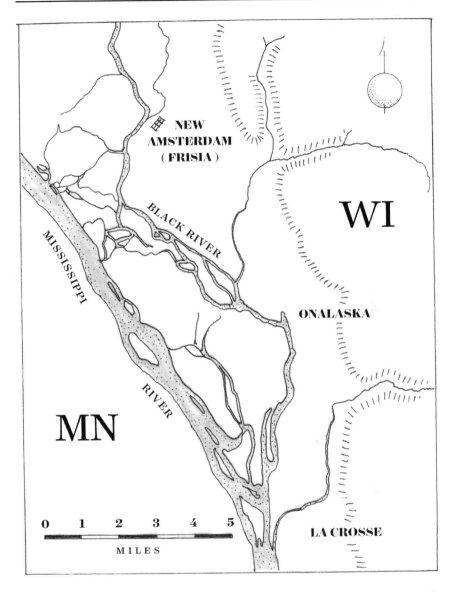

A portion of La Crosse County showing the maze of water courses north
of La Crosse city in the 1850s. The colony of Frisia was established
on the Black River, facilitating transport of its lumber production
(*map by Kenneth A. Schaaf and Jon Schaaf*)

July 20, a beautiful summer morning, a crew set out for Onalaska. There they purchased a quantity of food provisions, selected the tools and nails they would need, ordered a wagonload of lumber, and hired a German driver to deliver it. They spent the night in his home.

On Thursday morning, they all set out for the new home site—Bonnema, the crew members, the surveyor, and the wagon driver with his load of lumber. The first six miles passed with ease on an established dirt road. The last two miles, however, required cutting a new course. Each time a stream was encountered, it became necessary to build what Haagsma called "a Swiss bridge." The men would cut two, three, or four large trees, place them across the stream, and then lay a series of smaller logs across them, parallel to the stream, thus making bridges as they went along. Sometime around midday, their destination was reached, and the surveyor was able to call out, "Here is your land, and on this tree, you will see the mark of the line that runs straight through it."[65] At once the lumber was unloaded and the driver and surveyor released to return to Onalaska.

"There we stood," wrote Haagsma, "on a gentle hill amid a countless multitude of trees, in a beautiful field in July."[66] Nearby flowed the Black River, farther was the Mississippi, and in the far distance, the bluffs of Minnesota.

The reflection lasted only a moment. Quickly the men picked up their tools to build their first shelter, racing the sun as they went. Haagsma called the structure a "tent," although any resemblance to such a fabric shelter was limited to its overall shape. First a long trench was dug, and over it was placed a roof of planks nailed to a long ridgepole. By sunset the first shelter was

---

[65] Haagsma, *Frysia, of schets der Friesche volksplanting in Noord-Amerika* (Bolsward: P. M. Feenstra, 1855), 12.

[66] Ibid.

Haagsma's "tent" or temporary dwelling as it appeared in his 1855
publication on the settlement (*courtesy Tresoar*)

nearly finished. Haagsma tells us, it was not fancy, just "practical architecture."[67]

In total exhaustion and joyous satisfaction, they lay their heads down on a bed of grass, hoping for sweet rest. Not knowing what wildlife might roam in the dark, axes and hammers were kept at their sides, reminiscent of the first night on the beach on Grand Bahama Island. Unfortunately, they suffered the same fate in their new home as they had experienced on the island—a night-long attack, cursed by "muskitos" from above and what appeared to be ants from below. Sweet dreams would not be possible. After a futile struggle, the crew built a large bonfire, filled their pipes with tobacco, and in true Dutch fashion, spent the night smoking.

The following morning, Haagsma tells us, the sound of the hammer rang through the forest, where, other than the tent of the wandering Native American, no building had ever stood. Soon two huts were ready for occupancy.

[67]   Ibid., 13.

In De Jager's third article, he begins to build a case for emancipation for the black race. Based on statements he had heard from his Galena guests, he compared the abusive treatment received at the hand of the ship's crew members with the kindness shown by their black hosts. "The shipwrecked were made to feel at home in the quarters of the Negroes," wrote De Jager. "They were cared for with tenderness and love. You see here that the Negroes, if they are free and not bound by slavery, are acting as human beings and as Christians."[68]

In his fourth post, De Jager publicly calls Dutch consul Toewater to task for his unsympathetic treatment of his countrymen when passing through Saint Louis.[69] And in his final attempt to persuade his readers, De Jager makes a broad appeal for assistance. "Dear Countrymen," he concludes, "be so good and help those poor people, many lost everything."[70]

We have no further indication that De Jager's appeal for justice and financial support was ever acted upon. All too quickly, the need was forgotten.

---

[68] De Jager, *De Hollander*, July 27, 1853.
[69] Ibid., August 3, 1853.
[70] Ibid., August 10, 1853.

Consecrated to human freedom, the land awaits
the sober culture of devoted men.
Louisa May Alcott

Frisia

Spread across the northern states, from New England to Wisconsin, during the mid-nineteenth century, was a belt of utopian communities. Spawned by social, political, and religious dissatisfaction in Europe, they took full advantage of the freedom offered to them in the United States. Most of these communities were the inspiration of romantic idealists—perfectionists—determined to establish a living environment without the ills of conventional towns and cities—a return to the Garden of Eden.

The Fruitlands commune was begun with lofty intentions, the vision of American educator Amos Bronson Alcott and British reformer Charles Lane. Louisa May Alcott never took her father's effort seriously, later referring to Fruitlands as "transcendental wild oats." William Harrison, in his introduction to Alcott's book on the experiment, declares that, although the founders were serious in their purpose, the commune had a "zany side," attracting

199

"some freaks, cranks, and near lunatics."[71] Established in June of 1843, on one hundred acres of Massachusetts countryside, the entire band took residence in a single farmhouse. Into this setting wrote young Alcott, "Beauty, Virtue, Justice, and Love might live happily together, without the possibility of the serpent entering in."[72]

But community rules were harsh and severe. Lane insisted on an early rise for all, the taking of a cold bath, followed by a music lesson, all before a "chaste repast of fruit and bread." Then on to "healthful labor," from which Lane would take leave. At day's end, there would be "social communion, prolonged till sunset, when we retire to sweet repose."[73] The strictest of vegetarians, they abstained not only from eating flesh but also from the consumption of all animal products, whether for food or for clothing, and even from the use of animals for field work and manure.

"The sun and evening sky do not look calmer than Alcott and his family at Fruitlands," neighbor and landowner Ralph Waldo Emerson wrote in his journal. "I will not prejudge them successful. They look well in July. We will see them in December."[74]

Fruitlands did celebrate Christmas, but by then all knew its demise was imminent. Lane left on January 6 to join a nearby community of Shakers, a sect more in line with his views on celibacy. A week later, Alcott, his wife Abigail, and their four little women, now heavily encumbered in debt, packed up their few belongings and moved into three rooms rented from a neighbor. Alcott and Lane's unrealistic expectations and internal bickering brought the experiment to an end.

---

[71] Amos Bronson Alcott, *Transcendental Wild Oats and Excerpts from the Fruitlands Diary*, with an introduction by William Henry Harrison (Harvard, MA: Harvard Common Press, 1981), 4.
[72] Alcott, *Transcendental*, 29.
[73] Ibid., 35.
[74] Ralph Waldo Emerson, *Journal of Ralph Waldo Emerson* (Boston: Houghton Mifflin, 1909-14), 6:420-21.

Bonnema's dream, originally named Frisia, the Latin form of Friesland, was not a social experiment. His vision was entirely pragmatic—the establishment of an agrarian community made up of farmers, woodcutters, carpenters, tradesmen, and merchants from the original band of Frisians, as well as others from the Netherlands that might wish to join them along the way. Private ownership of land, home, and business was a common goal; before leaving Friesland, there was the hope that they would be able to purchase property, build their homes, and reap a harvest— all within the same year. They were ignorantly optimistic, with no idea of what lay ahead.

Although we find no mention of community rules of personal conduct, there were expectations. Bonnema continued to provide financing for housing and living expenses, with the understanding that, in time, he would be reimbursed. Haagsma would oversee the accounts, although he discretely revealed nothing in his journals on this matter. Until all could live independently, survival required sharing living space. One of the long huts built on arrival was designated for Bonnema, Haagsma, and all of the single men and women—believed to total twenty-one. The other hut was for the families, estimated to be thirty-five persons. For both groups, it must have been a bitter reminder of their weeks of confinement at sea. Haagsma tells us more about what the furnishings were not, rather than what they were. There were no mirrors, no mahogany tables, no soft sofas, no fine bedsteads—all those things had been left behind. What few items they had were handmade, simple, and functional—long rustic benches and tables. Beds were nothing more than a pile of hay covered at night by a sheet.

With amazing speed on the part of Broer Haagsma in Frisia and printer/bookhandler Sipke Houtsma in Harlingen,

Haagsma's account of the Frisians' journey across the Atlantic went on sale in Friesland on August 19. Profits realized from the forty-cent copy price were designated for Haagsma's father, the cow doctor, through Haagsma's friend, Pieter Runia.

"The men diligently worked on," recorded Haagsma, "with the sweet hope of soon being in possession of a better house."[75] In three months' time, there were six homes, in addition to a carpenter's shop and a blacksmith's shed. On September 30, Haagsma reported to the *Sheboygan Nieuwsbode* with some reluctance, "Our company has been diminished by several persons, due on the one hand to loss by death [on board ship] and by others leaving for other places. Together our group numbers twenty men, thirteen women, and four children."[76]

Fall was exceptionally beautiful, warmer than what the Frisians could remember experiencing in the Netherlands. Before winter, they had the pleasure of plowing the ground for the next growing season. Daytime temperatures through December were almost springlike, although many days began with a heavy frost or a thin layer of snow. "Many times I stood in the middle of the prairie," wrote Haagsma, "and felt compelled to admire the scene before me. The high, white bluffs, like silver shining in the brilliant sunshine, mixed gracefully with areas where the snow had melted, and contrasted with the pine evergreens—that undulated plain— that beautiful forest—all along the meandering river bank, the dramatic work of a proficient and worthy Master."[77]

In early January of 1854, the weather suddenly changed as heavy snows moved in from the west. By the middle of the

---

[75]   Haagsma, *Frysia*, 16.

[76]   Either Haagsma miscounted the number of children, or the newspaper erred. There were probably two dozen children in Frisia at the time. *Sheboygan Nieuwsbode* (November 15, 1853), 2.

[77]   Haagsma, *Frysia*, 17.

month, temperatures dropped to thirty degrees below zero, and the normally free-flowing Mississippi became totally ice covered. February remained cold but less severe than the previous month; by March, the men found the ground suitable for working.

Eighteen months after their arrival in Wisconsin, Haagsma submitted a report on the colony to bookbinder/printer Pieter Martens Feenstra in Bolsward, Friesland. *Frysia, of schets der Friesche volkplanting in Noord-Amerika* (Frisia, or sketch of the Frisian settlement in North America) was written primarily to encourage other Frisians to join the Wisconsin colony. Here Haagsma made an honest attempt to inform his countrymen as to what they could expect to find in America. It was also around this time that the settlement was renamed New Amsterdam, perhaps to broaden its appeal to more Hollanders. To this end, there was only marginal success. Census records and property ownership maps show that in twenty years' time, a little more than a dozen Dutch families joined the original homesteaders. But during the same period, one quarter of the original group left for other locations.

It is difficult to determine if the ambitious town plan for New Amsterdam was Bonnema's vision or that of his wife, Louise. For one thing, it was published eleven years after Bonnema's demise. In it we find that the streets named after the town's founder, his brother, and his grandparents are all misspelled. It shows a grid of eleven streets forming twenty-five blocks and 184 building lots. Only seven of the streets were built, and, of the proposed lots, it is doubtful if more than two dozen were originally built upon.[78]

---

[78] Population figures for New Amsterdam are also difficult to determine. Some historians (H. Lucas, Y. Poortinga), perhaps concluding from the published town plan, suggest there were up to two hundred homes in New Amsterdam. Karsten makes reference to there being between four- and five hundred persons at its height. Normally federal census records are reliable sources for this information; in the case of New Amsterdam, however, the 1860, 1870, and 1880 enrollment figures include with New Amsterdam

There are several explanations for the meager success of Frisia/New Amsterdam. Certainly the calamitous journey had had a major impact on those who came in 1853. Many must have questioned if anything good could come from that which had begun so badly. Admittedly, there were subscribers to the contract who, from the start, had intended to remain part of the colony for the minimum time they felt obligated but who considered the shipwreck as a sure release from any commitment. Others, soured by the hardship of the first years and resultant dissension, were eager to move on. The very location, although originally attractive and promising, proved unsustainable. Within twenty years, the forests around New Amsterdam were depleted, and any effort to replenish them would take decades to realize. Those who turned to agriculture found the sandy soil relatively unproductive. When Bonnema returned to grain production, the source of his success in Friesland, he was met with a weak Chicago market and failed to return a profit.

Rev. John H. Karsten, former pastor of the Oostburg, Wisconsin, Reformed Church, saw another factor in New Amsterdam's failure to prosper—the lack of spiritual leadership.[79] The Seceders, who had arrived a few years earlier, were led from the pulpit by men like Albertus C. Van Raalte (Holland, MI), Maarten A. Ypma (Vriesland, MI), and Hendrik P. Scholte (Pella, IA). New Amsterdam, although comprised of Christian families, lacked a uniting spiritual leader. That Bonnema could open a bar and a dance hall on Main Street without a challenge gives some indication of the spiritual temperature of the colony.

---

portions of Holland Township and North Onalaska. It is extremely doubtful there were ever two hundred homes in the village proper. The 1973 United States Geological Survey map of the area shows only thirty-three homes in the village.

[79] Karsten, "A Half Century of Dutch Settlement in Wisconsin, 1847-1897," in *Dutch Immigrant Memoirs and Related Writings*, ed. H. S. Lucas (Assen, Netherland: Van Gorcum, 1955), 2:139.

Dutch historian/sociographer Jacob van Hinte came to a similar conclusion. "The unifying strength of a common religion, whether embodied or not in a religious leader, was lacking. Mere ethnic ties, so strong particularly among Frisians, were not enough to allow them to tackle in unison the difficulties related to the move from one country to another."[80]

In van Hinte's view, "Frisia . . . died entirely."[81]

It was not until fifteen years after their arrival that the proposal was made and acted upon to meet on Sunday mornings for worship and the reading of a sermon prepared in Dutch.[82] The administration of the Lord's Supper and baptism would need to await a visiting minister.[83] The denominational banner shifted from Presbyterian to Reformed Church in America as pastors came and went. In 1879, the year the church building was completed, and again in 1880, the Classis of Wisconsin (RCA) made urgent appeals at the Particular Synod of Chicago on behalf of the church for a minister who could preach in both Dutch and English. But the number of people in New Amsterdam remained low, their finances stretched thin, and by their own admission, they were divided in opinion. The congregation finally voted in 1884 to transfer their affiliation to the Presbyterian denomination.

The community of New Amsterdam remains today an unincorporated village. You can drive through it in five minutes. The homes are modest; there are forty, perhaps fifty at most. You will not find Oepke Bonnema's house on Main Street, nor will

---

[80]   Van Hinte, *Netherlanders*, 303.

[81]   Ibid., 167.

[82]   The suggestion came from Frisian-born Reinder Keizer, an outsider to New Amsterdam, who had emigrated from Het Bildt in 1848, settling first in central Wisconsin and then moving to the Onalaska area during the 1860s. Keizer led the effort in 1870 to organize a church in New Amsterdam, being joined by six families that had survived the *William and Mary* shipwreck and others who came later.

[83]   Rev. Peter Lepeltak (RCA), during his ministry in Greenleafton, Minnesota, would on occasion make the one-hundred-mile horseback ride to New Amsterdam. He is reported to have baptized sixteen children on one of his visits.

you find his hotel, bar, dance hall, grocery store, or sawmill. They are all gone, as are the other early buildings. Main Street is no longer the main street; today the primary thoroughfare is County Road Xx. You will, in fact, have difficulty finding any evidence of those who left their homes in Friesland more than 160 years ago, survived a horrible shipwreck en route, ascended the Mississippi, and made their homes here. There is no tulip festival in the spring, no annual Founders Day parade in July, no windmill replicas on front lawns, and no wooden shoes on a sign that says "Welkom to New Amsterdam." When Henry S. Lucas visited New Amsterdam in the 1940s, in preparation for his history of the town, he had difficulty finding anyone who could converse in Dutch or Frisian. He concluded, "Exposed to American influences, which poured into the community from every side, it was impossible to continue the old Frisian and Dutch ways. Old forms of life and thought faded, and new ones were substituted. A new amalgam came into being."[84]

Canadian James Kooistra visited New Amsterdam in the spring of 2006 in search of the village's origins. In town, the only evidence he found was Oepka [sic] Street, Harmon [sic] Street, Jelle Street, and Sternford [sic]—four roads named after Bonnema's family. Then driving three miles northeast to Green Mound Cemetery, he found stone memorials bearing the names of many who had made the journey in 1853. Bonnema's tall stone is there, as well as more modest markers for the Chalsmas, Kooistras, Stienstras, Westerhuises, and a few more. Silent witnesses.

But in town, there is one memorial that is not silent. On the corner of John and Harmon Streets stands the New Amsterdam Presbyterian Church, where every Sunday morning, the church bell still calls the community to worship. It may have taken the

---

[84] Lucas, "The Founding of New Amsterdam in La Crosse County," *The Wisconsin Magazine of History* 31 (Madison: State Historical Society of Wisconsin, 1947), 58.

Dutch settlers some years to establish, but it remains today as New Amsterdam's single landmark, with a timeless, universal message: "God is our refuge and strength, an ever present help in trouble" (Psalm 46:1).

PART V

Epilogue

From all reports found, it is believed that the *William and Mary* sank somewhere between ten and twenty miles west of the northwestern tip of Grand Bahama Island and lies at the depth of nineteen hundred feet. She rests undisturbed in perpetual night, well beyond the reach of amateur divers and the interest of professional salvagers and is no threat to coastal navigation.

With the passage of more than 160 years since the ship's demise, one wonders if any articles taken on the *William and Mary* might still be extant—a pocket knife passed down from father to son, a Dutch Bible carried out of Friesland, a piece of jewelry worn by one of the women, perhaps even Tuininga's fork. Of the Frisian survivors, the ship's crew, and the rescuers, could there be any living descendants in possession of family legends, stories of their connection to the lost ship? Could they still be found after five or six generations? That was something I wanted to know.

Rescuer: Robert Sands

The rescue of the 164 passengers on the stricken *William and Mary* made wrecker Robert Sands of Abaco Island an immediate hero. The first two newspaper notices of the wreck appeared in Nassau, just eleven days after the event. The *Bahama Herald* announced to the island community, "Through the noble exertion, chiefly of Mr. Sands, master of the wrecking schooner *Oracle*, the lives of these emigrants have been providentially saved."[1] Likewise, the *Nassau Guardian* posted, "Capt. Sands has doubtless been instrumental in saving the lives of all on board and . . . deserves the warm appropriation of the humane and a generous reward from the British and American governments."[2]

It was Major D'Arcy, the commandant of the troops in Nassau, that appealed to the London-based Royal National

[1] *Bahama Herald* (May 14, 1853), 2.
[2] *Nassau Guardian*, May 14, 1853.

213

Institution for the Preservation of Life from Shipwreck for special consideration. Although the operations of that office were previously limited to the shipwrecks along the coasts of the United Kingdom, when the organization met in July of 1853, it was open to making an exception.

On August 5, the *Royal Cornwall Gazette* published, "The silver medal of the institution was voted to Mr. Robert Sands, . . . in consideration of his noble exertions in saving, under Divine Guidance, 190 lives from the emigrant ship *William and Mary*."[3] The expanded number of lives saved was not the only embellishment. Sands was reported to have seen the *William and Mary*'s collision with the reef and immediately made headway to her rescue. Having arrived, it was he who immediately initiated the pump operation. Further, once the last passenger was safely removed, the ship immediately sank. All of theses statements are in conflict with reports made by eyewitnesses. While all those rescued were no doubt grateful to be removed from the sinking vessel and placed safely on the beach of Grand Bahama Island, many were displeased that their personal belongings were left behind and then confiscated by their rescuers.

In early September, the institution's medal arrived from England and was placed in the custody of Major D'Arcy until arrangements could be made for presentation to Mr. Sands in the presence of his crew. Finally, on Monday, October 31, 1853, Lieutenant Governor C. R. Nesbitt made the award in the Government House in Nassau.

> Captain Sands, I have much pleasure in seeing you for the purpose of presenting to you, in the presence of Major D'Arcy, commanding the troops, and other gentlemen here assembled, the silver medal of the Royal National

---

[3]   *Royal Cornwall Gazette, Falmouth Packet, and General Advertiser*, Truro, England (August 5, 1853), 7.

Silver medal of the Royal National Institution for the Preservation of Life from Shipwreck. Designed in 1824 by British engraver William Wyon, the medal is slightly smaller than a silver dollar. On the reverse side is the phrase, "Let not the deep swallow me up," taken from Psalm 69:15 (*courtesy of Downies*)

Shipwreck Institution, voted to you by the beneficent body, in approbation of your exertions in saving from drowning the passengers of the ship *William and Mary*, bound from Liverpool to New Orleans.[4]

Nesbitt did not fail to convey to Sands the sentiment of the Duke of Newcastle, Her Majesty's secretary of state for the colonies, that Sands' actions should be viewed as an "example of generosity and courage shown to the numerous body of . . . fellow colonists engaged in an occupation so trying to the character as that of wrecking."[5]

Upon receiving his award, the record shows that Captain Sands expressed his gratitude: "In the performance of the services he rendered, he acted upon feelings which arose out of sentiments early inculcated by example of his parents."[6]

---

[4]   *The Life-boat, or Journal of the National Shipwreck Institution* (London: C. Knight, 1854), 87.
[5]   Ibid.
[6]   Ibid.

One might assume that on an island as isolated as Abaco, the public file on Sands' life would soon come to a close. We know that by 1857, he had experienced a rescue of sorts, leaving the wrecking trade and turning to carpentry. But in 1903, a full fifty years after his notable effort, his name unexpectedly surfaced once again. On July 30 of that year, the schooner, *William H. Van Name*, Captain C. B. Flowers at the helm, sailed up the Chesapeake Bay to its berth in Baltimore harbor. On board was a team of twenty-four scientists, who, under the auspices of the Geographical Society of Baltimore, had just completed a two-month expedition to the Bahama Islands. Taking advantage of the proximity of the islands to the United States and their relative isolation, they undertook surveys in a broad range of disciplines, including health and sanitation. It was under the guidance of Dr. Clement A. Penrose, vice director and surgeon, that a medical survey was conducted on each of the islands visited. Now back in Baltimore, they began to unload from the schooner's cargo hold all their specimens— containers of birds, jars of reptiles, boxes of seashells, cartons of drawings and photographs, and file cases of medical records.

When a reporter interviewed Dr. Penrose as to what he had found in the Bahamas, attention was quickly directed to what had been discovered at Hope Town on the Island of Abaco. It was there that Dr. Penrose and his assistants encountered a high incidence of leprosy, blindness, and other physical and mental maladies.[7]

Two years later, when his complete findings were published, Penrose wrote:

> In Hopetown [sic] we have an ideal illustration of what a small and restricted community of human beings will do. Here is an experiment conducted by Nature, as it were, to show what will result from close intermarrying.[8]

[7]   *The Sun*, Baltimore, MD (August 3, 1903), 6.
[8]   Penrose, *Sanitary Conditions in the Bahama Islands* (New York: MacMillan, 1905), 413.

With the assistance of three islanders, including Samuel Malone, a cousin of Robert Sands, Penrose was able to produce a table on the Malone family, tracking the spread of the disease. Penrose concluded that leprosy was introduced to the settlement through Robert Sands' parents, Charles Sands and Eliza Malone Sands. Charles eventually died of leprosy. Although three of Robert's siblings contracted the disease, as well as several of their children, Robert and his nine children were spared.

Robert Sands died in 1892, at the age of seventy-two. Having such a large family, it is reasonable to expect that many in the Abacos might trace their ancestry to him. To learn more, I contacted the Wyannie Malone Historical Museum in Hope Town. Named after Sands' maternal grandmother, its specific mission is "To preserve Hope Town's past for the future." The museum had immediate success in identifying several descendants, but to my chagrin, when contacted, none had any knowledge of their forefather, the rescuer, Robert Sands. Over and over, this would be the response from descendants of those connected to the *William and Mary* shipwreck. There were rare exceptions. A resident of the Florida Keys, whose grandparents had left the Abacos in search of vocational opportunities, returned to Hope Town in her quest for information on her ancestors. She attended one of the museum's annual heritage events and made a profound personal discovery. There in one of the displays she saw the name of her great-grandfather, Robert Sands.

"I saw a newspaper on the wall and recognized his name. I had heard about the wrecking business, and it wasn't good. But he saved a lot of lives. I thought it was wonderful; pretty amazing."[9]

---

[9]　Marlene Wilson, interview by Kenneth A. Schaaf, July 31, 2015.

Survivors: Hendrik Kas and Grietje Jansonius

It was a bitterly cold day when Hendrik Kas said goodbye to his parents, his three brothers, and his two sisters and left Friesland. And it was a rather warm day in July when he arrived in Wisconsin, picked up pen and paper, and began to write:

> Waarde Ouders, Broeders en Zusters! Dear Parents, Brothers and Sisters! I can inform you that by God's grace, I am still healthy and well.[10]

On several pages, and in considerable detail, with well-chosen words, Hendrik Kas thoughtfully informed his family of his trip experience from Lowestoft, England, to La Crosse, Wisconsin. "The trip was quite difficult as everyone can truthfully

[10] Kas, transcribed and translated letter, undated, in the collections of Heritage Hall, Calvin College and Seminary, Grand Rapids, MI.

say," Hendrik wrote. "But I do believe that if God will give us health, we will soon recover."[11]

Hendrik Kas did recover and soon established himself in the New Amsterdam/Onalaska area. He purchased 120 acres, built a home, and served as the village notary. One year after his arrival, his sister, Geertje, joined him, and two years later, his youngest brother, Willem, arrived. In business Hendrik became a dry goods merchant in La Crosse. And when Hendrik married, his bride came from among the *William and Mary* passengers; he mentioned her name in his letter to his family. Grietje Jansonius had been an orphan since the age of nine; her life in Menaldumsdeel was that of an unfortunate farm servant. She was twenty when she left Friesland, twenty when she and Hendrik were married, and twenty-one when the first baby came. In their seventeen or so years of marriage, she and Hendrik parented seven children.

We do not know the exact date or circumstance, but in the early 1870s, Hendrik was left a widower, with children ranging in age from about eighteen down to three. Nor do we know how he learned of Trijntje Wiersma, a widow with three children living in Zeeland, Michigan, some 450 miles away. But in May of 1878, Hendrik and Trijntje were married; Hendrik relocated to Zeeland, with just one of his children, and began working there as a farmer. Over the next four years, Hendrik would father two more children, daughters Grace and Sadie.

We believe it was sometime during the 1890s when Hendrik died. The 1900 federal census for Zeeland, Michigan, lists Trijntje, or Kate, as she became known, as a widow, living with her daughter, Sadie, an eighteen-year-old "telephone girl." Ten years later, the record shows Kate still living with Sadie, sometimes called Sarah, who was now married to Cornelis DeKoster, an express agent. This couple would raise two sons, Franklin and Lester.

[11]   Ibid., 3-4.

It is in Lester that we see traces of Hendrik's character. Lester chose for himself a life of letters. He served for many years as a professor of speech at Calvin College and as the director of the library at the college and seminary. During the 1970s, he was the editor of the *Banner*, the voice of the Christian Reformed Church, then published weekly. The author of more than a dozen publications, he is regarded by one of his former students, Dr. Harry G. Arnold, to be "a brilliant man, well-read in philosophy, theology, and church matters, an apologist for the Christian faith."[12]

In March of 2013, I had opportunity to interview Lester's widow, Ruth, and daughter, Leslie. Neither of them had ever heard Lester speak of his grandfather, Hendrik Kas, and his first wife, Grietje Jansonius, or their dramatic rescue at sea. While Lester covered many topics in his writing career, apparently, his origins were not among them. But he did come close. In 1956, in an erudite essay on evil, he made reference to a group of people who encountered the unexpected on their voyage to America.

> Most people might find it difficult or impossible to define with any precision the idea of "evil" at all. But they know that anxiety is real. Like the heedless passengers on the great *Titanic*, they have felt the . . . impact of their world's collision with the Unknown; they acutely sense that something is amiss deep down beneath the surface of life, and they dimly suspect that for all his glittering speed, modern man cannot outstrip his nemesis, whatever it may be.[13]

It is doubtful if Lester ever knew of his grandfather's fateful journey. And it is equally doubtful that he was ever aware that in the library he directed was a translated copy of the letter his grandfather wrote on God's grace so many years ago.

---

[12] Harry Arnold, e-mail exchange with Kenneth A. Schaaf, March 24, 2013.
[13] Lester DeKoster, *All Ye that Labor: An Essay on Christianity, Communism, and the Problem of Evil* (Grand Rapids, MI: Eerdmans Publishing, 1956), 10.

Survivors: Beinze Rienks and Metje van der Ploeg

The way Broer Haagsma saw it, Beinze and Metje were two of the singles on board the *William and Mary*. Beinze was twenty-five, from Het Bildt, and with the single men. Metje was twenty-two, also from Het Bildt, and with the single women. Perhaps they knew each other. A letter now in the possession of the Rienks family tells a different story. According to the letter, Beinze was a young gardener working on the estate of a wealthy Frisian sea captain; he fell in love with the captain's daughter, his only child, and, against her family's wishes, they married and ran off to America. The family's vast fortune fell into the hands of strangers.[14]

Social historians love family legends; they provide plausible information, clues to what might have happened. This is what we

[14] Letter written by John Emry, a great-great-grandson of B. C. Rienks, on December 8, 1990, to Beryl Rienks, of Grand Junction, CO.

know (during the nineteenth century, the Dutch kept remarkably thorough vital statistics): registers of births, marriages, deaths, wills, and military records. Through advancements made in digitization, many of these records are accessible today. So what does the record show for this young couple? First of all, it clearly notes that Metje was not an only child; she was one of eight. Second, while three documents note her father being a skipper, six others show him as a small farmer or workman. Third, the family's wealth is very likely overstated; when Metje's father died in 1846, at the age of forty-seven, his occupation was given as a house painter. Neither he nor his wife left an estate. There was no vast fortune. Finally, no record has been found that verifies Beinze and Metje were married before leaving Friesland.

The legend does go on to include their ill-fated voyage—a shipwreck in the West Indies and the loss of all their possessions. They saved nothing but the apparel they were wearing and the Bibles to which they clung. Once having arrived in the United States, they worked on a farm in the East for one whole year without pay, since the paper they received proved to be worthless— no doubt the contract they had with Bonnema. To think of "the East" as referring to the eastern portion of the country is highly improbable; more likely it is relative to where the couple established their home in Dubuque, Iowa, in 1855.

Dubuque, on the Mississippi's western bank, was the area Bonnema had originally intended to settle before moving farther upriver. When Beinze and Metje Rienks, now Benjamin and Martha, relocated to Dubuque County, they purchased farmland some ten miles west of the Mississippi River in Center Township and built a log home. It was here that their children were all born, three girls and six boys. Martha died here at age thirty-nine, when her youngest was still an infant.

For three years, the daughters picked up their mother's tasks of cooking, sewing, cleaning, and childcare. A woman in the community did the wash once a week. Finally, in 1874, a stepmother entered the scene: German born, forty-two-year-old Elizabeth, along with her two children. It was a move of desperation and one all too common during the nineteenth century, both on the frontier and back in Holland. Fortunately, in the case of Benjamin and Elizabeth, it was mutually beneficial; the outcome pleased both parties and their children.

With such a large family, it is not surprising to see them pulling up stakes and venturing out on their own; certainly Benjamin's seventy-five or so acres could not sustain all of his children, nor were there sufficient options for marriage. Around 1884 two brothers left the homestead for Greeley, Colorado. When their letters of encouragement were received back home, the girls soon headed to Greeley to open a dressmaking shop. Finally, in the late 1880s, the three youngest brothers left Iowa for Greeley, purchased farms, and one by one, took Colorado brides.

In January of 2012, I had a conversation with Beryl Rienks, a retired coal miner living in Grand Junction, Colorado. Beryl is a great-grandson of Benjamin and Martha Rienks. Like so many other descendants of *William and Mary* survivors, he knew nothing of either the shipwreck or the hardships experienced by his great-grandparents until the day he received a letter from a distant cousin that told him of a family legend—part truth, part fiction—of a young couple and their trip to America. Beryl, here is the full story.

Survivors: Antje Kooistra and sons

Very few women would care to trade places with Antje Kooistra. By age thirty-seven, she had lost one son in Friesland, two young sons at sea, and her husband in Nassau. On arrival in Frisia/New Amsterdam with twelve-year-old Sake, eleven-year-old Tiete, and eight-year-old Symon, her only means of survival and contribution to the community was her work as a seamstress. At first the boys worked at farming with the other men of the colony and their sons, but the work was hard, and the sandy soil was not particularly productive. After a short time, Antje decided to leave the group and move with her boys into a log cabin in La Crosse. Two years later, she moved again, this time toward the village of Onalaska, into an even more primitive shelter, one with a dirt floor and a roof made of willow branches covered with wild rice plants.

In an effort to fit into the American culture, the Kooistra family did what so many immigrants felt compelled to do—they changed their names. Antje became Anna; Sake became Silas; Tiete somehow became Tector, and Symon was changed in spelling. All gave up their Frisian surname for a more Anglicized "Coster," although Coster is also a Dutch name.

Life on the frontier was harsh, and early death was common. Anna died in La Crosse in 1862, at the age of forty-six. She was buried in the Old Campbell Cemetery, where a red granite stone erected years later by her great-grandson marks the Coster plot. Anna's son, Simon, died at age twenty-two and is buried next to her.

Proof of Silas's assimilation came on March 10, 1862, the day he enlisted in Company B of the Wisconsin Volunteer Infantry and went off to defend the Union in the American Civil War. Whether motivated by conviction of the cause or a desire for adventure, we will never know. It took only six months before he was involved in heavy action. In 1862 he fought in the battles of Second Bull Run in Manassas, Virginia; South Mountain in Frederick County, Maryland; and Antietam in Sharpsburg, Maryland. In 1863 he saw action in Chancellorsville, Virginia, and Gettysburg, Pennsylvania. It was on the first day of fighting at Gettysburg that the twenty-one year old took a lead ball to his right thigh, breaking the bone. He was taken to Gettysburg Courthouse Hospital where surgeons amputated his leg. Twenty-nine days later, he died of blood poisoning. Silas's final resting place in Gettysburg is only yards from where President Lincoln presented his well-known dedication four months later.

The same year that Silas went off to war, his younger brother, Tector, embarked on his own journey, one that would engage him for the next sixty years and take him to many cities across the country. Tector began working for the Milwaukee Railroad, initially in the roundhouse operation, but, for most of his career, he worked as an engineer, crisscrossing the Chicago, Milwaukee, St. Paul & Pacific Railroad system.

Silas Coster of Company B,
Wisconsin Volunteer Infantry
(*courtesy Pearl Coster*)

In October of 1924, the *La Crosse Tribune and Leader-Press* interviewed Tector on his still-fresh recollections of the ordeal his family experienced some seventy-one years earlier. He spoke of waves that at one moment would tower over them like mountains and threaten to sink them and the next moment catapult them high above dark caverns and gallons of brine that swamped the deck and splashed down through their living space and into the hold below. Visions that are indelible, that wake you up in the night, memories that will not stop.

Tector married in 1873 and over the next eight years fathered four children, including a son he named after his brother Silas. Son Silas followed Tector in a career working for the Chicago, Milwaukee, St. Paul & Pacific Railroad. When Silas married, he and his wife had one son, Roy. Memories of the shipwreck that Tector told to his grandson, Roy, during the late 1920s and early 1930s kept the *William and Mary* story alive in the Coster family. Tector Coster died in August of 1933 and is believed to have been the last survivor of the *William and Mary* shipwreck.

One of my pleasures in 2013 was exchanging information with Pearl Coster, widow of Roy, formerly of La Crosse. Pearl is a retired teacher, an energetic historian, and protective curator of the Coster family documents, including a tintype made of young Silas Coster shortly before the battle of Gettysburg. At age ninety-seven, she was amazingly resourceful in our phone and email communications and constant in her encouragement.

Survivor: Izaak Roorda

If a prize was to be awarded or a premium paid for shear determination, Izaak Roorda would certainly qualify for that honor. Although most of the other Frisian survivors of the *William and Mary* traveled an estimated 6,885 miles before arriving at their final destination, it has been calculated that Izaak Roorda traveled 23,730 miles before he finally reached "home," a distance close to that of traveling around the earth at the equator. His story is most unique, much of it carefully recorded by Roorda himself.

Izaak was the fourth son born to house painter Epke Roorda and his wife Frouke. Of their eleven children, he was the one selected to leave the family nest for America. On the day following the *William and Mary*'s collision on Isaac Rock, twenty-one-year-old Izaak managed to escape the ship in the overloaded long boat. Later that day, Izaak, his two companions, and the others were rescued by the ship *Pollux* heading to Liverpool. Here they arrived on June 6, 1853, a full ten weeks after leaving the city on the *William and Mary*. "Words cannot describe," wrote Roorda, "my feelings of happiness and thankfulness of having again reached shore after so many weeks on the ocean."[15] During his entire time on the *Pollux*, Roorda was shoeless and confined to the deck; his only protection from the elements being an old piece of sailcloth.

In Liverpool, he and his two companions returned to the same German boarding house they had stayed in months earlier. Over a period of twelve days, Roorda, Ulbe Bergsma, and Oene Wagenaar visited the company that had arranged their original voyage and were able to receive a refund of thirty florins for the failed journey. Through the efforts of the Netherlands consul, they were also given money for their room and board while in Liverpool, arrangements and fare for their return to Friesland, and a small amount for traveling expenses. With considerable detail, Roorda tells of their arrival in Rotterdam, of being surrounded by news reporters, receiving train tickets for Amsterdam, and then finally his reunion with his father, mother, sisters, and brothers two days later.

In what appears to be a demonstration of maturity rarely found in someone his age, Izaak determined to turn his calamitous experience into profit. With the facts still clear in his mind, he at once wrote his story, had it printed in pamphlet form, and offered it for sale to a curious Frisian public. Any profit realized was set aside for his return fare to America.

One year later, Roorda was found living in Pella, Iowa, the very successful colony established in 1847 by Seceder Hendrik Scholte. Letters to his family must have been enthusiastic; by June of 1855, his brothers, Anne and Weiger, had joined him in Pella. Two years later, their parents and four more of their siblings arrived just weeks before the marriages of Izaak and Weiger to sisters Boukje and Trijntje Buwalda.

[15]   *Roorda Family History* (Des Moines, IA: [privately published, n.d.]), 26.

By 1861 Izaak's brother, Anne, married yet another Buwalda sister, and for a time, it appeared that Izaak and his family had found their home and settled in contentedly. But then came the war. Izaak's brother, Hendrik, enlisted in the Seventeenth Iowa Volunteers Infantry. The record of his service is brief: mustered in April of 1862 and died of illness in Corinth, Mississippi, on August 19, 1862. In all likelihood, he never saw battle action.

We have no clear explanation for what happened next. Perhaps it was a lack of understanding of what the war was about, a fear that the war in the South and East might eventually reach into Iowa, or possibly another issue entirely. Whatever the cause, it was important enough for them to take drastic action. In 1864 Izaak and several of his brothers and sisters, with their families and friends, picked up stakes and moved across the country just about as far as they could go.

The first leg of their trip was by train, from Pella to New York City. From New York, they took a ship to Panama, crossed the isthmus by train, and once on the Pacific, they took another ship to Oregon. Here they spent five years farming in the Oregon City area.

In 1869 the Roordas and their friends decided to return to Pella, this time taking a ship to San Francisco where they were able to connect with the newly completed transcontinental railroad. The Union Pacific provided a direct route back to Iowa. For Izaak and Boukje, they were home at last. Here they purchased farmland, raised their nine children, and found a faith community in the Reformed Church.

In July of 2011, I spoke with Howard Van Zante, a great-grandson of Izaak Roorda. Like his great-grandfather, his grandfather, and his father, Howard is also a farmer, still in the Pella area, a deacon in the Reformed Church community there. He is a serious man who measures his speech and works hard. I was immediately drawn to his character. His wife is an operating room nurse in the local hospital, and they have three sons. I asked him if he had ever heard that he had an ancestor who was rescued in a shipwreck on his way to America and was surprised to hear his reply. He told me that perhaps ten years earlier, at a family reunion, his father had mentioned that a relative, his name forgotten, was shipwrecked when their boat hit a coral reef. None of the details had been passed down in the story. I asked him what he had told his sons about the shipwreck. "Nothing yet," he said.[16]

---

[16]   Howard Van Zante, interview by Kenneth A. Schaaf, July 12, 2011.

Survivor: O. H. Bonnema, community planner

The entrepreneurial passion that had appeared so early in the life of Oepke Bonnema in Friesland, soon asserted itself in La Crosse County, Wisconsin. After staking his initial land claim, he laid out a town plan. Here he built his home and a general store. He opened the first post office, established himself as the postmaster, and began delivering mail twice a week to the residents of Holland Township. He donated one acre of land for the establishment of a school, built a hotel, designated it as a stagecoach stop, and brought to the village a tavern and dance hall. He is conspicuously absent in the construction of the church in New Amsterdam.

In 1856 Bonnema began buying additional acreage, and in ten years' time, he held deed to over one thousand acres. Taking advantage of the vast forestland and access to water, he built a sawmill on the bank of a branch of the Black River. He is said to have purchased a steamboat to move his lumber to market in Saint Louis. And drawing on his experience and success in Friesland, he began to grow wheat for the Chicago market.

Politically, one might expect to find Bonnema's name in the annals of Wisconsin or certainly La Crosse County. Instead, he was content to keep his attention close to home, serving as the treasurer of Holland Township for many years.

Despite Bonnema's driving commercial ambition, life did not go as planned. In 1856 he married Ytje Stienstra, the sixteen-year-old daughter of Johannes and Riemke Stienstra, fellow *William and Mary* passengers. Their marriage was childless and ended in separation before Ytje's twentieth birthday.[17] In 1860 Bonnema married again, this time to Swiss-born Louise Spangler, twenty-one, a pastor's daughter. It too, proved to be childless.

Nor did his financial investments do well. The timber trade started out well, but in 1868, Bonnema was sued by a fellow lumberman and sold the sawmill to cover his losses. After building a second mill, the regional timber supply ran out, and the mill ceased operations. His expectations for New Amsterdam as a viable community never materialized; the hotel saw few patrons. Many of the Frisians that he had brought to the United States abandoned the effort, some before the establishment of the town, some a few years after. An appeal was made to others in the Netherlands to join in the effort, but other than his brother, Harmen, and perhaps a dozen families, the colony showed little growth as a Dutch community; census records show clearly that most residents of the region were of Norwegian ancestry.

Jelle Bonnema, brother of Oepke and Harmen, believed it was a mistake for his siblings to resettle in America. "If they had only remained in the Netherlands," the senior brother is reported to

---

[17] Ytje Stienstra continued living in the New Amsterdam community, married a second time in 1863, and gave birth to one child. She married again in 1869 and had two more children.

have said, "then they would certainly have become rich, especially in the years 1860-1880, since the price of grain increased so much locally while it decreased in America."[18]

Oepke H. Bonnema died in New Amsterdam on March 20, 1895, at the age of sixty-nine. The following day, a brief obituary, with both his first and his last names misspelled, appeared in the *La Crosse County Record*. No mention was made of his wife. It concluded with, "He brought considerable wealth with him from Holland but lost it in unfortunate business transactions."[19] He was buried next to his brother in nearby Green Mound Cemetery. Louise never remarried; she died twenty years later.

[18] Van Hinte, *Netherlanders in America*, 167.
[19] *La Crosse County Record* (March 21, 1895), 2.

Survivor: B. B. Haagsma, record keeper

It is from the writings of Broer Baukes Haagsma, the cow doctor's son, that we learn so many of the details of the Frisian travelers, far more than from any other single source. When making his Atlantic crossing, Haagsma was a youthful twenty-two—bright, alert, and inquisitive. From his hand, we have *Lotgevallen van den Heer O. H. Bonnema en zijne togtgenooten*, the forty-page account of the 1853 voyage; his *Frysia, of schets der Friesche volkplanting in Noord-Amerika*, a forty-nine-page sequel on the establishment of Frisia/New Amsterdam; plus several of his letters written en route to family at home.

Most likely, his sense of obligation to Oepke Bonnema kept Broer Haagsma in Frisia for the first year or two. But for the young bookkeeper, the small community could not keep his interest for long. He remembered the energy level of Saint Louis, the continuous coming and going of people through the city, some

LOTGEVALLEN
VAN DEN HEER
O. H. BONNEMA
EN
ZIJNE TOGTGENOOTEN,
OP REIS
UIT FRIESLAND
NAAR DE
VEREENIGDE STATEN
VAN
NOORD-AMERIKA.

BESCHREVEN DOOR ZEDs. BOEKHOUDER
B. B. HAAGSMA,
(VOORHEEN ONDERMEESTER TE ANUM.

MET EENE KAART

Uitgegeven ten voordeele van den Vader des Schrijvers,
DOOR
P. RUNIA.

Te HARLINGEN bij
S. HOUTSMA. Boek- en Steendrukker.

Title page of Broer Haagsma's account of the Frisians' journey to the United States (*courtesy Tresoar*)

moving downriver, others northbound, many heading westward, either on the Missouri or by wagon. Haagsma also remembered the ill treatment their company received from the Dutch consul when they arrived in the city in 1853, convinced the consul could have done much more for the travelers.

It is no surprise then to find Haagsma in the "Gateway to the West" in 1855. There he was employed as a bookkeeper for Crow, McCreery & Company (later Crow, Hargadine, and still later, Hargadine, McKittrick), a drygoods firm that would employ him for the next forty-five years.[20] But Haagsma became better known in Saint Louis for his appointment by King Willem III of the Netherlands as the Dutch consul for the states of Missouri, Iowa, and Illinois, a post abandoned by Frederick Toewater upon the start of hostilities in the American Civil War. On December 11, 1862, President Lincoln and Secretary of State William Seward, officially recognized Haagsma in his position, a post he held until

[20]   *Gould's Saint Louis City Directory*, Saint Louis, MO, 1864-1907.

his death.[21] In that role, he was the representative of the Dutch government in the Mississippi Valley and an advocate for Dutch immigrants passing through Saint Louis or settling in states or territories west of the Mississippi River.

Although he was successful in his business endeavors, his personal life was a great disappointment. In November of 1866, at the age of thirty-five, Haagsma traded his bachelor life for the companionship of Miss Mina Schmitke, an eighteen-year-old, Prussian-born immigrant. During the couple's thirty-four-year marriage, they changed residences in the city twenty-one times, nine times in their last decade together. By 1900 we find them living separately and acknowledging their divorce. Nine years later, Mina lived alone in San Francisco, where she remained for the rest of her life.

Broer and Mina had one child, Albert, who upon his marriage became the father of Bertram Louis, Haagsma's only grandchild. Born with deforming kyphosis (hunchback), Bertram would live only to age twenty-three.

The early 1900s were years of decline for Haagsma. In 1901, when the queen of the Netherlands visited the United States, it was Haagsma's younger brother, Ysbrand, who took the limelight with his Dutch impressions at a reception of the Holland Society in Chicago. In 1904 Haagsma was recognized by the press as the resident official for the Netherlands' participation in the World's Fair in Saint Louis. But it was the vice consul, Gerrit H. ten Broek, to whom Queen Wihelmina conferred knighthood for his work with the fair. Two years later, being found quite feeble in body and hard of hearing, Haagsma's consular duties had to be assumed by ten Broek.

In 1907 we find seventy-six-year-old Haagsma residing at 911 Warren Street, a red brick duplex boarding house five blocks

---

[21]   *Daily National Intelligencer*, Washington, DC (December 11, 1862), 3.

Broer Haagsma's last residence as it appeared about
2010, at 911 Warren Street, Saint Louis, Missouri.
The building has since been demolished
(*courtesy Jon Schaaf Photography*)

from the Mississippi. On Sunday, August 25, his son, Albert,
visited him. By now, the senior Haagsma's hearing was so poor,
the only way father and son could communicate was by way of
paper and pencil.

"He sometimes became very much discouraged,"
Albert told a reporter, "and I would try to draw him out of
his despondent moods."

"I wrote to him that I would get him a new home,"
Albert continued, "and try to make him more comfortable."

"This is no home," his father wrote. "I do not want the
railroads, the street cars, the noise, and smoke. I have a fine
home in the mountains, among the trees and the birds and
the flowers. I want to go there."[22]

The conversation went on for an hour, the only sounds
being their breathing and the pencil scratching the paper.

[22]   *Saint Louis Post-Dispatch* (August 29, 1907), 1.

The following day, Albert returned to the boarding house but found his father missing. Neighbors reported seeing the elderly man standing on the street corner, looking into the sky, and walking about in confusion. Two days later, the body of an elderly man was found in the river, at the foot of Carr Street, some twenty blocks south of Warren. Albert was convinced it was that of his father.

On August 30, 1907, the *New York Tribune* reported, "Consul found in river: death of Broer B. Haagsma of St. Louis thought accidental."[23] His remains were buried that afternoon in St. Peter's Cemetery in Saint Louis, "among the trees and the birds and the flowers."

[23] *New York Tribune* (August 30, 1907), 3.

Survivors: Johannes Tuininga and family

For the Tuininga family, life in Friesland was not as bad as that experienced by some of the other travelers. It was home, familiar, a church community, blessed with many of the simple pleasures of life. "Their lives were serene, and the children healthy," wrote Anna Tuininga Brown years later. "They were quite poor, and grandfather was discontented because of the low wages he received."[24] So when word of Bonnema's offer came, the Tuininga family made the decision to leave. Although they knew their choice meant saying goodbye to their family in Friesland, they never realized it would result in releasing all their possessions, and costlier still, the lives of a son and a daughter.

Once they arrived in the woods of Wisconsin, they found life in New Amsterdam was not the Utopia they had hoped it would

[24] Brown, *Life Story of John Tuininga*, 188.

be. Housing was exceptionally primitive, nothing like what they had left behind. Food was in short supply; there was no church, and efforts at working together were failing. According to Anna, her grandfather, "had grown weary of the bickerings, quarrelings, and petty jealousies rife in the colony and would have no further association with them."[25]

So Johannes took his wife, Trijntje, his son, Jan, and daughters, Sjouke and Albertje, crossed the Mississippi, and settled on 160 acres of land in La Crescent, Minnesota. Despite it being hilly and heavily wooded—so different from what they had known in Friesland—Johannes was determined to make it work. With the help of his son, he built his own home, barn, and eventually other outbuildings. They cleared the land, planted fields, and in time, added another two hundred acres.

Daughters Sjouke and Albertje took Dutch husbands from the other side of the river, but Jan remained unmarried well into his thirties. Then one day, in the German church he attended, Jan met an English girl, Elizabeth. He proposed; she reluctantly accepted (there were no other offers), and they married. Over the next seventeen years, she gave birth to eight children. Anna, the third born, candidly revealed, "Their union was not very happy."[26] A common practice of the Dutch was to visit together after Sunday services. Jan loved this time since it meant long conversations over coffee with those with whom he had much in common. Not so for Elizabeth; her preference was in the opposite direction, toward her parents and her relatives in the English community.

According to Anna, Jan's health since the shipwreck had not been robust. About the age of fifty, he began a physical decline with bouts of pneumonia. Jan died in June of 1897, just short of his sixtieth birthday.

---

[25]   Ibid., 189.
[26]   Ibid., 192.

"There was a large funeral, for papa had many friends," Anna wrote. "On that day, grandmother asked grandfather to raise her up in bed so she might watch the funeral procession disappear over the hill. Tears rolled down her cheeks, and she cried in anguish, 'Jan, my son, come back to me.'"[27]

In little more than a decade of Jan's death, all four of his sons had left the farm to settle in the state of Washington. John, Albert, and Arthur had become house carpenters, while Charles entered the timber trade working in a sawmill.

In 1934 Anna recorded her very sensitive account of her family's fateful journey to America and early life on the Minnesota frontier. She woefully ended with:

> Today the valley is changed. Its beauty and glory have disappeared. The people who use to live there are gone. The mill wheel is silent, and the old woolen mill burned down long ago; the small English settlement deserted and the houses falling apart in decay. The little German church has been pulled down; it was sold for the lumber in it. The old Tuininga farm looks bleak and desolate. The creek is drying up, and willows like weeds grow everywhere. Farm buildings are in ruins, hardly an original building left, except the rambling old farmhouse mama insisted on having built.[28]

In August of 2012, I spoke with two of Jan's great-grandchildren, both now in their seventies. "Have you ever heard the account of how the Tuininga family came to the United States in 1853? Have you ever heard the story of your family being shipwrecked?" Without a second's hesitation, each responded "no" to both questions. Like many of those who lived in the colony only a short time, when they left the Midwest, they also left behind their heritage. Once relocated, everything was forgotten.

[27] Ibid., 194.
[28] Ibid., 194.

Seaman: John D. Best

There is one thing that we must all admire in the character of *William and Mary* crew member John D. Best—his ability to carry on despite the hardship and trauma that came his way. When he was a child growing up in Bath, Maine, his parents were told he had weak lungs and probably would not live to manhood. When the boy heard this, he resolved to go to sea and overcome this weakness. At fifteen, and without parental approval, he shipped out on John Patten's *Caspian*. Feeling no ill effect, in the fall of 1852, at age sixteen, he left Bath again, this time on the *William and Mary*. When its westbound voyage ended in shipwreck, Best was able to return to New York with Captain Stinson and several others of the crew, where he signed onto the *John C. Calhoun*, another ship registered in Bath. That voyage ended in shipwreck just five days later in the Bay of Fundy. Having returned safely to Bath, in November of 1853, he went out on the ship *Clinton*, bound for Turk's Island, in the Bahamas. Here, while at anchor, the ship encountered a storm, split in two, and sank. Once again, he was rescued and eventually made his way back to Boston. On his next ship, the *Franconia*, he served as second mate on one voyage and mate for another. When he began experiencing difficulty with the captain, he decided to leave the sea, travel up the Mississippi, and try working the Great Lakes in the grain trade. Here he became captain of the bark *Chicago Board of Trade*.

In 1865, after ten years on the Great Lakes and now married to a former schoolmate from Bath, Best came ashore for good and established a ship chandlery trade in Chicago. The business prospered and grew. Then came October 8, 1871, the day a careless flame destroyed some 17,500 buildings in the city, including the business of John Best. He lost everything.

When he began experiencing asthmatic symptoms, friends recommended relocation to Colorado. In 1872 Best, with his wife and four small children, moved to Denver, where he established a produce business. Here, as in Chicago, a fast-moving fire destroyed his trade, but this time, he was able to secure a loan for $20,000 and quickly rebuild. He moved to a larger facility on Market Street, and over the next decade, he established a grain, hay, flour, and feed store on Nineteenth Street. As the business continued to grow, sons Charles F. and John W. joined their father in the enterprise. And like so many others in Denver with entrepreneurial interests and a willingness to take risk, he became a principal in a mining venture in the mountains. With a capital stock of $2.5 million, he and two others incorporated the Geneva Consolidated Silver Mining and Smelting Company, operating several mines in Clear Creek County, sixty-four miles outside of Denver.

Adversity continued to follow. First, there was a business lawsuit. Worse yet was the loss of two of his children: his eleven-year-old daughter, Lucretia, in 1873, and his twenty-five-year-old son, John W., in 1899. This was followed in quick succession by the deaths of both his mother and his wife. John D. went on. By now his profits had assured him of a comfortable style of living. The 1910 federal census shows him as a gentleman of seventy-four, retired, with his niece serving as his housekeeper, an Irish cook preparing his meals, and a young groundsman, all living in his home at 707 Corona Street and East Seventh Avenue. And it became his habit to annually return to the East to visit his wife's brother in Bath. There, one Saturday evening in the fall of 1914, he slipped into eternity. Charles Best accompanied the body of his father by train back to Denver where he was buried in the family plot in Riverside Cemetery. Although there is no evidence that John D. Best in his years in Denver ever had any exchange with Timothy R. Stinson, his former captain, it is more than curious that their graves are in the same section of the same cemetery and only forty paces apart.

In November of 2011, I located a great-granddaughter of John D. Best. Because of her father's interest in family history, she was aware of her ancestor's involvement with the *William and Mary*. In fact, her father had kept over the years a collection of newspaper clippings related to John D. Best, including one with the only known illustration of the *William and Mary*. All of these, she was open to sharing. "I do feel a bit guilty though being related to one of the crew that basically abandoned all those poor passengers," she confessed.[29] I assured her that it is difficult to judge the action of a teenage boy, especially when his captain led the way. As Best matured, he demonstrated remarkable leadership and decision-making skills, in addition to an uncanny ability to always bounce back after experiencing adversity.

---

[29] Kari Steigelmar, e-mail exchange with Kenneth A. Schaaf, November 17, 2011.

Survivors: Sjoerd Bekius and Maartje Schaaf, cousins

Despite their common background in Friesland, the traumatic experiences they shared on their journey, and their agreed-upon Michigan destination, once in America, the lives of Sjoerd Bekius and Maartje Schaaf took very different directions.

In an address before the Newcomen Society in 1964, Daniel Bryant referred to Sjoerd Bekius as "a restless soul in search of his promised land."[30] It is difficult to determine how restless Bekius may have been in 1853, but it is certain that, when he made his crossing, he entered a land flowing with milk and honey. His first home was in Zeeland, Michigan, near his uncle, Pieter Schaaf, Maartje's father. In 1855 he married Tiertje Berkompas, a young woman who had arrived in 1847 on the *Vesta* with Maartje's family. The young couple settled in Beaverdam and began farming, and

[30] Bryant, *Journey to the Promised Land: The Story of Bekins Van & Storage Co.* (New York: Newcomen Society of North America, 1964), 9.

Sjoerd Bekius, ca. 1860
(*courtesy Donna Bekius Breems*)

within the year, they welcomed their first child. Over the next twenty-four years, twelve other children would follow. Sjoerd enjoyed a marriage of fifty years; he was content in his life of husband, father, farmer, and member of the Beaverdam Reformed Church. When he died in 1907, at the age of seventy-six, he had sixty-nine grandchildren. On his gravestone, emblematic of his faith, were placed the words of Psalm 17:15 (in Dutch), "As for me, I shall behold Thy face. I shall be satisfied, when I awake, with Thy likeness."

We may assume that Maartje first lived in Zeeland, with either her father and brother or her married sister. But finding neither work nor marriage prospects in so small a community, she moved on to nearby Grand Rapids, a newly incorporated city of some three thousand persons. Here she met Leendert van der Stolpe, a farmer and himself a recent arrival from the Netherlands. They married in 1858 and soon began their family. Maartje and Leendert had five children together: the first died at age eleven; another died at two months; a third child died without record; and two daughters lived to adulthood. In 1864 they purchased thirty-seven acres of farmland in Section 1 of Wyoming Township, on the southwest edge of Grand Rapids, and began selling their produce in the city. Maartje had barely twenty-one years of marriage with Leendert, when she died at age forty-eight. At the time of her death, both of her daughters were still young women; she never knew the men they would marry, and she never saw her six grandchildren.[31] Curiously, the stone over her grave in the Fulton Street Cemetery in Grand Rapids says Maude rather than Maartje.

The Bekius sons were an ambitious lot; we do not know who first thought of it, but one of them cleverly suggested their name would sound more American if they inverted the u to make an n; from that day, Bekius became Bekins. It was Sjoerd's son, Martin, who conceived the idea of buying a team of horses and a wagon and establishing the Bekins Van Lines. When the concept proved successful in Sioux City, Iowa, he drew his younger brothers into the business and established another branch of the company in Omaha, Nebraska. In 1895 Martin moved the company headquarters to Los Angeles. In time, the family company went national, then worldwide; the Bekins name became virtually a household word. Today, if you spend any time on the interstate highways, you will see their large white vans with the Bekins name in green letters.

In 1947, on the one hundredth anniversary of Tiertje Berkompas Bekins' arrival in the United States, the Bekins family published its first edition of *Bekins Blue Book*: the family of Sjoerd Bekius. Copies of the book, containing accounts of Sjoerd and several other survivors of the *William and Mary*, are certainly on the bookshelf of many Bekins family members. Many in the family attended biannual reunions, held at various locations around the

---

[31] Two years after Maartje's demise, Leendert married again and fathered another child. When his second wife died, Leendert married a third time at age seventy-eight. As a retired farmer, he lived comfortably off the gradual sale of his land; he died at age eighty-five.

country. In June of 1982, the Bekins family held its reunion back in Het Bildt, Friesland.

Few have ever heard of Maartje Schaaf van der Stolpe. The farm that she and her husband once poured themselves into is today an urban neighborhood of small homes sandwiched between two commercial corridors. The parallel tracks of the former Grand Rapids-Indianapolis Railroad and the Grand Rapids-Valley Railroad, along with US-131, all intersect what was once their productive farm; every day thousands driving in and out of Grand Rapids, unknowingly cross over what was once their dairy pasture. The only hint of its former use appears on a sign strapped to a utility pole on busy Grandville Avenue SW, between a tire shop on one corner and a taco stand on the other: Stolpe Street.

In 2011 I had a conversation with a great-grandson of Maartje and Leendert van der Stolpe and with a great-great-grandson of Sjoerd and Tiertje Bekius. Both men were amiable and open to share what they knew of their individual family histories. Neither had any knowledge of an ancestor being involved in a shipwreck. The Schaaf/van der Stolpe descendant disclosed that an incident in 1925 had put a rift in the family, one that had virtually eliminated any contact with his grandmother, Maartje's daughter. The Bekins heir, though proud of his family name and identification, is now four generations separated from the shipwreck. Both men are far removed from what happened more than a century and a half ago to have any recognition of an impact on their lives today.

Survivors: Sjoerd Tjalsma and family

When I was born, my Frisian grandmother's only comment was, "Kennet. Dats a naam?" Why not Minne like my grandmother's father? Or Yde and Watse, her uncles? Perhaps Siebe, or Daam, or some other good Frisian name?

When the Frisian travelers arrived in 1853, they too brought with them some strange names. Names that were spelled in a variety of forms in Friesland were soon totally misspelled on the frontier. Tjalsma quickly went to Chalsma, and has stayed that way ever since. Sjoerd, a common name in Friesland, did not have a chance here. The 1860 census taker recorded Sjoerd as Hugh; the 1870 and 1880 census takers wrote Seward. In one of the newspapers, Sjoerd is given the name Jewett; a cemetery record used Shurad. Sjoukje soon became Susan, so much easier to spell and pronounce. Their son Tjalling, named after his grandfather, went to Challing, which then evolved to Charles. So it is a little strange that, when Seward and Susan's ninth child was born a year after their arrival in Wisconsin, the Frisian name Flaaske was given. By the 1870 census, Flaaske had become Caroline.

Charles was sixteen when he arrived in New Amsterdam, and like his father and brothers, he immediately engaged in farming. When it came time for him to marry, it is no surprise to find him taking Susan Tuininga, another survivor of the *William and Mary*, as his bride. The couple became part of the church community in New Amsterdam and raised two children, Anna and Jacob.

Jacob followed in his father's path; he married (Ella), purchased 120 acres of farmland two miles South of New Amsterdam, became part of the church family, and raised three children: Wesley, Bessie, and Victor.

And Victor did the same; he married (Maude), purchased two hundred acres of farmland one mile southeast of New Amsterdam, took his place in New Amsterdam Presbyterian Church, and raised his family as those before him. When Victor died in 2004, at the blessed age of 103, land developers took an immediate interest in his farmland estate. In the words of *La Crosse Tribune* reporter Joe Orso, "It could have been a strip mall. You could have turned west on McHugh Road off Hwy 53/35 and in less than three minutes been in a food court. Or it could have been an industrial park. Instead, the sixty-one acres in the town of Holland will remain what nature started developing them into . . . years ago: sand prairie."[32] In 2007 the Mississippi Valley Conservancy completed the purchase of the farm, declared it the Holland Sand Prairie State Natural Area, and transferred ownership to the town of Holland.

In September of 2012, I spoke by phone with a son of Victor, a great-grandson of *William and Mary* passengers Charles and Susan Chalsma. He was the first in his family to leave the farming

[32]   Orso, "Holland sand prairie hits some milestones," *La Crosse Tribune* (September 6, 2007).

profession, choosing instead to become a building contractor. It was his mother, Maude, who first told him about the *William and Mary* tragedy when he was a teenager. Having grown up in the New Amsterdam area, and having attended the New Amsterdam Presbyterian Church as a boy, he is far more familiar with his unique heritage than most great-grandchildren of the shipwreck's survivors. Still he guards his privacy, is modest in his position, and reluctant to disclose his family's involvement in establishing the village of New Amsterdam. I cannot help but think that is probably how Sjoerd Tjalsma would have viewed his role on the frontier as well.

Former Captain: Timothy R. Stinson

There is a longstanding expectation that, in the event of a maritime disaster, a vessel's master will remain with a ship until all passengers and crew are removed. So when the captain of the Italian cruise liner, *Costa Concordia*, abandoned his ship on January 13, 2012, in advance of his passengers, people immediately held him in contempt all across Italy. Similarly, in 1991, when the cruise ship *M/V Oceanos* was caught in a storm gale on the west coast of Africa, its captain drew strong criticism when he issued an abandon ship order and then immediately left on the first available helicopter. A musician, hired to entertain the passengers, took responsibility for seeing that the 160 remaining passengers were safely evacuated. In 1965, when the cruise ship *Yarmouth Castle* caught fire in the Caribbean, the captain of a rescue ship was outraged to find the *Yarmouth*'s master was one of the first to flee the sinking vessel; he forced the captain back to his ship until all its passengers were cared for.

In literature, we have Conrad's *Lord Jim*, the story of a young first mate who abandoned his stricken ship, *Patna*, and its eight hundred passengers when the ship's loss seemed inevitable. After being tried and stripped of his papers, Jim went into a self-imposed asylum on a Malay island where he could forget his past and hopefully regain the respect of society.

So what happened to Captain Stinson? Was he ever charged and brought to trial? Was he convicted?

In a desperate attempt to escape the shame of his cowardice, the dereliction of his duty, and the near-certain possibility of prosecution, Timothy Stinson fled Maine with his wife, Thankful, and his young son, Charles. The only clue as to his whereabouts came from *William and Mary* owner, John Harward, when he disclosed that Stinson had left to visit his brother "in the West." Although Stinson did have two brothers, neither of them lived any farther west than the Kennebec River Valley. The captain disappeared, and under the heavy weight of guilt, he chose to go into exile. Like those whom he had recently abandoned at sea, now he was in need of rescue. He needed a place to find peace—with God, with family, and within the community.

His location for the next six years remains a mystery.

We can be certain that there were letters from Timothy to his family in Maine—letters without a sender's name or address—although none is known to be extant. No information has been found on Thankful Stinson; we assume that she died sometime between 1853 and 1858. On April 15, 1859, in Christian County, Illinois, Timothy Stinson married twenty-five-year-old Lucy E. Call. The following summer, the couple is found renting a home in Pana, Illinois, a mining and railroad town in the center of the state. Here Stinson began a new trade—house painting. But with only 160 houses in a relatively new village, work was scarce. The following year, Lucy gave birth to a son, Edward, born not in Illinois but across the river in Iowa.

By the time of the 1870 federal census, Timothy, Lucy, Charles, and Edward were residing in Warsaw, Illinois, a town of 3,583 persons on the Mississippi River. Timothy, now fifty, and Charles, twenty-one, are both listed here as house and sign painters.

Several things may have influenced Stinson to make his next move: health reasons, the advice of friends, or what he read in the paper about Denver, Colorado, the exciting new "Queen City of the Plains" and the business opportunities it would present. House painters in Denver could expect to be paid between $3.50 and $5.00 per day.

Denver was founded in 1858 when a few nuggets of gold were discovered near the confluence of the South Platte River and Cherry Creek. When Stinson arrived a dozen or so years later, it was still a town of dusty dirt roads filled with pioneer wagons, miners, and Native Americans—but very few women. The total number of residents at the time was less than five thousand. British traveler Isabella Bird arrived not long after Stinson, and she was not impressed with what she saw.

> I looked down upon the great City of the Plains, the metropolis of the Territories. There the great braggart city lay spread out, brown and treeless, upon a brown and treeless plain, which seemed to nourish nothing but wormwood and Spanish bayonet. The shallow Platte, shriveled into a narrow stream with a shingly bed six times too large for it, . . . [was] fringed by shriveled cottonwood.[33]
>
> There were men of every rig: hunters and trappers in buckskin clothing; men of the Plains with belts and revolvers,

---

[33] Bird, *A Lady's Life in the Rocky Mountains: An Annotated Text*, ed. Ernest S. Bernard (Norman, OK: University of Oklahoma Press, 1999), 152.

in great blue cloaks, relics of the war; teamsters in leathern suits; horsemen in fur coats and caps and buffalo-hide boots, with the hair on the outside, and camping blankets behind their huge Mexican saddles; Broadway dandies in light kid gloves; rich English sporting tourists, clean, comely, and supercilious looking; and hundreds of Indians on their small ponies, the men wearing buckskin suits sewn with beads, and red blankets, with faces painted vermilion and hair hanging lank and straight, and squaws much bundled up, riding astride with furs over their saddles.[34]

Streets in the oldest section of Denver were established parallel to Cherry Creek and diagonal to the cardinal points. On Champa Street, between C and D (today 12th and 13th Avenues), in a neighborhood of one- and two-story brick and wood-frame boarding homes, Stinson moved his wife and two sons.

We do not know where it happened or when, perhaps in Pana or Warsaw and maybe soon after arriving in Denver, but somewhere along the line, Stinson's trail of guilt led him to find forgiveness in Jesus Christ. Painters have ample time to think as they work; days of covering distressed buildings with fresh paint moved him to consider his condition before his Creator. There is evidence that Stinson's life changed; even his name, Timothy (Greek *Timotheos*), meaning "honoring God," took a new significance. In 1872 he attended the Congregational Church, a few blocks from where he lived, and in June of that year, he served as a delegate at the annual Sunday school convention in Greeley, Colorado. On New Year's Day, 1873, he made public profession of his faith in Christ and joined the First Presbyterian Church, along with Lucy.[35]

---

[34]   Ibid., 155.
[35]   Son Charles continued attending the Congregational Church, where he served as the Sunday school librarian. When several of the city churches organized what was known as the Railway Union Mission Sunday School, Charles served as its chorister.

The *Denver City Directory*, published annually by Corbett, Hoye & Company (later Corbett & Ballengers), was primarily a business publication. It provided the names of each head of household, their profession, sometimes the name of their employer, and their home address. Timothy Stinson's name first appeared in the 1873 issue and followed every year thereafter until the time of his death. In its first appearance, he was:

Stinson, T. R. painter, r. ss Champa, bet. C & D[36]

Today these old directories serve as our best source of information not only of Timothy's work but also in tracking his constant shifting of residence, a trait frequently associated with those living in boarding or rental facilities. In 1874 he moved the family several blocks to the east, to 342 Wasoola (today Court Place); in 1875 they moved nearly twenty blocks directly south to 9 Broadway; in 1879 they moved to 307 Twenty-First Street, a shift some twenty-five blocks to the north. (Curiously, during the time the Stinsons resided on Twenty-First Street, John Best, former seaman on the *William and Mary*, lived only one block away.) In 1882 Timothy and Lucy made another move downtown, this time to 95 Evans (today Cherokee), and five years later, a move uptown to 1240 Evans. (Today their former home site is a parking lot in what is known as the Golden Triangle in the heart of Denver.) In 1890 it was once again downtown, to 51 Second Avenue West, only to be followed the next year by a move to a home on Denver Avenue (today W. Denver Place), in the Boulevard/Highlands area far to the north and west.

From his earnings, Timothy made several investments. In 1874 he purchased two large lots in the Potter Highland section on the north side of the city; Charles purchased a single lot next to his father's at the same time. Three lots may sound

---

[36]   *Denver City Directory* (Denver, CO: Corbett, Hoye, 1873), 200.

L. R. CHITTENDEN.   T. R. STINSON.

CHITTENDEN & STINSON,

PLAIN AND DECORATIVE

Paper Hanging,

Calcimining,

Painting,

Graining.

Corner 15th and Lawrence Sts.

(Under People's Savings Bank.)

Advertisement placed by Stinson and his business partner in the *Denver Daily Times* in the spring of 1877 (*courtesy Library of Congress*)

insignificant, but in actuality, they comprised three quarters of a city block, between West Thirty-Fourth and West Thirty-Fifth Avenues and Alcott and Bryant Streets. The area was promoted as having cleaner air and water than the rest of the city. Its major drawback, however, was that the location was so far away from downtown Denver that no one wanted to move there. When purchased in 1890 by real estate broker H. G. Wolff, an organizer of the Highland Street Railway Company, each lot was subdivided into six home sites.

In an unusual move for the time, Lucy Stinson also purchased land, two lots on what today is Grant Street in the heart of downtown Denver. When she sold the property in 1881, she received the rather large sum of $3,000.

In 1878 Timothy, Charles, and fellow painter Ledru Chittenden are found to be the owners of the Great Eastern Mine, a tellurium and free gold mine located on Hoosier Hill in the Gold Hill Mining District of Salina, Colorado. Its 210-foot main shaft picked up a vein of ore four feet wide and six inches thick, paying a reported average yield of $200 per ton.

Like many in Denver, Timothy also got caught up in the Leadville silver rush in the late 1870s. In January of 1880, he, Chittenden, and ten other investors filed Mining Application No. 430 for what was called the Edith Mine in the California Gulch Mining District. Unfortunately, the 1880s saw a decline in the value of silver. There is no evidence that their investments paid a significant dividend, if any at all.

Timothy and Lucy's son, Edward, had other ambitions. He was a serious student and well liked by all who knew him. At the age of sixteen, he made public his faith in Christ and became a member of First Presbyterian Church. In order to attend high school in Denver at that time, it was necessary to pass a two-day written entrance examination. Edward was one of twenty-five successful candidates and began school in the fall of 1878.

If Timothy and Lucy Stinson displayed any pride in Edward's high school achievements, they had every reason to do so. The *Rocky Mountain News*, Denver's first newspaper, published the young man's speaking accomplishments on the debate team and in lyceum declamations. During the summer between his freshman and sophomore year, Edward began a part-time position as mail clerk for the *Rocky Mountain News*, a job he continued into the school year. In September he was elected treasurer of the school football club. But in late October, he took ill. Being of strong constitution, his recovery was certainly expected. His illness was diagnosed as typhoid, but rather than improve, he declined with each passing week. On Wednesday morning, November 26, the day before Thanksgiving, to the shock of his parents, classmates, and newspaper staff, Edward died.

At a time when city newspapers posted obituaries for well-known public figures only, the *Rocky Mountain News* published two lengthy articles on their nineteen-year-old staff member.

> The death of Edward A. Stinson, which took place yesterday, is an event which will be generally regretted by all who knew

the young man and were familiar with his many manly qualities. Ed was the only son of T. R. Stinson, a well-known resident of this city, and was a typical Colorado boy. . . . Some months ago, he was added to the city department of the *News*, and during his short connection with the paper gave promise of developing into a vigorous and graceful writer. Ed was the embodiment of good nature and gentleness and was a general favorite among his associates in the *News* editorial rooms.[37]

At two o'clock on Saturday afternoon, the funeral procession left the Stinson home on Twenty-First Street for the short walk to the church. The service was conducted by the family's former pastor, Rev. Dr. Willis Lord, seventy, a man known as a ripe scholar, with all the graces of a courtly gentleman. The filled church heard the singing of the high school glee club and the church choir. Dr. Lord praised the Christ-like attributes of Edward and extended the sympathies of the congregation to his bereaved parents. At the conclusion of the service, there was the long procession northward to Riverside Cemetery, Denver's new and only cemetery, to a burial plot previously purchased by Charles Stinson.

Having experienced the loss of a stillborn grandchild and the death of Edward, Timothy did what ancient Abraham did for his family—he purchased a burial site that would serve his family for years to come. In the fall of 1881, Timothy bought a large lot in Block 5 in Riverside Cemetery. At the center of the lot, he had installed a tall, white marble column on a square base. We believe a decorative urn originally capped it, but over the years, the upper portion has been lost; the once-glistening stone is now

---

[37] *Rocky Mountain News*, Denver, CO (November 27, 1979), 8. In the same issue appeared a resolution formulated by the high school lyceum, extending "heartfelt sympathies to the bereaved parents whose affliction seemed to be greater than they can bear."

sugarized, its shortened shaft closely mimicking a broken ship's mast. Once the lot was purchased, Stinson had the remains of his granddaughter and son reinterred here. In 1883 Timothy's granddaughter, four-year-old Ida Jean, was buried here, and in 1887, Lucy's father, Stephen Call, was buried in the family lot. One day, they would all be brought here.

Over the years, the Central Presbyterian Church remained an important part of the Stinson family. Despite the Stinsons' frequent relocations, the family continued to attend Central. And they continued their affiliation when the church moved from its original building on Fifteenth Street to one on the corner of Eighteenth and Champa, then in 1892, to a large, new facility at Seventeenth and Sherman.[38]

In those early years, the congregation was composed of Denver's elite. The Stinsons, however, were not part of the city's upper socioeconomic class; they had shied away from any leadership role. Timothy appears nowhere in the church records as an officer; he had never served as an elder, deacon, or trustee. Yet here the Stinsons participated in worship, contributed to the needs of the fellowship, received the Lord's Supper, and grew in their faith.

The one-time mariner never returned to the sea but remained always in view of the snow-capped Rockies. He continued working into his seventies. He died of heart failure on Saturday, March 24, 1894, in his home on Denver Avenue. He was seventy-four. His funeral was held the following Tuesday at Central Presbyterian

---

[38] Denver historian Phil Goodstein wrote, "Of all the magnificent church buildings on Capitol Hill, none matches the beauty of the interior of Central Presbyterian." *Ghosts of Denver: Capitol Hill* (Denver: New Social Publications, 1996), 129. When I visited the church that Timothy Stinson had attended some 120 years ago, I saw what Goodstein meant. The large, wood-paneled lobby, with its decorative fireplace, stained-glass skylight, and staircases to the balconies above, resembles the foyer of a grand theater. The sanctuary is even more impressive, with rows of tiered theater seats, perimeter box seats, and an elaborate array of organ pipes. Large stained-glass windows bathe the entire auditorium in a soft, golden light.

Captain Stinson's tombstone in
Riverside Cemetery, Denver
(Courtesy Mark de Nooy)

Church, conducted by his pastor, Dr. John N. Freeman. His body was laid to rest in the family lot in Riverside Cemetery. He was survived by Lucy, his wife of thirty-five years; his son, Charles; his daughter-in-law, Lou; and his granddaughter, Luella. There is no record in Denver of a last will and testament.

As I had done for many of the survivors of the *William and Mary* shipwreck, I searched for a living descendant of Timothy Stinson. After months of investigation, I discovered three, all great-great-great-grandsons of Stinson, all close in age. Two grew up within two miles of where the captain last lived; another was born and raised in California. One was named Timothy. Although it is very doubtful if any had even the slightest knowledge of their ancestor and his involvement in the *William and Mary* shipwreck, all three declined my invitation for an interview. I honor their desire for anonymity.

A Final Word

When I try to picture what our Frisian travelers looked like, I immediately think of my relatives—my grandparents, parents, aunts, and uncles. They share a common heritage and, in the absence of photographs, give faces to those in the story. A few were tall, most were short, some lean, others a bit stout. All were unmistakably Dutch.

When I was a boy, Sunday was our day for gathering as a family. It was coffee after the morning service or tea in the afternoon. That is when individual personalities were best seen, when family news, thoughts, and opinions flowed easily around the kitchen table. Conversations were generally light, moved quickly from one topic to another, and were frequently interjected by volleys of laughter. Certainly each household had its share of problems, but these were matters that seldom entered the discussion, at least not in front of the kids. Nor did my uncles,

271

almost all of whom had served in the war, ever talk about that chapter of their lives, although such memories still would have been fresh in their minds. I should not be surprised then that the Frisian survivors were similarly reluctant to speak of their ordeal crossing the Atlantic.

Like many of the Frisian travelers, my relatives had a strong God sense, attended similar services, sang from a similar psalter. They subscribed to the Heidelberg Catechism, knew the wording of Lord's Day I by heart, "What is your only comfort in life and death?" Yet each person was so very different. One would pray like the minister, another offer only silent prayer without even a spoken "amen." Some could argue doctrine; most did not want to talk about it, at least not in family gatherings. I most admired those who, though having experienced their share of life's storms, hung to the resolve that "Without the will of my heavenly Father, not a hair can fall from my head." Their walk with the Lord was such that, in the middle of each tempest, they fully expected that peace would follow.

I rather think it was the same on board the *William and Mary*. As the ship listed precariously, drifting without captain or crew, some cried, some gave up hope, some prayed, and a few cursed. I am particularly thankful that in the search for documentation, a handful of letters were uncovered that openly testified of God's grace and mercy. No one, of course, was really aware of the full extent to which that was true. Had God not provided the Bahamian rescuers when He did, a few hours later, the Gulf Stream would have carried the Frisians outside the vision of Sands and his crew, and they would have been lost with the vessel. I see the graciousness of God in providing the welcoming arms and generous spirit of the people of Grand Bahama Island and New Providence Island and how He provided for the Frisians' spiritual, physical, and material needs while there. I am amazed at how God moved them on to the United States and prevented their exposure to the deadly cholera outbreak soon to hit Nassau. Once in New Orleans, God again opened the hearts of people to provide aid before quickly moving the refugees on their way up the river, beyond the reach of the worst epidemic of yellow fever in the city's history. But they never knew.

For those living during the mid-nineteenth century, especially those who crossed the Atlantic, nautical imagery was commonly understood. As such, it frequently found its way into the hymnody of the period—in songs like "My Anchor Holds," "Jesus, Savior, Pilot Me," and "Master, the Tempest is Raging." Seven years after the sinking of the *William and Mary*, William Whiting wrote a poem that would become known as the navy hymn, sung by both the US Navy and the British Royal Navy. But today, most of us do not go to sea. The metaphorical terminology appears archaic. Yet the truth remains: we are all in peril; we are all in need of the Eternal Father to save us.

Eternal Father, strong to save,

Whose arm hath bound the restless wave,

Who bidd'st the mighty ocean deep

His own appointed limits keep;

Oh, hear us when we cry to Thee,

For those in peril on the sea!

Appendix

Officers and Crew of the William and Mary

Those who were picked up by the *Reuben Carver* and taken to New York:

Captain Timothy (T. R.) Stinson, 32, of Bowdoinham, ME
First Mate Samuel B. Welsh of Boston, MA
Second Mate Loami Ross, 18, of Litchfield, ME
Seaman Stephen W. Purington, 24, of Bowdoinham, ME
Seaman Nicholas Card, 18, of Bowdoinham, ME
Seaman John D. Best, 17, of Bath, ME
Seaman Henry Moore of New York, NY
Seaman Edward Weeks, 18, of Portland, ME
Cook _____ Williams of England

Those who were picked up by the *Pollux* and taken to Liverpool

Seaman Isaac M. Ridley, 21, of Harpswell, ME
Seaman Lemuel Preble, 37, of Woolwich, ME
Seaman Thomas Allen, 27, of Baltimore, MD
Seaman Joseph Roe, 21, of Portugal

Those who stayed with the *William and Mary* until rescued

Steward William Busby of London, England
Seaman Patrick or William Ward of Philadelphia, PA
Seaman Samuel B. Harris, 24, of Providence, RI
Passengers' cook Peter McDonald

Passenger List of the William and Mary

Drawn from B. B. Haagsma and records from the *Time*, *Rover*, *Clyde*, *Pollux*, and other sources

Passengers from the Netherlands

Unless noted otherwise, they were transported from Nassau to New Orleans on the schooner *Time*

1. Algera, Tjipke Dirks (25, a farmhand of Franekeradeel)
2. Balkstra, Jan Jans (29, a rope maker of Harlingen)
3. Balkstra, Antje (née van Slooten, 26, of Harlingen)
4. Bekius, Sjoerd Douwes (23, a butcher of Nieuwe Bildtzijl, Het Bildt)
5. Bergsma, Ulbe Andries (25, of Kimswerd; returned to Liverpool on the Pollux)
6. Bonnema, Oepke Haitzes (28, a grain merchant of Kimswerd)
7. de Boer, Hendrikus Gerrits (29, a blacksmith helper of Harlingen)
8. de Boer, Anna (née Spoelstra, 31, of Harlingen)

9. de Jong, Herke Jolkes (43, a carpenter's helper of Harlingen)
10. de Jong, Anna Aleides (née Voortallen, 31, of Harlingen)
11. de Jong, Luutske (7, of Harlingen)
12. de Jong, Cornelius (7, of Harlingen)
13. Gersema, Jelle de Vries Hermanus (24, a baker's helper of Kimswerd)
14. Graafsma, Bauke Douwes (40, a workman of Wonseradeel)
15. Graafsma, Klaaske Aukes (née Tichelaar, 29, of Wonseradeel)
16. Graafsma, Beitske (9, of Wonseradeel)
17. Graafsma, Trijntje (1, of Wonseradeel: died at sea on Apr. 5)
18. Haagsma, Broer Baukes (22, an assistant teacher of Wonseradeel)
19. Heemstra, Sytske Martens (23, of Sint Annaparochie, Het Bildt)
20. Hofman, Dirk Dirks, of Barradeel (26, died at sea on Mar. 30)
21. Hofstra, Bertus (30, a tailor of Menaldumsdeel)
22. Hollander, Pietje (28, of Wonseradeel)
23. Jansen, Jan Willems (23, unemployed, of Franekeradeel)
24. Jansonius, Grietje Jans (20, a farm servant of Manaldumsdeel)
25. Kas, Hendrik Jans (27, a wagon maker's hand of Franekeradeel)
26. Kooistra, Jacob Sakes (45, a carpenter's helper of Wonseradeel: died in Nassau on May 16)
27. Kooistra, Antje Tiettes (née Piekema, 37, of Wonseradeel)
28. Kooistra, Saki (12, of Wonseradeel)
29. Kooistra, Tiete (11, of Wonseradeel)
30. Kooistra, Symon (8, of Wonseradeel)

31. Kooistra, Baukje (2, of Wonseradeel: died at sea on Apr. 12)
32. Kooistra, Marinus (1, of Wonseradeel: died at sea on Apr. 18)
33. Kuiken, Dirk Cornelis (25, a miller's hand of Het Bildt)
34. Molenaar, Gerrit
35. Ploegsma, Cornelis Jakobs (31, of Franekeradeel)
36. Rienks, Beinze Cornelis (25, a farm hand of Het Bildt)
37. Rienks, Hendrik (of Het Bildt)
38. Roorda, Isaak Epkes (21, of Dantumawoude: returned to Liverpool on the Pollux)
39. Salverda, Peter Ages (32, a workman of Franekeradeel)
40. Schaaf, Maartje Pieters (23, a farm servant of Het Bildt)
41. Sikkema, Rients Sikkes (33, a workman of Barradeel)
42. Sikkema, Ymkje Sytzes (née Nauta, 32, of Barradeel)
43. Sikkema, Maaike (3, of Barradeel: died at sea on Apr. 29)
44. Sikkema, Sikke (3 months, of Barradeel: died at sea on Apr. 7)
45. Spanjer, Hendrik (35, of Menaldumadeel died at sea on Apr. 2)
46. Stienstra, Johannes Dirks (38, a workman of Franekeradeel)
47. Stienstra, Riemke Heekes (née Nijdam, 34, of Franekeradeel)
48. Stienstra, Ytje (11, of Franekeradeel)
49. Stienstra, Lieuwe (15, of Franekeradeel)
50. Stienstra, Dirk (9, of Franekeradeel)
51. Tjalsma, Sjoerd Tjallings (43, a boatman of Kimswerd)
52. Tjalsma, Sjoukje Lykles (née Hoogterp, 40, of Kimswerd)
53. Tjalsma, Lyckle (19, of Kimswerd: died at sea on Apr. 18)
54. Tjalsma, Tjalling (16, of Kimswerd)

55. Tjalsma, Sjouke (15, of Kimswerd)
56. Tjalsma, Klaas (12, of Kimswerd)
57. Tjalsma, Jacob (9, of Kimswerd)
58. Tjalsma, Dirk (6, of Kimswerd)
59. Tjalsma, Sjoerd (3, of Kimswerd: died on Mississippi River on June 26)
60. Tuininga, Johannes Jans (40, a workman of Barradeel)
61. Tuininga, Trijntje Alberts (née de Haan, 39, of Barradeel)
62. Tuininga, Jan (15, of Barradeel)
63. Tuininga, Sjouke (12, of Barradeel)
64. Tuininga, Antje (10, of Barradeel: died at sea on Apr. 3)
65. Tuininga, Albertje (8, of Barradeel)
66, Tuininga, Gerrit (3, of Barradeel: died at sea on Mar. 30)
67. van der Ploeg, Jan Martens (65, a market gardener of Westdongeradeel)
68. van der Ploeg, Baukje Jans (38, a laborer of Westdongeradeel)
69. van der Ploeg, Marten Jans (34, a laborer of Westdongeradeel)
70. van der Ploeg, Metje Sapes (22, a farm servant of Het Bildt)
71. van der Tol, Peter Jans (29, of Franekeradeel: died near Nassau on May 11)
72. van der Veer, Johannes Koenraads (56, an instrument maker of Leeuwarden)
73. Wagenaar, Oene Martinus (34, of Heerenveen: returned to Liverpool on the Pollux)
74. Wesselius, Siebren Riekeles (56, a workman of Barradeel)
75. Wesselius, Marijke Klases (née Hamer, 47, of Barradeel)
76. Wesselius, Grietje (23, of Barradeel)
77. Wesselius, Antje (15, of Barradeel)

78. Wesselius, Sjoerd (12, of Barradeel)
79. Arijen Gerrits Westerhuis (38, a workman of Barradeel)
80. Westerhuis, Jeltje Jakobs (née Knol, 42, of Barradeel)
81. Westerhuis, Japke (14, of Barradeel)
82. Westerhuis, Hanne (12, of Barradeel)
83. Westerhuis, Jakob (10, of Barradeel)
84. Westerhuis, Rinske (4, of Barradeel: died at sea on May 2)
85. Westerhuis, Sipke (6 months, of Barradeel)
86. Zwicht, Dirk (32)

Non-Dutch passengers

(Transported from Nassau to New Orleans on schooner *Rover*)

87. Alby or Abbey, Catherine (40)
88. Archer or Orchard, Sally (40, a widow, of Ireland)
89. Archer or Orchard, Thomas (10, of Ireland)
90. Archer or Orchard, John (8, of Ireland)
91. Bowly or Bones, Johanna (21, of Kilkenney, Ireland settled in New Orleans)
92. Brooks, Joseph (22, of England, settled in Texas)
93. Brooks, Mary (22, of England)
94. Brown, John (45, a civil engineer of New Lanark, Scotland,)
95. Brown, Jean (35, of Scotland)
96. Brown, John (16, of Scotland)
97. Brown, Wilson (14, of Scotland)
98. Brown, George (12, of Scotland)
99. Burke, James (50)
100. Burns, Catherine (50)
101. Burns, Henry (15)
102. Donnelly, Bridget (23, of Ireland, settled in New Orleans)

103. Doyle, Daniel (26, of Ireland)
104. Flyn, Mary (37, of Ireland)
105. Flyn, Bridget (9, of Ireland)
106. Flyn, John (7, of Ireland)
107. Flyn, Mary (4, of Ireland)
108. Flyn, Ellen (40, of Ireland)
109. Flyn, Mary (13, of Ireland)
110. Flyn, Margaret (11, of Ireland)
111. Forest, James (24, of Ireland)
112. Gibbon, Honor (30)
113. Gibbon, Bridget (10)
114. Gibbon, Judy (8)
115. Herron, Patrick (28, of Ireland)
116. Kelly or Kelty, Mary (26)
117. Kelly, Catherine (22, of Ireland)
118. Martin, Ann (18, of Ireland, going to Galena, IL)
119. McCluskey, Andrew (50, of Ireland, wished to settle in Wisconsin)
120. McCluskey, Mary (48, of Ireland)
121. McCluskey, Patrick (22, of Ireland)
122. McCluskey, May (18, of Ireland)
123. McCluskey, Rosey (16, of Ireland)
124. McCluskey, Thomas (his name did not appear on the Rover list)
125. McCluskey, Bridget (15, of Ireland)
126. McCluskey, Peter (13, of Ireland)
127. McCluskey, Andrew (12, of Ireland)
128. McCluskey, Johannes (12, of Ireland)
129. McCluskey, Patrick (6, of Ireland)
130. Milligan, Honora (33)
131. Milligan, Thomas (18)
132. Milligan, Mary (8)
133. Milligan, John (5)

134. Nicholls, Alex (21, of Ireland)
135. Nowland, Margaret (25, of Ireland)
136. Ryan, Margaret (35)
137. Ryan, Mary (12)
138. Ryan, John (10)
139. Ryan, Ellen (7)
140. Sullivan, John (50)
141. Sullivan, Johanna (50)
142. Sullivan, James (16)
143. Sullivan, John (10)
144. Sullivan, Margaret (12)
145. Sullivan, Julia (4)
146. Sullivan, William (4)
147. Tobin or Forban, Ellen (17)
148. Tobin or Forban, Ellen (15)
149. Walsh, Margaret (25, of Ireland)

Non-Dutch passengers
(Transported from Nassau to New Orleans on schooner *Clyde*)

150. Ansley, A. (28)
151. Bush, James (50)
152. Callaghan, Dennis (26)
153. Doherty, Edward (26)
154. Doyle, D. (26)
155. Farnish, S. (24)
156. Fitzpatrick, W. (23)
157. Fitzpatrick, Ann (20)
158. Fitzpatrick, Hugh (20)
159. Fitzpatrick, Phillip (21)
160. Ham____, P. (38)
161. Kime, R. (24)
162. Lumon, F. (40)

163. Morhood, G. (17)
164. Palard, Heinrick (25, of Berlin)
165. Scaby or Sealy, Pat (21)
166. Soutes, Randolph (18)
167. Stewart, Luke (57, of England, going to St. Louis)
168. Stewart, Isabella (50, of England)
169. Stewart, Isabella (16, of England)
170. Stewart, Ann (7, of England)
171. Stewart, Elias or Alice (5, of England)

Non-Dutch passengers
(Rescued by the *Pollux* and transported to Liverpool)

172. Abbey, James
173. August, Henry H.
174. Baggan, Owen
175. Boyle, Bridget
176. Cain, Patrick
177. Diamond, John
178. Flinn, Thomas
179. Gannon, John
180. Haungs, Florian
181. Higgins, Bridget
182. Kilty, Patrick (25, of Ireland)
183. McGuire, Catherine
184. Miller, Ebenezer
185. Ryan, Rose
186. Ryan, Patrick
187. Shiel, William
188. Stewart, John
189. Welch, Elizabeth
190. Welch, John
191. unknown German boy

Remaining passengers from the William and Mary, *about whom little is known:*

192. Bonne, M. Aime (of France)
193. Cavanagh, Luke (intended to go to New Orleans)
194. Diamond, Mrs. John (died in Nassau of yellow fever)
195. Father of Mrs. Diamond (reported to have drowned)
196. Mother of Mrs. Diamond (unknown disposition)
197. Sister of Mrs. Diamond (reported to have drowned)
198. Sister of Mrs. Diamond (unknown disposition)
199. Sister of Mrs. Diamond (unknown disposition)
200. Child of Mrs. Diamond (18 weeks, reported to have died at sea)
201. Dolan, John (35, intended to go to New Orleans)
202. McDonald, Peter (was the passengers' cook, last seen in Nassau)
203. O'Brien, _____ (38, of Ireland)
204. unknown passenger
205. unknown passenger
206. unknown passenger
207. unknown passenger
208. unknown passenger

Selected Bibliography

Adams, Silas. *The History of the Town of Bowdoinham, Maine, 1762-1912.* Fairfield, ME: Fairfield Pub. Co., 1912.

Bacot, John. *The Bahamas: A Sketch.* London: Longmans, 1869.

Baker, William Avery. *A Maritime History of Bath, Maine, and the Kennebec River Region.* 2 vols. Bath, ME: Marine Research Society of Bath, 1973.

Barrett, P. J. H. *Grand Bahama.* Harrisburg, PA: Stackpole Books, 1972.

Bekins Blue Book Centennial Celebration: The Family of Sjoerd Bekius, Known as Bekins in America. n.p.: Bekins, 1947.

Bethell, A. Talbot. *The Early Settlers of the Bahamas and Colonists of North America.* 3rd ed., rev. Nassau, 1937.

Bignell, Philippa. *Taking the Train: Railway Travel in Victorian Times.* London: Her Majesty's Stationery Office, 1978.

Blunt, Edmund M. *The American Coast Pilot: Containing Directions for the Principal Harbors, Capes, and Headlands on the Coasts of North and South America*. 16th ed. New York: E. & G. W. Blunt, 1850.

Butterfield, Consul Willshire. *History of La Crosse County, Wisconsin: Containing an Account of its Settlement, Development, and Resources*. Chicago: Western Historical Co., 1881.

Carrigan, Jo Ann. "Yellow Fever in New Orleans, 1853: Abstractions and Realities." *Journal of Southern History* 25, no. 3 (1959): 339-53.

Cleveland, Lewis F. *General Description of the City of Nassau and Island of the New Providence, Bahamas, West Indies*. New York: W. Baldwin, 1871.

Conclin, George. *Conclin's New River Guide, or a Gazetteer of All the Towns on the Western Waters*. Cincinnati: J. A. and U. P. James, 1852.

Cumings, Samuel. *The Western Pilot: Containing Charts of the Ohio River and the Mississippi*. Cincinnati: G. Conclin, 1848.

Denver City Directory. Denver: Corbett, Hoyle, 1873-1880; Corbett & Ballenger, 1881-1891; Ballenger & Richards, 1892.

Dodge, Steve. *Abaco: The History of an Out Island and its Cays*. 2nd ed. Decatur, IL: White Sound Press, 1995.

Drysdale, William. *In Sunny Lands: Outdoor Life in Nassau and Cuba*. New York: Harper and Bros., 1885.

Evans, Thomas J. *Geology of La Crosse County, Wisconsin*. Madison: Wisconsin Geological and Natural History Survey, 2003.

Fenner, Erasmus Darwin. *History of the Epidemic Yellow Fever at New Orleans, La. in 1853*. New York: Hall, Clayton, 1854.

Galema, Annemieke. *Frisians to America, 1880-1914: With the Baggage of the Fatherland*. Groningen: REGIO-PRojekt Uitgevers, 1996.

Goodstein, Phil H. *Denver Streets: Names, Numbers, Locations, Logic*. Denver, CO: New Social Publications, 1994.

Haagsma, Broer B. *Frysia, of Schets der Friesche Volkplanting in Noord-Amerika*. Bolsward, Friesland: P. M. Feenstra, 1855.

——. *Lotgevallen van den Heer Bonnema en Zijne Togtgenooten op Reis Uit Friesland Naar de Vereenigde Staten van Noord-Amerika*. Harlingen, Friesland: S. Houtsma, 1853.

Ives, Charles. *The Isles of Summer; or Nassau and the Bahamas*. New Haven, CN: Ives, 1880.

James, Leslie. *A Chronology of the Construction of Britain's Railways, 1778-1855*. London: Ian Allan, 1983.

Karsten, John H. "A Half Century of Dutch Settlement in Wisconsin, 1847-1897." *Dutch Immigrant Memoirs and Related Writings*, selected and arranged for publication by Henry S. Lucas. Assen, Netherlands: Van Gorcum, 1955.

Kemp, Peter, ed. *The Oxford Companion to Ships and the Sea*. London: Oxford University Press, 1976.

Lemmen, Loren. "The Wreck of the William and Mary." *Origins* 13, no. 2 (1995): 2-9.

Lewis, Henry. *The Valley of the Mississippi*. St. Paul: Minnesota Historical Society, 1967.

Lloyd, James T. *Lloyd's Steamboat Directory and Disasters on the Western Waters*. Cincinnati: J. T. Lloyd, 1856.

Lucas, Henry S. *Netherlanders in America: Dutch Immigration to the United States and Canada, 1789-1950*. Grand Rapids, MI: Eerdmans, 1955.

——. "The Founding of New Amsterdam in La Crosse County." *Wisconsin Magazine of History* 31, no. 1 (1947): 42-60.

McAleer, Jinny. *The Genealogy of Wyannie Malone, American Loyalist and Early Settler of Hope Town, Abaco, Bahamas*. Wilmington, NC: Broadfoot, 1998.

Penrose, Clement A. *Sanitary Conditions in the Bahama Islands*. New York: MacMillan, 1905.

Pinkham, Fred D. *Stinson Genealogy*. 2 vols. Bath, ME: F. D. Pinkham, 1975.

Poortinga, Y. "Emigraesje ut Westerlauwersk Fryslan nei en Festiging yn 'e Foriene Steaten (Oant Likernoch 1900 ta)." *Friesisches Jahrbuch* 32 (1958): 89-109.

Ritchie-Noakes, Nancy. *Liverpool's Historic Waterfront: The World's First Mercantile Dock System.* London: Her Majesty's Stationery Office, 1984.

Roorda, Izaak. "Shipwreck of the Sail Ship William and Mary." *Roorda Family History*, privately published in Des Moines, IA, n.d.

A Sailing Directory for the West India Islands: Containing Instructions For Navigation Among the Islands of Porto Rico, Hayti, Jamaica, Cuba, & c., and For the Various Ports in the Bay of Honduras and the Gulf of Mexico. 6th ed. London: James Imray, 1851.

Schroeder, J. B. *Report to the Deutsche Gesellschaft, June 13, 1853.*

Spence, Jeoffry. *Victorian and Edwardian Railway Travel.* London: B. T, Barsford, 1977.

Swierenga, Robert P. *Dutch Emigrants to the United States, South Africa, South America, and Southeast Asia, 1835-1880: An Alphabetical Listing by Household Heads and Independent Persons.* Wilmington, DE: Scholarly Resources, 1983.

——. *Dutch Emigration Records, 1847-1877: A Computer Alphabetical Listing of Heads of Household and Independent Persons.* Kent, OH: R. P. Swierenga, 1974.

——. *Dutch Immigrants in U.S. Ship Passenger Manifests, 1820-1880: An Alphabetical Listing by Household Heads and Independent Persons.* Wilmington, DE: Scholarly Resources, 1983.

——. *Faith and Family: Dutch Immigration and Settlement in the United States, 1820-1920.* New York: Holmes and Meier, 2000.

Twain, Mark. *Life on the Mississippi.* New York: Harper and Bros., 1899.

Van Hinte, Jacob. *Netherlanders in America: A Study of Emigration and Settlement in the Nineteenth and Twentieth Centuries in the United States of America.* General editor, Robert P. Swierenga, chief translator, Adriaan de Wit. 2 vols. Grand Rapids, MI: Baker Book House, 1985.

Van Raalte, Albertus C. *Voices from North America*. Grand Rapids, MI: Heritage Hall, 1992.

Wharton, Thomas Kelah. *Queen of the South: New Orleans, 1853-1862: The Journal of Thomas K. Wharton*. New Orleans: Historic New Orleans Collection and New York Public Library, 1999.

Wood, Peter H. *Weathering the Storm: Inside Winslow Homer's Gulf Stream*. Athens: University of Georgia Press, 2004.

Newspapers

Bahama Herald. Nassau
Bangor Daily Whig & Courier. Bangor, ME
Bath Independent. Bath, ME
Boston Atlas
Boston Daily Evening Transcript
Brooklyn Daily Eagle
Burlington Free Press. Burlington, VT
Charleston Daily Courier. Charleston, SC
Charleston Mercury. Charleston, SC
Chicago Tribune
Daily Morning News. Savannah, GA
Daily National Intelligencer. Washington, DC
Daily Orleanian. New Orleans, LA
Daily Picayune. New Orleans, LA
Daily Saint Louis Intelligencer
Denver Post
Denver Daily Times
Eastern Times. Bath, ME
Hartford Daily Courant. Hartford, CT
De Hollander. Holland, MI
Illustrated News. New York, NY
La Crosse County Record. La Crosse, WI

La Crosse Tribune and Leader-Press. La Crosse, WI

Leeuwarder Courant. Leeuwarden, Netherlands

London Times. London, England

Liverpool Mercury. Liverpool, England

Maine Cultivator and Hallowell Gazette

Missouri Republican. St. Louis, MO

Morning Chronicle. London, England

Morning Courier and Enquirer. New York, NY

Nassau Guardian. Nassau, Bahamas

New Hampshire Statesman. Concord, NH

New York Daily Times

North American and United States Gazette. Philadelphia, PA

Rocky Mountain News. Denver, CO

Royal Cornwall Gazette, Falmouth Packet, and *General Advertiser*.
    Truro, England

St. Louis Post Dispatch. MO

Savannah Daily Georgian

Sheboygan Nieuwsbode. Sheboygan, WI

Sun. Baltimore, MD

Weekly Herald. New York, NY

Weekly Mirror. Bath, ME

Index

Abaco Island, 79, 80, 99, 107-8,
  138, 213, 216-17
Abenaki tribe, 27, 43
Aigburth, England, 38
A & J Dennistoun & Company,
  151
Alcott, Abigail, 200
Alcott, Amos Bronson, 199, 200
Alcott, Louisa May, 199
Algera, Tjipke, 164
Allen, Thomas, 46, 90
Amazon River, 89
America, 225, 232, 234, 236
American Coast Pilot (Blunt), 47
American consul, 36, 112-13, 119
Amsterdam, 11, 232
Andover Theological Seminary,
  MA, 63
Androscoggin River, 30, 43
Andros Island, 138

Anglican Church of Christ, 120
Antietam (Battle of), 228
Arkansas River, 171
Arnold, Harry G., 221
Arrowsic Island, ME, 43
Arrowsic, ME, 146
Arum, Friesland, 15
Aspinwall, Panama, 164
Atlantic Dock Company, 125
Audubon, John James, 165, 175
Augusta, ME, 44
Aunt Phillis's Cabin (Eastman), 50

Bacot, J. T. W., 115
Bahama Herald, 111, 213
Bahama Islands, 77, 102, 138
  map, 216, 250
Bahamas Air Sea Rescue Associa-
  tion (BASRA), 98
Baker, William Avery, 31, 44

Balize, LA, 148
Balkstra, Anna, 9, 164, 180
Balkstra, Jan, 9, 164, 180
Ballard, Eliza Jane (née Stinson), 147
Ballard, Mary (née Stinson), 146
Baltimore, MD, 98, 216
Bangor Daily Whig & Courier, 129
Banner, 221
Barcelona, Spain, 164
Barradeel, Friesland, 8
Barratt, P. J. H., 102, 105
Bath, ME, 32, 44, 46, 249, 251
Bath Weekly Mirror, 140
Baton Rouge, LA, 166
Bay of Fundy, 249
Beauford, SC, 48
Beaverdam, MI, 253
Beaverdam Reformed Church, 254
Bekins Blue Book, 255
Bekins, Martin, 255
Bekins, Sjoerd Douwes.
    See Bekius, Sjoerd Douwes
Bekins, Tiertje, 253, 255
Bekins Van Lines, 255
Bekius, Douwe Alerts, 11
Bekius, Sjoerd Douwes, 10, 73, 77, 84, 87, 98, 106-7, 135, 164, 193, 253, 254 image
Bekius, Tiertje (née Berkompas), 253, 255
Bergsma, Ulbe, 86, 90-91, 169, 192, 232
Berry Islands, 80, 138
Best, Charles F., 250
Best, John D., 45, 90, 128, 130, 249, 265
Best, John W., 250-51
Best, Lucretia, 250
Bijlsma, Pieter, 193
Bird, Isabella, 263
Birmingham, England, 36
Black River, 192, 196, 235
Blunt, Edmund March, 33, 47, 80-81, 108

Boell, F. W., 171
Bolsward, Friesland, 203
Bonnema, Haitze Eeltje, 6
Bonnema, Harmen, 7, 236
Bonnema, Jelle, 7, 236
Bonnema, Louise (née Spangler), 203, 236-37
Bonnema, Oepke Haitzes, 6-8, 11, 15, 21, 37, 41, 67, 86, 132, 153, 164, 180, 183, 190-91, 193-94, 196, 201, 203-6, 224, 235, 239, 245
Bonnema, Stijntje (née Fopma), 6
Bonnema, Stijntje (second wife), 7
Boston Daily Evening Transcript, 140
Boston Journal, 130
Boston, MA, 98, 127, 132, 168, 173, 250
Bowdoin College, ME, 63
Bowdoinham, ME, 28, 30, 41, 44-45, 127, 129, 146-47, 169
Boyce & Company, 48
Brassey, Annie, 120
Breadalbane, Marquis (John Campbell) and Marchioness of, 123
Brewster, William, 24
British Consulate, 153, 155
British Naval Yard, 110
British railway, 22
Brooklyn Daily Eagle, 128
Brooklyn, NY, 128
Brooks, Joseph, 81, 85, 93
Brown, Anna (née Tuininga), 245
Brown, Captain, 148
Brunswick, ME, 30, 43
Bryant, Daniel, 253
Bryant, William Cullen, 39
Burlington Free Press, 132
Burlington, IA, 186
Busby, William, 92, 112
Byron, Lord, 24

Cairo, IL, 174
California, 270

Call, Stephen, 269
Calvin College, 221
Card, Nicholas, 45, 90
Carrigan, Jo Ann, 158
Carthage, IL, 186
Cathance River, 44-45
Cathedral of St. Peter, St. Paul, and St. Andrew, 23
Cay Sal Banks, 139
Central Presbyterian Church, 269, 270
Chalsma, Anna, 258
Chalsma, Bessie, 258
Chalsma, Charles, 258
Chalsma, Ella, 258
Chalsma, Flaaske (Caroline), 258
Chalsma, Jacob, 258
Chalsma, Maude, 258
Chalsma, Seward. *See* Tjalsma, Sjoerd
Chalsma, Sjouke (Susan) (née Tuininga), 246, 258
Chalsma, Victor, 258
Chalsma, Wesley, 258
Chamberlayne, William John, 120, 135
Chancellorsville, VA, 228
Charity Hospital, 158
Charleston Daily Courier, 48-49
Charleston Mercury, 49-50
Charleston, SC, 46-47, 139
Charlotte, Saharia, 121
Chassahowitzka River, 129
Cherokee Sound, Abaco, 99
Cherry Creek, 263-64
Chesapeake Bay, 216
Chicago, IL, 194, 204, 236, 241, 250
Chicago, Milwaukee, St. Paul & Pacific Railroad, 228-29
Chipman, H. N., 120, 133, 137
Chittenden, Ledru, 266
cholera, 6, 60, 99, 116, 186-87, 273
Christian County, IL, 262

Christian Reformed Church, 221
Cincinnati, OH, 148
City Fire Insurance Company, 33
Civil War, 171, 182, 228, 233, 240
Claytor, W. R., 166, 172
Clear Creek County, CO, 250
Clemens, Samuel (Mark Twain), 170, 180, 186
Cleveland, Lewis F., 115
Cobb, Edward, 91, 119
Colorado, 250
Colton, Calvin, 7
Columbus, Christopher, 120
Committee for the Relief of the Emigrants per the *William and Mary*, 111
Conclin's *New River Guide*, 156, 167, 170, 173-74
Concord, ME, 44
Cone, Rev. C. C., 45
Confidence-Man, The (Melville), 165
Congregational Church, 264
Conrad, Joseph, 262
Conroy, Mrs., 158
Cooper River, 48
Corbett & Ballengers, 265
Corbett, Hoye & Company, 265
Corinth, MS, 233
Coster, Anna (née Antje Kooistra), 227
Coster, Pearl, 230
Coster, Roy, 229
Coster, Silas (né Sake Kooistra), 227-28, 229 image
Coster, Silas (son of Tector Coster), 229
Coster, Simon (né Symon Kooistra), 227-28
Coster, Tector (né Tiete Kooistra), 228-29
"Crescent City" (New Orleans), 151
Cromwell, Oliver, 23
Crosby Channel, 51, 57

Crow, Hargadine, 240
Crow, McCreery & Company, 240
Cunningham, Samuel, 134
Cushing, Caleb, 25

Daily Evening Transcript (Boston), 126
Daily Missouri Republican, 162, 168, 183
Daily Morning News (Savannah), 131
Daily Orleanian, 169
Daily Picayune (New Orleans), 130, 150, 153, 155-56, 166
Dana, Juliette Starr, 175
Danby, Robert, 66
D'Arcy, Major, 213-14
Darling, Lucy (née Sargent), 113
Darling, Timothy, 113, 134
Davenport, IA, 188
Davis, Jefferson, 25
de Boer, Anna (née Spoelstra), 9, 164
de Boer, Hendrikus, 9, 164
Decker, Wilbur F., 33
de Jager, Hermanus, 189-90, 192, 198
de Jong, Anna Voortallen, 9, 164
de Jong, Cornelius, 9
de Jong, Herke, 9, 164
de Jong, Luutske, 9
DeKoster, Cornelis, 220
DeKoster, Franklin, 220
DeKoster, Lester, 220-21
DeKoster, Ruth, 221
Dennis, Leslie (née DeKoster), 221
Denver City Directory, 265
Denver, CO, 250-51, 263-65
Deutsche Gesellschaft, 152, 159
Deutsche Zeitung, 155
Diamond family, 194
Dickens, Charles, 37, 175, 178
Drysdale, William, 109
Dublin, Ireland, 187

Dubuque, IA, 191, 224
Dunn, Charles, 50
Dutch consul, 179, 198, 232, 240

earthquakes, 173
Eastern Times (Bath, ME), 181
Eastman, Mary H., 50
East River, 125
economy, Frisian, 4
Edith Mine, 267
Elbe, River, 40
Elbow Key, 80, 107
Ellet, Elizabeth Fries, 189
Ely Cathedral, 23
Ely, England, 23
Emancipation Proclamation, 157
Embargo Act, 43
Embden, ME, 44
Emerson, Ralph Waldo, 36, 200
Emery, Captain, 119
emigrants, origin of, 10
Evening News (Saint Louis), 181

faith: expressions of, 28, 66, 85, 92, 97-98, 101-2, 113, 122, 135-36, 179, 198, 202, 205, 207, 219, 221, 233, 254, 258, 264, 267, 269, 272
Farmingdale, ME, 146
Feenstra, Pieter Martens, 203
Fenner, Erasmus Darwin, 158
Ferdinand Kennett & Company, 153
Fever River, 188
Fillmore, Millard, 65
First Presbyterian Church, 264, 267
Florida, 78
Flowers, C. B., 216
Fopma, Jelle Louws, 6
Fort Brighton, Merseyside, 38
Fort Charlotte, Nassau, 109, 121
Fort George, ME, 43
Fort Pinckney, SC, 48
Fort Rosalie, MS, 167

Fort St. Philip, LA, 151
Fort Sumter, SC, 48, 50
Franekeradeel, Friesland, 9
Frederick County, MD, 228
Freedom, PA, 167
Freeman, John N., 270
Freeport, Grand Bahama Island, 101
Freeport, IL, 193
Friesland (NL), 3, 10 map, 25, 38, 40, 64, 100, 136, 152, 169, 181, 191-92, 201-4, 206, 211, 219, 224, 227, 232, 235, 245, 253, 256-57
Frisia community, 201, 227, 239
Fruitlands community, 199, 200
Frysia, of schets der Friesche volkplanting in Noord-Amerika (Haagsma), 203, 239
Fugitive Slave Law, 63
Fulton Street Cemetery, 255

Galena and Chicago Union Railroad, 193
Galena, IL, 180, 182, 188, 192-93, 198
Garden Key, FL, 139
Gast, Leopold, 181
"Gateway to the West," 240
Geneva Consolidated Silver Mining and Smelting Company, 250
Geographical Society of Baltimore, 216
George III (king), 121
Gereformeerd Kerk, 5
German Society, 152, 159
Gersema, Jelle, 164
Gettysburg (Battle of), 228, 230
Gettysburg Courthouse Hospital, 228
Gettysburg, PA, 228
governor's mansion, 120
Graafsma, Bauke, 9, 64, 164
Graafsma, Klaaske, 9, 164

Graafsma, Trijntje, 64
Grand Bahama Island, 78, 91, 101, 105, 107, 130, 139, 197, 211, 214, 272
Grand Junction, CO, 225
Grand Rapids-Indianapolis Railroad, 256
Grand Rapids, MI, 179, 193, 254-56
Grand Rapids-Valley Railroad, 256
Great Eastern Mine, 266
Great Grimsby, England, 40
Great Isaac Rocks, 36, 77n, 80-81, 83, 127, 132, 138 map, 231
Great Lakes, 250
Greeley, CO, 225, 264
Green Mound Cemetery, 206, 237
Gregory, John, 116, 123, 133, 186-87
Groggon, William, 121
Guildford, Surry, England, 28
Gulf of Mexico, 89, 141, 148, 171
Gulf Stream, 78, 89, 91-92, 97, 139, 272
Guthrie, James, 25

Haagsma, Albert, 241-42
Haagsma, Bauke Broers, 13
Haagsma, Baukjen, 14
Haagsma, Bertram Louis, 241
Haagsma, Broer Baukes, 13, 38, 41, 45, 57, 59, 61, 64, 74, 77, 80, 84, 97, 101, 103, 107, 109, 113, 120-21, 136-37, 141, 149-50, 153, 155, 164, 167, 169-70, 174-75, 179, 181, 188, 190, 194, 201, 223, 239
Haagsma, Fokeltje, 14
Haagsma, Mina (née Schmitke), 241
Haagsma, Ysbrand, 241
Hall, A. Oakey, 147

Hall, Francis, 140
Hamburg, Germany, 40
Hannibal, MO, 186
Hargadine, McKittrick, 240
Harlingen, Friesland, 3, 6, 17, 19, 40, 201
Harrison, William Henry, 199
Harris, Samuel, 45, 92, 112
Hartford Daily Courant, 126
Hartley, Jesse, 36
Harward, David, 30
Harward, George, 28, 30
Harward, Hannah, 30
Harward house, 31 image
Harward, John, 28, 30, 32 image, 41, 45, 48, 50, 129, 140, 168, 262
Harward, Letitia, 28
Harward, Otis, 30
Harward, Thomas, 30
Harward, Thomas (doctor), 28
Harward, William, 28
Harward, William (born in Bowdoinham), 30
Hawthorne, Nathaniel, 36
Heemstra, Sytske, 164
Heidelberg Catechism, 272
Helena, AR, 172
Henry IV (king), 190
Henry of Navarre, 190
Het Bildt, Friesland, 10, 193, 223, 256
Highland Street Railway Company, 266
H. M. Commissariat Department, 112
Hofman, Dirk, 60-61
Hofstra, Bertus, 164
Hog Island, Nassau, 108
Hole-in-the-Wall, Abaco Island, 80
Holland, 237
Hollander, De (Holland, MI), 190, 192
Hollander, Pietje, 164

Holland, MI, 204
Holland Sand Prairie State Natural Area, 258
Holland Society, 241
Holland Township, WI, 235
Holland, WI, 258
Hong Kong, British Territory, 66
Hope Insurance Company, 33
Hope Town, Abaco Island, 79, 99, 216-17
Houtsma, Sipke, 201

Icarian community, 186
Illinois, 240
Illustrated News (NY), 130
Imray, James, 150
Indian Wars, 27
Ingersoll, Joseph R., 123
Ingraham, J. H., 70
Iowa, 191, 233, 240, 263
Iowa Territory, 186
Irving, Washington, 121
Isaac, John Raphael, 35
Isaac Rock. *See* Great Isaac Rocks
Ives, Charles, 70

James M. (victim of yellow fever), 158
Jansen, Jan, 164
Jansonius, Grietje, 164, 220-21
Jefferson, Thomas, 145
Jesuits Bend, LA, 151
Jesus College, 121

Kalamazoo, MI, 194
Karsten, John H., 204
Kas, Geertje, 220
Kas, Grace, 220
Kas, Hendrik Jans, 133, 136, 164, 219
Kas, Sadie (Sarah), 220
Kas, Willem, 220
Keizer, Reinder, 205
Kemp, Captain, 133, 137, 139, 141, 146, 150-51

Kennebec River, 27, 30, 33, 42-44, 146

Kennebec River Valley, 29 map, 43, 262

Kennebunk, ME, 107

Key West, FL, 139

Kimswerd, Friesland, 8, 15, 169

King's Chapel, 28

Kingston, Jamaica, 131

King, William, 25

Kooistra, Antje, 9, 71, 118, 164, 227

Kooistra, Bauke, 67, 71

Kooistra, Jacob, 9, 38, 67, 71, 107, 118

Kooistra, James, 206

Kooistra, Marinus, 71

Kooistra, Sake, 227-28, 229 image

Kooistra, Symon, 227-28

Kooistra, Tiete, 59, 84, 101, 118, 227

Kuiken, Dirk, 164

La Crescent, MN, 246

La Crosse County Record, 237

La Crosse County, WI, 195 map, 235

La Crosse Tribune, 258

La Crosse Tribune and Leader-Press, 229

La Crosse, WI, 192, 219, 227, 230

Lancashire, England, 51

Lane, Charles, 199, 200

Lane Seminary, OH, 63

Latrobe, Benjamin, 145

Leadville, CO, 267

Leeuwarden, Friesland, 170, 181

Leeuwarder Courant, 8, 11, 14, 169-70

Leguest, Pierre Laclede, 177

Le Havre, France, 69, 164

leprosy, 217

Levinge, R. G. A., 154

Lewis, Winslow, 145

Life on the Mississippi (Twain), 170

Lincoln, Abraham, 157, 168, 228, 240

Little Abaco Island, 79

Little Isaac. *See* Great Isaac Rocks

Liverpool, England, 12, 22-24, 35, 48, 64, 74, 77, 92, 98, 107, 127, 142, 148, 155, 169, 187, 215, 231-32

Liverpool Mercury, 24, 36, 51

Loggerhead Key, FL, 139

Londonderry, Ireland, 42

London, England, 23, 122, 170, 213

Lord Jim (Conrad), 262

Lord, Willis, 268

Los Angeles, CA, 255

Lotgevallen van den Heer O. H. Bonnema en zijne togtgenooten (Haagsma), 239

Louisiana Purchase, 145

Louisiana Staats Zeitung, 155

Louis IX, Saint, 177

Louis XV (king), 177

Lowestoft, England, 11, 18, 21, 23, 219

Lucas, Henry S., 206

Macao (Portuguese Territory), 66

MacKay, Alexander, 178

Madison, James, 173

Magnus, Charles, 171

Magoun and Clapp, 32

Magoun, David C., 48

Maine, 262

Maine Cultivator and Hallowell Gazette, 45

Malassez, Charles T., 111, 120, 122, 132-33

Malone, Ephraim, 99

Malone, Samuel, 217

Malone, Wyannie, 79, 99

Maloney, Daniel, 146

Malta, Italy, 164

Manassas, VA, 228

Manchester, England, 22, 36, 51

Margaret R. (victim of yellow
    fever), 158
Marion, John, 49
Massachusetts, 200
Matanilla Reef, 79
Mather, Cotton, 42
Maury, Matthew Fontaine, 89
McDonald, Peter, 113
McIntyre, Captain, 92
Melville, Herman, 36, 165
Memphis, TN, 172
Menaldumsdeel, Friesland, 220
Merrymeeting Bay, 27, 30, 44
Mersey, River, 35, 38, 51, 57 image
Michigan, 192, 253
Michigan Central Railroad, 194
Miller, Ebenezer, 83, 86
Milwaukee Railroad, 228
Minnesota, 191-92, 196, 247
Mississippi River, 37, 89, 118,
    139, 141, 145, 149, 165, 167,
    171, 178, 190-92, 196, 203,
    206, 224, 241-42, 246, 250, 263
Mississippi Valley, 241
Mississippi Valley Conservancy,
    258
Missouri, 240
Missouri River, 177, 185, 240
Moffett, Pamela (née Clemens),
    180
Moffett, William A., 181
Molenaar, Gerrit, 164
Moore, Henry, 45
Mormon community, 186
Morning Chronicle (London), 123
Mosquito Point, Grand Bahama
    Island, 102
Mr. Romer's Baptist Church, 134
Mure, William, 153, 155, 169

Napoleon, AR, 170-71
Nassau Guardian, 112, 119, 141,
    170, 213
Nassau Harbor, 110 image

Nassau Harbor, 124 map
Nassau, New Providence Island,
    79, 101, 107-8, 115, 120, 131,
    133, 137, 142, 155, 178, 186-87,
    213-14, 227, 273
Natchez, MS, 166-67
Native Americans, 188, 197
Nauvoo, IL, 186
Navy Bay, Panama, 131
Nederlands Hervormde Kerk, 5
Nelson, Horatio, 38
Nesbitt, C. R., 214
Netherlands, 201-2, 236, 254
Netherlands consul, 179, 198,
    232, 240
New Amsterdam Presbyterian
    Church, 206, 258
New Amsterdam, WI, 203, 220,
    227, 235-36, 239, 245, 258
New Brunswick, Canada, 43
Newcastle, 5th Duke of (Henry
    Pelham Fiennes Pelham-Clin-
    ton), 186, 215
Newcomen Society, 253
New England, 199
New Inland Mutual Marine In-
    surance Company, 34
New London, CT, 42
New Madrid, MO, 173
New Orleans as it is, 157
New Orleans, LA, 37, 57, 64, 77,
    92, 98, 107, 111, 118, 122, 137,
    139, 148, 150-51, 163-64, 169,
    177-78, 187, 190, 215, 273
New Providence Island, 116, 272
Newton, Isaac, 24
New York Commercial Advertiser, 140
New York Daily Times, 5, 91, 126,
    128-29, 132, 140
New York Morning Courier and
    Enquirer, 141
New York, NY, 69, 98, 125, 127-
    28, 132, 150, 159, 170, 181, 233
New York Tribune, 129, 243

New York Weekly Herald, 169
Nichols, James C., 34, 48
Nickerson, Captain, 128
Nieuwe Diep, North Holland, 11, 18
Nora, IL, 193
North Atlantic Ocean, 44
Northcroft, G. J. H., 93
Northeast Pass, 148
North of Europe Steam Navigation Company, 11
Norths Cay, 109
Northwest Providence Channel, 80, 108, 127, 138
Norwich, England, 23
Nottingham, England, 23

Ohio River, 167, 174, 177
Old Campbell Cemetery, 228
Oldenburg, Germany, 152
Omaha, NE, 255
Onalaska, WI, 192, 196, 220, 227
Oostburg Reformed Church, 204
Oostburg, WI, 204
Oregon, 233
Oregon City, OR, 233
Orso, Joe, 258

Pacific Ocean, 233
Pana, IL, 262, 264
Panama, 233
Passengers Act of 1852, 56, 187
Patten, John, 249
Pejepscot Company, 43
Pella, IA, 204, 232-33
Penobscot tribe, 27
Penrose, Clement A., 216
Perry, Matthew Calbraith, 65-66
Peterborough, England, 23
Philadelphia, PA, 24, 181
Philips, H. S., 163
Physical Geography of the Sea, The (Maury), 89
Pierce, Franklin, 25

Pilkington, John, 37, 51
Pinder (emigration officer), 187
Pinkham, Ethelyn, 44
Pinkham, Fred, 44
Pius IX (pope), 64
Plaquemine Parish, LA, 150
Ploegsma, Cornelis, 164
Ponce de León, Juan, 105
Portland, ME, 127
Prairie La Crosse, WI, 191
Prebble, Lemuel, 45, 90
Purington, Albert, 147
Purington, Charles, 147
Purington, Fanny, 45
Purington, Jane, 147
Purington, Mary, 147
Purington, Minerva, 147
Purington, Nathaniel, 45, 147
Purington, Stephen W., 45, 59, 80, 87, 169
Putnam, George H., 39

Queen City. *See* Saint Louis, MO
"Queen City of the Plains" (Denver), 263
"Queen of the South" (New Orleans), 151
Quincy, IL, 186

Reedham, England, 23
Reed, Walter, 159
Reformed Church, 204, 233, 254
Revolutionary War, 43, 99, 108, 130
Richmond, ME, 146
Ridley, Isaac, 45, 90
Rienks, Beinze (Benjamin), 164, 223
Rienks, Beryl, 225
Rienks, Elizabeth, 225
Rienks, Hendrik, 164
Rienks, Martha (née Metje van der Ploeg), 164, 223
Rigg, J. Linton, 108

Riverside Cemetery, 251, 268, 270
Robert & Williams, 125
Rockford, IL, 193
Rock Island, IL, 188
Rocky Mountain News, 267
Roe, Joseph, 90
Roorda, Anne, 232
Roorda, Boukje (née Buwalda), 232-33
Roorda, Epke, 231
Roorda, Frouke, 231
Roorda, Hendrik, 233
Roorda, Izaak Epkes, 4, 8, 18, 39, 56, 60, 73-74, 79-80, 85-86, 90-92, 118, 169, 192, 231
Roorda, Trijntje (née Buwalda), 232
Roorda, Weiger, 232
Ross, Loami, 45, 90, 128
Rotterdam, 232
Royal Cornwall Gazette, 214
Royal National Institution for the Preservation of Life from Shipwreck, 214
Runia, Pieter, 169, 202
Russell, Robert, 147

Sabbath School at St. Andrews, 134
Sagua la Grande, Cuba, 91, 125
Saint Louis, MO, 153, 163, 165-66, 171-72, 174, 177, 188, 198, 236, 239
Salina, CO, 266
Salt Cay Banks, 139
Salt Lake City, UT, 186
Salverda, Peter, 164
Sands, Charles, 99, 217
Sands, Eliza, 99
Sands, Elizabeth (née Malone), 217
Sands, Richardson, 98
Sands, Robert, 98-101, 107, 112, 140, 187, 213

Sands, William, 98
San Francisco, CA, 233
Sargent, John Singer, 113
Sass, R. F., 183
Savannah Daily Georgian, 131
Savannah, GA, 131, 170
Savannah Republican, 140
Sawyer, Thomas, 131
Schaaf, Maartje Pieters, 10, 164, 193, 253. See also van der Stolpe, Maartje
Schaaf, Maartje Sjoerds, 11
Schaaf, Pieter Sjoerds, 10, 253
Schaafsma, 193
Schaafsma, Feye, 9, 39
Schaafsma, Siementje, 9, 39
Scholte, Hendrik P., 204, 232
Schraard, Friesland, 13, 15
Schroeder, J. B., 151, 153, 159
Scott, Walter, 38
Seceder movement, 5, 11, 204, 232
Second Bull Run (battle of), 228
Settlement Point, Grand Bahama Island, 101-2, 107
Seventeenth Iowa Volunteers Infantry, 233
Seward, William, 240
Shaker community, 200
Sharpsburg, MD, 228
Sheboygan Nieuwsbode, 202
ship fever, 6, 60-61
Sikkema, Maaike, 74
Sikkema, Rients, 8, 64, 74, 133, 164, 193
Sikkema, Sikke, 8, 64
Sikkema, Ymkje, 8, 133, 164, 193
Sioux City, IA, 255
slavery, 25, 51, 63, 109, 156, 159, 166, 198
slaves: Adam, 157; Ben, 157; Ed, 157; Hachen, 157; Ned, 157; Suzana, 156
small pox, 6

Smith, Hyrum, 186
Smith, Joseph, 186
Smyth, James Carmichael, 121
South Mountain (Battle of), 228
South Platte River, 263
Spanjer, Hendrik, 61
Spear, J., 49
Spinney, Ruth (née Stinson), 146
Springfield, IL, 168
St. Andrews Benevolent Society,
    Committee of, 133
St. Andrews Presbyterian Kirk,
    113, 134
Steinfort, Botje Harmens, 6
St. George's Channel, 51
Stienstra, Johannes, 9, 164, 236
Stienstra, Riemke, 9, 164, 236
Stienstra, Ytje, 236
Stinson, Caroline, 147
Stinson, Charles Nathaniel, 45,
    130, 169, 262, 266, 268, 270
Stinson, David, 44
Stinson, Edward A., 263, 267
Stinson, Elizabeth, 43
Stinson, Hannah Hunter, 147
Stinson, Henry Clay, 147
Stinson, Ida Jean, 269
Stinson, James, 42-43
Stinson, James Jr, 43
Stinson, James (son of William),
    43
Stinson, Jane, 42
Stinson, John, 43-44, 146
Stinson, Lou, 270
Stinson, Lucy E. (née Call), 262,
    264, 266, 270
Stinson, Luella, 270
Stinson, Mehitable (née Reirdan),
    44, 147
Stinson, Thankful (née Puring-
    ton), 45, 130, 147, 169, 262
Stinson, Timothy Reirdan, 42,
    44-45, 50, 66-67, 73, 77-78,
    80-81, 84, 91, 112, 125, 140-41,

146, 168, 181, 190, 194, 249,
    262
Stinson, William, 43
Stirrup Cay, 80
Stowe, Calvin, 63
Stowe, Harriet Beecher, 49, 63
St. Peter's Cemetery, 243
Straits of Florida, 97
St. Sophia, LA, 151
Swiss bridge, 196
Sybesma, Mettje Nammes, 10

ten Broek, Gerrit H., 241
Thompson, Sarah (née Stinson),
    147
Thomson, John, 110
Times (London), 5
Tjalsma, Lyckle, 71
Tjalsma, Sjoerd, 9, 38, 71, 164,
    180, 185, 257
Tjalsma, Sjoukje (Susan), 9, 71,
    164, 180, 185. *See also* Chalsma,
    Sjouke (Susan) (née Tuininga)
Tjalsma, Tjalling, 258
Toewater, Frederick R., 179, 198,
    240
Tokyo, Japan, 65
Tony Beacon, 109
Trollope, Francis Milton, 174
Tuininga, Albert, 247
Tuininga, Albertje, 246
Tuininga, Antje, 61, 64
Tuininga, Arthur, 247
Tuininga, Charles, 247
Tuininga, Elizabeth, 246
Tuininga, Gerrit, 60
Tuininga, Jan, 246
Tuininga, Johannes, 8, 39, 60,
    102, 164, 211, 245
Tuininga, John, 247
Tuininga, Sjouke, 246, 258
Tuininga, Trijntje, 8, 60, 100,
    164, 246
Turk's Island, 250

Twain, Mark (Samuel Clemens), 170, 186
typhoid, 267
typhus, 6

Uncle Tom's Cabin (Stowe), 49, 63
Union Pacific Railroad, 233
United Kingdom, 214
United States, 199, 224, 236
United States consul, 36, 112-13, 119
United States vs. Daniel Maloney, 146

van der Ploeg, Baukje Jans, 9, 164
van der Ploeg, Boutje, 164
van der Ploeg, Jan Martens, 9, 164
van der Ploeg, Maartje, 164
van der Ploeg, Marten Jans, 9, 164
van der Ploeg, Metje, 164, 223-24
van der Stolpe, Leendert, 254, 256
van der Stolpe, Maartje (Maude) (née Schaaf), 253-56. *See also* Schaaf, Maartje Pieters
van der Tol, Pieter, 108
van der Veer, Johannes Koenraads, 58, 164
van Hinte, Jacob, 205
Van Raalte, Albertus C., 15, 204
Van Zante, Howard, 233
Vendue House, 109, 120
Verrill, Alpheus Hyatt, 121
vessels: *Albert*, 34 image; *Ambrose*, 69; *Asa Fish*, 98; *Ben Campbell*, 182; *Bengal*, 127; *Ben West*, 182, 185, 188, 189; *Brunette*, 180; *Canada*, 63; *Caspian*, 249; *Charles Crocker*, 165; *Chicago Board of Trade*, 250; *City of Norwich*, 11, 18; *City of Philadelphia*, 24; *Clara*, 182; *Clinton*, 249; *Contest*, 106; *Conway*, 131;

Costa Concordia, 261; *Crosby*, 57; *Eclipse*, 166; *E. S. Jane*, 98; *Flushing*, 44; *Formby*, 57; *Franconia*, 250; *Gallant*, 175; *Geo. Collier*, 182; *Grace*, 98; *Grand Turk*, 153, 161, 170, 178, 185; *Isabel*, 182; *Jesiah Lawrence*, 182; *John and Albert*, 30; *John C. Calhoun*, 249; *John Simonds*, 182; *Jonathan Cummings*, 148; *Jupiter*, 40; *Kate Kearney*, 182; *Levee*, 190-91; *Maccallum*, 42; *Martha Jewett*, 182; *Merry Meeting*, 28; *Michigan*, 182; *Minnesota*, 175, 180; *Mississippi*, 65; *Naples*, 31; *National Eagle*, 164; *New Lucy*, 182; *New St. Paul*, 181; *Northampton*, 57; *Oceanos*, 261; *Oneco*, 98, 119; *Ophir*, 127; *Oracle*, 98, 101, 106, 112, 213; *Osborne*, 107, 139; *Patna*, 262; *Patrick Henry*, 182; *Pilot*, 149; *Pollux*, 92-93, 98, 118, 231; *Porpoise*, 148-49, 151; *Prince*, 157; *QEII*, 69; *Rankin*, 98; *Reuben Carver*, 91, 119, 125, 128; *Rhine*, 31; *Roscius*, 146; *Rover*, 122, 132-33, 137, 148-49, 151, 153; *Royal Sovereign*, 98; *Smith Tuttle*, 128; *St. Ange*, 181; *Statesman*, 152, 164; *St. Louis*, 181; *St. Nicholas*, 181; *Time*, 50, 122, 132-33, 137, 141, 148-54; *Titanic*, 37, 221; *Tonquin*, 31; *Vassalborough*,, 30; *Vesta*, 253; *Wabash*, 31, 48; *William and Mary* (see separate entry); *William and Mary* (1718), 42; *William H. Van Name*, 216; *Yarmouth Castle*, 261
Vicksburg, MS, 157, 168
Victoria, MS, 170-71
Victoria, Queen, 64, 113, 122-23
Vos and Brown, 37
Vriesland, MI, 193, 204

Vrouwen Parochie, 193

Waddenzee, 17, 108
Wagenaar, Oene, 86, 90-91, 169, 192, 232
Ward, Patrick, 92
Ward, William, 46, 112
War of 1812, 44, 149
Warsaw, IL, 263-64
Washington, 247
Washington, DC, 181
Washington, George, 116
Washington, Lawrence, 116
Waterloo, LA, 166
Weale, Edward, 131
Webster, Daniel, 132
Weekly Herald (New York), 140
Weekly Mirror (Bath), 129
Weekly Northwestern Gazette (Galena), 189
Weeks, Edward, 45, 90
Welsh, Samuel, 45, 56, 67, 127-28
Wesselius, Marijke, 8, 164, 193
Wesselius, Siebren, 8, 87, 164, 179, 193
Wesselius, Tjalling, 193
Westerhuis, Arijen, 8, 78, 164
Westerhuis, Jeltje, 8, 78, 164
Westerhuis, Rinske, 78
Westerhuis, Siebren, 39
Western Barracks, 112, 123
West Indies, 224
Wharton, Thomas Kelah, 158
White Star Line, 37, 51
Whiting, William, 273
Whitman, Walt, 174
Wiersma, Trijntje (Kate), 220

Wihelmina, Queen, 241
Willem I (king), 5
Willem II (king), 5
Willem III (king), 240
William and Mary, 31, 41, 46-47, 55, 61, 63, 65-66, 70, 78, 87 image, 90, 92, 98, 100-102, 106, 110, 112, 117-19, 125, 131, 137, 139, 147, 150, 155, 161, 168, 179, 181, 186-87, 190, 192, 194, 211, 213, 215, 220, 223, 225, 229, 231, 236, 249, 251, 255, 258, 262, 265, 270, 272
Wilson, Henry T., 37, 51
Wisconsin, 191-92, 199, 203, 219, 245, 258
Wisconsin Volunteer Infantry, Company B, 228
Wolff, H. G., 266
Wonseradeel, Friesland, 9, 13, 188
World's Fair of 1904, 241
World War II, 272
Wyannie Malone Historical Museum, 217
Wyoming Township, MI, 255

yellow fever, 66, 152, 158, 273
Ypma, Maarten A., 204

Zeeland, MI, 220, 253
Zina Hyde & Company, 32
Zuiderzee, 18
Zwicht, Dirk, 164

Made in the USA
San Bernardino, CA
02 July 2018